I0213708

THE JOURNEY

HOW AN OBSCURE BYZANTINE SAINT BECAME OUR SANTA CLAUS

DAVID PRICE WILLIAMS

 Published by Markosia Enterprises, PO BOX 3477, Barnet, Hertfordshire, EN5 9HN.
FIRST PRINTING, October 2017.
Harry Markos, Director.

Paperback: ISBN 978-1-911243-42-7
Hardback: ISBN 978-1-911243-41-0
eBook: ISBN 978-1-911243-43-4

Book design by: Ian Sharman

FRONT COVER PICTURE:
St Nicholas. 13th Century icon,
St Catherine's Monastery, Sinai

BACK COVER PICTURE
Upper church at Gemlier.

www.markosia.com

First Edition

For Luke, Joe and Zoe, Isabella and Charlotte,
all of whom at one time or another will
have believed in Santa Claus.

CONTENTS

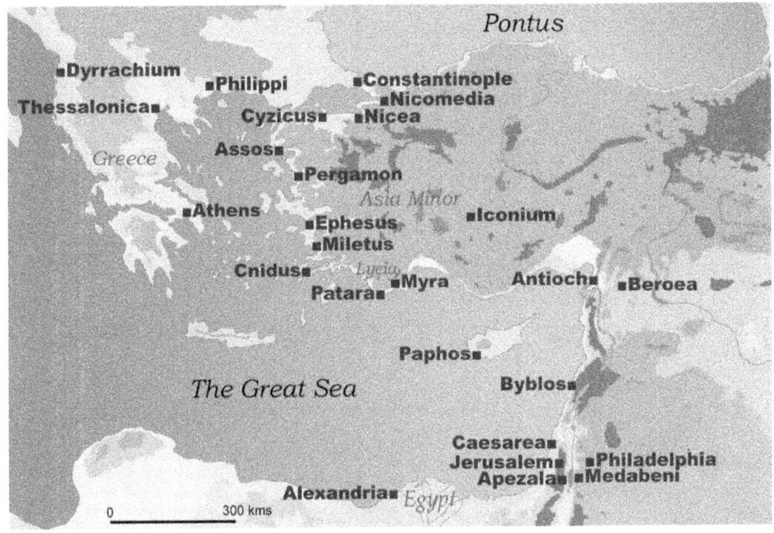
Pontus
Dyrrachium
Philippi
Constantinople
Nicomedia
Thessalonica
Cyzicus
Nicea
Assos
Greece
Pergamon
Asia Minor
Athens
Ephesus
Iconium
Miletus
Cnidus
Lycia
Myra
Antioch
Beroea
Patara
Paphos
The Great Sea
Byblos
Caesarea
Jerusalem
Philadelphia
Apezala
Medabeni
Alexandria
Egypt
0
300 kms

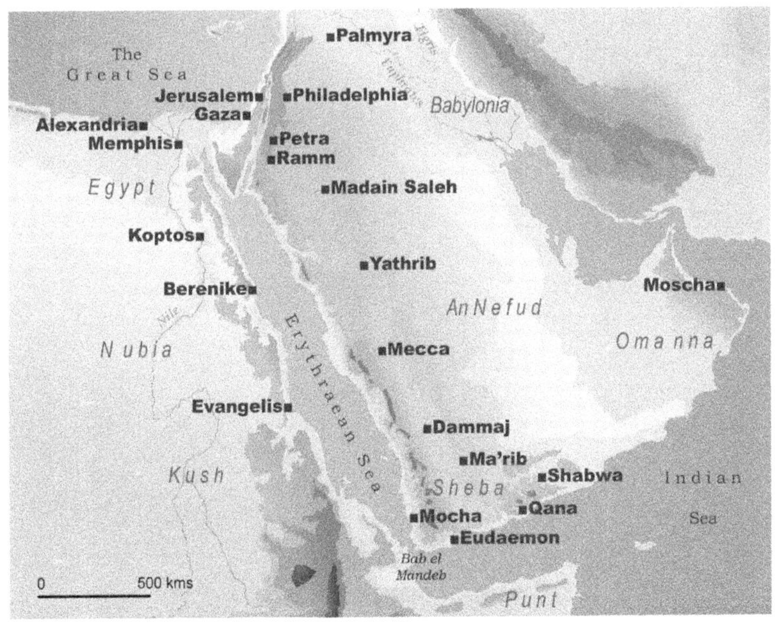
Palmyra
The Great Sea
Jerusalem
Philadelphia
Babylonia
Gaza
Alexandria
Memphis
Petra
Ramm
Egypt
Madain Saleh
Koptos
Yathrib
Berenike
Moscha
An Nefud
Nile
Omanna
Nubia
Mecca
Erythraean Sea
Evangelis
Dammaj
Ma'rib
Kush
Sheba
Shabwa
Indian Sea
Qana
Mocha
Eudaemon
Bab el Mandeb
0
500 kms
Punt

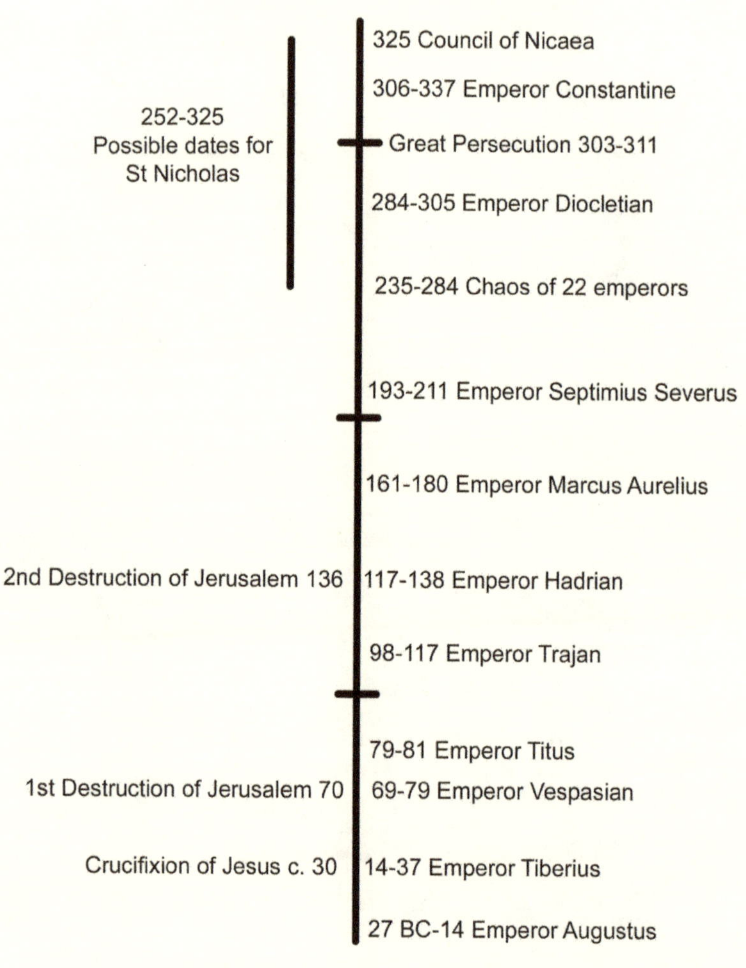
Dates AD - Anno Domini
325 Council of Nicaea
306-337 Emperor Constantine
252-325
Possible dates for
St Nicholas
Great Persecution 303-311
284-305 Emperor Diocletian
235-284 Chaos of 22 emperors
193-211 Emperor Septimius Severus
161-180 Emperor Marcus Aurelius
2nd Destruction of Jerusalem 136
117-138 Emperor Hadrian
98-117 Emperor Trajan
79-81 Emperor Titus
1st Destruction of Jerusalem 70
69-79 Emperor Vespasian
Crucifixion of Jesus c. 30
14-37 Emperor Tiberius
27 BC-14 Emperor Augustus

PART I

A MOMENT IN TIME

EPITAPH

AN INCIDENT ON PARTRIDGE ISLAND

The old man had been feverish for days now, his pale skin stretched like ancient parchment stitched with straggling tufts of white beard, his eyes sunk deep into their sockets. Andreas and his wife began to fear for his life. But each day, even as he seemed to grow frailer before them, he would insist on climbing to the summit of the island behind which they were sheltering from the winter storm. From here he would stand and gaze for hours far across the sea, south along the mountainous coast towards the place of his birth. Maybe he could sail there soon, he must have thought, back to his city, back to his old life. But the gales continued unabated, lashing the rocks below where he stood and howling among the high peaks of the nearby mainland. The flying spume of the surf thundered at the base of the cliffs, giving no indication of when they would ever be able to set sail from their refuge in the narrow sound where they were moored.

This day had begun like all the rest. The old man stood wistfully looking into the teeth of the wind, his eyes filling with tears. He remembered all his years since his childhood long ago. He had lived an eventful life, a life full of change and drama, a life for which he was deeply thankful and now, as the blustering storm tore the whispered prayers from his thin, cracked lips, he sensed he heard God calling him to another home. As the faint sunlight slanted through a gap in the wild sky and shimmered on the sea, he knew that his earthly work was finally over.

They had only left him for a few minutes in order to fetch a jar of water from the boat, but when they struggled back up the steep slope to the top of the island, they knew at once he had left them. His lifeless body, now an almost weightless rag, lay crumpled on the bare, wet limestone just below the highest point of the island, the wind plucking jerkily at his sodden robes. Although they had always known that he would not be with them for much longer, the sight of his insensible body supine in front of them, the man who had been their leader for so many years, moved them to a profound sorrow. Falling on their knees and tearing their rough shifts, they wailed into the buffeting wind, so alone now on that remote island. Even as they did so, the charging ominous clouds opened and an angled, watery sun shafted through the heavens again and touched the old man's corpse, for an instant illuminating in yellow-gold the place where he lay, catching the edges of his raiment almost like a halo.

In that moment Andreas knew what he must do. He would create a shrine to the old man's memory, a simple monument here on the top of the island exactly where he had been taken from them, to remember his life, to commemorate his great works and to honour the leader who had guided them through such troubled times. He would not be forgotten.

Later that day Andreas fashioned a rough cross from odd spars on the ship, lashing the cross piece together with old rope from the hold. He dragged it up to the summit where the ship's crew had already begun building a cairn out of the sharp limestone boulders. They carefully covered the old man where he had fallen, then piled more and more stones on top, making a high pyramid, high enough to be visible out at sea. They erected the cross in the centre of the cairn and threw more and more stones around it to make it firm. When it was finished, Andreas gave one last benediction and with an aching sadness they made their way down the hill to the ship.

By dawn the next morning the storm had blown itself out and a fresh breeze sent clouds scudding across the tops of the mountain ranges. Undoing the mooring ropes they heaved the stone anchors in-board one by one and hoisting the weather-beaten sail, they slowly edged the ship down the sound and around the edge of the island. What was it the old man had called this place, Andreas pondered? "Partridge Island," was that it?

The wind quickened and caught the rigging. The ropes stretched, the patched sail filled and pushed the vessel forward, water foaming at its prow, its old timbers creaking with the movement. The ship picked up speed, leaving a bubbling wake as she sailed south, finally quitting the island. With a heavy heart Andreas looked up at the dark outline, his thoughts a mixture of sweet memory and bitter despair. As the ship pulled further away, he could make out the summit and there against the sky stood the profile of the cairn, just as they had left it, with the cross pointing heavenwards as if to chart the old man's last journey.

Andreas recalled a moment from the previous day, after he had formed the cross, when he had taken a heated chisel from the embers of the fire in the tile-roofed galley and burnt the old man's name on the intersecting bar. Maybe one day others would remember this saintly old man with whom he had lived for so many years, through bad times and good. Maybe the whole world would come to know of him, the man who now lay buried on that remote windswept summit under the rude wooden cross which in rough Greek letters spelled out his name - ΝΙΚΟΛΑΟϹ – "Nicholas."

Andreas and his wife, who stood close beside him at the ship's rail, took one last look back then they turned to face each other searching for some comfort, lost in emptiness and grief; he had been the dearest friend to both of them. In the end inevitably the vessel drove through the sea and around the headland, out of sight of the island and into the bright day. At least, they consoled themselves, they had Nicholas' written account of his own life in their possession.

* * * * *

Who could have known then what we know now? Getting on for two millennia later, that saintly old man buried atop Partridge Island in 325 AD was to become perhaps one of the best-known figures of all time, his name echoing down the centuries even to this day - to wit our very own Santa Claus. What follows might be his story.

PART II

A STORY OF MY LIFE

CHAPTER ONE

IN THE BEGINNING

Even in those days long ago when I was young, Patara, the city of my birth, was such a bustling port, but then it was the centre of my boyhood universe. By that time it was already a thousand years old, built, so they said, by ancient Lycians to serve the great cities of the Xanthos Valley whose deep gorges stretched far back into the towering ranges of the Taurus Mountains. The river always ran a translucent jade and icy cold with the melting snows off the high peaks which shut our valley away from the interminable, high plains of Asia Minor.

Natives of the city often boasted that Alexander the Great had spent a few days here as he marched his army around the coast on his way to conquer the mighty Persian Empire some six hundred years ago. Certainly his Greek way of life has left its mark on our city. You only had to look at the magnificent colonnaded streets to see the Greek influence, their cool, pillared shade a real godsend on a hot summer's afternoon. As a boy I used to run through them on my way to the harbour at the mouth of the river to look at all the ships moored by the quaysides. They came from all round our sea and beyond, those vessels. I found it so romantic, so exciting. I was not to know then that my own journeying was also to take me far from home to places of which I had never dreamt, in search of excitement, yes, but as it turned out in search of enlightenment too, a journey which for me brought me to the very meaning of life itself.

When I looked at the sailors I saw such an array of nationalities just from the different styles of clothes they wore – light-skinned fair-haired men from the ports of the Adriatic, from Illyria and Dalmatia, dressed in colourful striped pantaloons and white smocks; dark-eyed Romans from Ostia, looking so austere in their black shirts and trousers; swarthy Arabs with pointed beards from the cities of Phoenicia and from the far-off Nile wearing rough, toe-length gallabiyahs. And there was a real mixture of languages – Latin was the language of the empire and spoken with varying degrees of competence. But Greek was our language and at least in Patara it was the language everyone used to conduct business. We had our own local dialect which was soft and colourful by comparison to the coarse shouts of the deck hands from the east. And then there were the men from the deserts of Arabia, who spoke together so quickly in a totally unintelligible guttural patois I sometimes wondered how they had learned such a difficult tongue. But when they spoke in Greek, which they had to do to make themselves understood, it was not especially good Greek; it was rather slow and strongly accented.

To me, my city seemed such a crossroads of goods in those days. You could see all the different cargoes being piled up on the quaysides, merchandise from all over the world. There were special ships from Syria that landed exotic silk from somewhere far to the east, beyond the edge of the earth someone once told me. It arrived in bales wrapped tightly in woollen sacks which from the outside looked distinctly uninteresting. But I had seen them carefully unwrapped in the special warehouses away from the dockside and they were absolutely magnificent. I remember seeing one merchant unrolling a bale and the vibrant colours of the fabric appeared to cascade all over the floor. The decorations on the individual bolts of cloth were fantastic, woven with beautiful mythical beasts in colours so bright they almost seemed alive. There were huge flowers and trees, all in greens, reds, whites and browns, all colours of the rainbow and so finely crafted you wondered, as they lay there glowing in the sunlight, if any human fingers could be nimble enough to produce such incredible pictures as they did.

The silk merchants were a rather aloof class and wealthy too. They would speak in reverential tones about the textures, the knot values and the prices, which seemed so out of this world they were like the very silk itself. I wondered who would wear such exotic fabrics, but it seemed there was an inexhaustible demand for this material among the endless rich matriarchs of the imperial capital, Rome and these appetites must be being passed on to their daughters too. I doubted I would ever see anyone dressed in such finery. Who would ever be able to afford such luxury where we lived?

There were other expensive cargoes. Every now and then a ship would be carrying spices from India – pepper, ginger and turmeric. They came in small wooden drums and when they had been offloaded they were lined up in rows on the flag-stones to be auctioned. Another cargo which fascinated yet frightened me a bit were the wild animals - the elephants, giraffes and other exotic beasts from Africa. They were sold to Rome to be killed in the arena for entertainment on public holidays, to celebrate the emperor's birthday or some other festival; we Greeks would never indulge in such barbaric sport as killing animals for amusement.They looked so dejected, being forcibly dragged off the ships to be kept in pens outside the city. I didn't much like the men who traded in these animals either. They always looked untrustworthy somehow and they were so cruel to their charges it's a wonder any of the animals survived the journey. But being boys it didn't stop us going out to the pens now and again to see if they had acquired anything we hadn't seen before.

But mostly the shipments with which the men on the quaysides were busiest were commodities being exported from our valley - timber, animal hides and agricultural produce from the fields of the Xanthos Valley to be sold to Rome and the other big Italian cities. There were forests of tree trunks which were brought down the river from up in the mountains, especially the huge pine trees with massive boles and long straight trunks used in the construction industry. Someone told me they built houses six and seven storeys high in Rome, tenements for the working classes they said; they needed endless wooden beams to hold the things up. I couldn't imagine how people lived like that, all existing on top of one another. And the same man told me these rickety buildings burnt down regularly, catching light with embers falling from cooking stoves or fires lit to keep people warm in the frosty Roman winters. That's why they needed so much timber I suppose, to rebuild the same pitiful apartments all over again.

I often saw bale after bale of animal hides too being stowed in ship's holds, roped together and swung up over the gunwales. They always stank because they were generally untreated – raw ox hides, sheep skins and goat skins, the latter used for the manufacture of parchment, which incidentally made Asia Minor famous after its invention in the city of Pergamon some centuries ago. I was told that it was the deliberate restriction on the supply of papyrus from Egypt that caused the Pergamon library to create the wonder writing material and now it's so widely used that Egypt has lost out.

Then there were the grain ships which carried wheat in huge quantities for the Roman army so that they could all have their daily bread in whatever far-flung outpost they had been billeted.

It was always feared that if they didn't get their ration of loaves every day, the legions would mutiny, especially since many of the soldiers had joined the army from foreign countries and were not necessarily loyal to the emperor. That was always a potential problem, in particular now when the empire was so weak and emperors arose and fell like skittles in an ale house.

Every June and July there would be a constant creaking of carts from the interior bringing the grain harvest down the roads on either side of the valley to the granaries near the harbour. They were massive buildings and by August they'd be full to overflowing with the threshed wheat ready for export. I knew many boys my own age whose fathers were involved in transporting the grain in bullock carts. They must have had innumerable mills and bakeries in Rome to process such a vast quantity.

The harbour and all its comings and goings were a source of endless fascination for me. I used to sit on the wall near the old bath-house and watch the ships being warped in from the outer roads in the bay. We had many slaves, mainly captured years ago from north of the Pontus, who would strain in long gangs on the ropes thrown to the shore, muscles stretched taut, as they pulled the heavy hulks around the breakwater and into their mooring positions alongside the harbour wall. The harbour inspectors and the gang masters would yell instructions to them, but they knew what they were doing and never made a mistake in their delicate manoeuvres. Each ship would be brought broadside on to the quay and then dragged sideways until it just touched the huge, roped-straw fenders hanging down to protect their hulls. The gangplanks would be pushed out and the unloading could begin.

We had military ships too calling at Patara, enormous galleys which carried legionaries from one part of the empire to another stopping for supplies or to fix some minor damage. We didn't normally see many soldiers where we were. Most people were only too happy to live in peace with the imperial administration, especially since everyone was making so much money out of them! When the galleys were out at sea, they looked like huge centipedes with the oars moving to and fro in unison, but in the harbour the oars were taken in-board and they had to be warped in with ropes just like all the rest. They were heavy, these troop ships, especially when fully loaded and the dock gangs had to haul extra hard to bring their hulks into their appointed place, usually with some over-dressed centurion or another, in full armour, bawling superfluous orders at them from the deck railing. Once they'd come to rest, the officers in charge would shout more orders to the men on the dock-side and then disembark. Arrogantly, in full dress and with sword hilts bouncing on their thighs, they swaggered over to the harbour buildings to arrange the official documents before sloping off to one of the wine shops along the front, not the most salubrious at the best of times it has to be said, where they would slake their thirst after their days at sea.

You should have seen the great variety of smaller craft that weaved in and out of our bay too, the small ships carrying barrels of pitch from half way down the Euphrates to be used in ship repairs. The crew always looked as though they'd just been climbing a sooty chimney, their hands, arms and faces covered in the black oily tar. They never seemed to be able to get clean again and most of the shopkeepers in the city wouldn't allow them to enter their premises in case they blackened the doors or counters. I always felt sorry for these poor malodourous souls whom no-one seemed to like. But I'm sure they wouldn't have felt the same if they were in a ship sinking for want of a few denarius-worth of waterproofing.

And there were the wine ships, elegant craft from Greece which were laden with hundreds of amphorae, full of sweet red wine from the Island of Samos up near Ephesus or the deep ruby wines from Cnidus, much appreciated by our wealthier citizens. You could always tell where the wine came from because all the wine jars were different shapes, depending on where they were made. There were always hotly contested arguments about which of the wines we imported in Patara was the best, although I always wondered if maybe it was the source of the water with which they diluted their wines that made the difference. There were those who would swear this spring water would bring out the best aroma, whilst others vehemently argued that it was that one from further up the valley, or that the best flavour could be got by cooling the wine, adding ice brought down during the winter from the mountains and stored in one of our ice houses.

The shallower parts of the river mouth were crowded with other tiny craft, especially the fishing boats that would go out during the night and come back just after dawn to land their catch for our market before the sun was up. We had a plentiful supply of fish, from red and grey mullet to huge grouper with their big ugly mouths, long-snouted barracuda, silvery sea bass and colourful bronze headed bream, not to mention buckets of cuttlefish, octopus and hard-shelled flapping cray fish. They were whisked from the bottom of the rowing boats up to the fish market and, apart from a few buckets of sardines, they had usually all been sold before breakfast and the market washed down for the day.

* * * * *

I must have been about seven or eight years old when my father Aquila engaged a tutor for me.

"What that boy needs is some discipline," he ruled. "Let him learn something useful instead of spending so much time at the harbour all day long!"

So, much to my discomfort, for the next few years I had to spend every morning learning Latin irregular verbs, reading the plays of Aeschylus, the dialogues of Plato and Pliny's 'Naturalis Historia', or reading Xenophon's 'Anabasis' or Herodotus 'Histories'.

"Discourse on the metaphysical nature of Socrates' responses in 'Crito'," I would be asked.

I would usually mumble some nonsense or another; after all, what did I know about metaphysics. Then I would be rapped hard over the knuckles for being a dunce, or for not paying attention, or for gazing out of the open doorway at Irene the maid cleaning the courtyard outside. What did I care at my age about Greek philosophy? It was hundreds of years ago. I was often dreaming about the afternoon, directly after our mid-day meal, when I could go fishing with my friend Demetrius. We often did that. But the mornings always dragged, particularly when I had to read Homer aloud to my tutor with the original pronunciation and rhythm.

"No, no, no!" he would bellow at me. "Will you pay attention, Nicholas? This is Agamemnon's most important speech, you dolt!" clouting me around the ear at the same time for good measure.

I tried to plead with my father, but to no avail. He wanted his son to be better educated than he. And so it was that I grew up schooled in the Classics while he remained an untutored countryman who through native resourcefulness and hard work had become wealthy. Yes, by any standards of the market place he was a successful businessman.

It hadn't always been like that. He had been born into relative poverty in a small hamlet outside Patara where his parents, my grandparents, had been basket-makers. They used the willow wands from the trees growing in the marshlands down by the river to make hampers and carriers for the commercial markets in the city. I never knew them; they died relatively young, having not really advanced. But through contacts, my father was apprenticed to a family of perfume makers who lived in the upper city. He was given all the menial jobs, like spending hours and hours on end picking rock-roses on the mountainside, or filling sacks with wild jasmine which could be boiled to extract the essence to make scent.

And that's how he got into the incense business. At first it was restricted to bleeding the terabinth trees which grew on the slopes above the river which he did for himself while he was collecting the flowers his employers wanted. He had to slash the bark with a sharp knife, a difficult task as the bark was hard and rough. He then had to wait a few days for the tiny beads of resin to ooze out of the cut and dry into hard little droplets, at which point he prised them off the tree into a waiting bowl. It was really back-breaking work, up early each morning and out on the hillsides finding the right trees to cut. He would spend every evening gathering his meagre harvest and sorting through the glaucous pellets, cleaning off any dust or flies that had got stuck to their surface until well after dark. It did not sell for a huge price down in the market. It was a much cheaper option than, say, frankincense. But he sold enough of it that slowly he began to make a substantial living. The advantage was that it didn't need processing, like the oils and unguents the perfume makers produced. He just needed a lot of it, which took all the spare time and effort he could put into it.

The day came when he felt he could go it alone, so he said farewell to the perfume business and set out on his own. Everyone wanted incense. They burnt it in braziers around the house to ward off evil spirits (and to disguise the household smells that hung around the rooms!) It was used in a prayerful way in the smaller temples, 'to ascend to the gods,' to placate their senses. And most importantly it was burned at every funeral, to enable the person's spirit to lift with it to the heavens, or so everyone believed. My father didn't care one way or the other, so long as people went on buying his little bags of dried resin. And the smell it exuded while it was smouldering was quite pleasant, I suppose. I was brought up with it so I can't really say I liked or loathed it. But it put food on the table and I didn't think anything about it.

Gradually, with hard work and long hours my father amassed quite a sizable amount. I never saw any of it when I was growing up. He always retained that village cunning with which he had been born and kept his cards very close to his chest and his gold well out of sight, suspecting everyone. My mother died when I was born which had made my father somewhat reclusive, so I knew little of his business affairs. Whilst I was a child he remained single, but once I had reached manhood he changed. Having come from such poverty, I think he needed someone to appreciate just how well he had done over the years. So, when I was at the end of my teens, he took a much younger wife.

He was already quite an old man by then, but Calista, the woman he married, was almost the same age as me. She was a country girl from up the Valley and my father had been prevailed upon to marry her by his friend and kinsman, Eugenios, a farmer from near Pinara. She was no doubt very pretty, but I was concerned that she didn't seem to have an idea in her head except how to present herself as the new wife of a wealthy man. She seemed solely interested in her hair and appearance and how much money she could spend on clothes, so I didn't have much to do with her. She had rustic good-looks, curvaceous and coquettish, and I think my father thought he could dress her up and make her his mascot, his mannequin who would demonstrate that he'd made something of his life after all that struggle. He could afford to show her off as an emblem, a symbol of the elevation in society he'd achieved.

She wasn't the least interested in befriending me. I was just an appendage that my father brought with him, something she'd have to put up with, so we rarely spoke. At meal-times I tended to eat in silence and at other times in the house she was too busy ordering our maid Irene around to care about me and what I might be doing. Irene on the other hand was a city girl who had earned her manumission from slavery and she felt harassed by this jumped-up village hoyden, but she couldn't say anything. Irene used to tell me quietly how miserable she felt, being bossed around by this nobody. When she wasn't doing that, Calista spent her time flirting with Chronos, a strapping young man who was my father's apprentice. I often heard them giggling together in the tablinum, our dining room, when my father was out haggling prices in the market.

"That Chronos is up to no good!" Irene would say. "He's far too interested in Calista, if you ask me. Your father should watch out for him."

But I felt unable to speak to him about it. To him I was only ever someone who would know nothing of the trials and pitfalls of married life. So I kept quiet and just watched and listened. One afternoon, I must have been in my early twenties, I came back early from the city. The sky was a bit overcast that day and there was a storm brewing out at sea. The harbour had shut up shop early against the bad weather, so there wasn't much going on. I was in the atrium at home and I heard voices the other side of the tablinum door.

“Oh, Chronos, take me with you.” It was Calista’s voice, pleading with Chronos in a cajoling voice. “I know you’re going to leave soon and you know I love you, don’t you? I don’t want the old man; he’s nothing to me. And listen, I can get his gold. I know where he keeps it. We can go far away from here and start a new life together, away from all this.”

The mention of gold seemed to have a galvanizing effect on Chronos. His usually sour attitude changed and he became obviously very interested in Calista’s proposition.

“Listen,” he said quietly, “don’t say such things out loud! Alright, I am going far away if you must know. I’ve got passage on a ship arranged. If you can get the gold, you can come with me, right? The ship’s leaving in two days’ time. Do you think you can do it in time?”

“I’m certain. I know just where he’s hidden it. He doesn’t think anyone knows. But I’ve seen where he puts it. I’ll get it, for sure!”

They made to leave the tablinum and I faded into another room so that they wouldn’t know I was there. I thought for a while, but I knew I had to tell my father. He would be furious at me for interfering, but I didn’t have any other option. So when he came home that evening, I suggested that I knew where he kept his money hidden and maybe others knew too. Did he think that it was such a safe place? As I expected he was not pleased, but I could see he gave the matter some thought. I had no idea where he'd actually hidden it, but hoped he would react to what I'd said. I couldn't do much more. Maybe he already suspected something was going on between Calista and Chronos. Maybe he'd heard talk about it, or he'd already felt something untoward was going to happen. Anyway, I'd done my bit. It was up to him.

As it transpired he did do something.

I learned later he had kept his gold pieces in a number of stout linen bags behind loose bricks in a soak-away just outside the kitchen. It seems that he took them out that night and replaced them with similar bags full of broken mosaic tiles from the garden at the back of the house. Where he then hid his hoard instead I didn't find out until after he died.

CHAPTER TWO

COMPLEXITIES OF THE EMPIRE

Chronos and Calista disappeared together that weekend, quitting our house without a word and leaving my father alone with me and our maid Irene. They took my father's business books with them, with all the names of his contacts overseas, the people to whom he sold incense.

My father found out more of what happened after the pair had left by asking his friends in the port. They said that they had seen the two run-aways speaking to a Rhodian sea captain in one of the wine shops and had gone aboard his ship the same afternoon. An hour or so later the gangs pulled on the ropes and the ship was warped out of the harbour and with sails raised it made off around the headland into the gathering dusk to travel towards the open sea. The heavily laden craft must have tacked along the mountainous coast of southern Lycia in the strong winds and effectively no-one from Patara ever saw her again.

It was perhaps six months later that we heard more about the fate of that ship and its passengers. It must have sailed through the night, because the following morning some villagers down the coast to the east of us said they saw it pass near Bird Island

and on towards the Great Cape some twenty miles away. It was tacking near a low rocky promontory which protruded aggressively from the mainland off its starboard beam. The boat reached towards it, but as it drew close to bear away from its cliffs a fiercely treacherous gust of wind from the high Lycian mountains must have caught the little vessel, because she span around and her stern cracked against the crags of the Cape. As the planking tore open, the heavy cargo must have dragged the hull beneath the waves because she sank instantly, seemingly with nearly all the crew. In a blizzard of expelling air bubbles, she would have plummeted downwards and presumably have come crashing to rest on the steeply shelving rocks deep below the surface.

As far as was ever discovered, there was only one survivor, a badly injured deck hand who told them what had happened. They had been carrying two passengers, so he had explained, a man and a woman, who had sat sullenly on the deck all night. Sometime after dawn the man had asked the woman for something from the bags she was carrying. She rummaged about in one of her baskets and had taken out one of number of small cloth sacks. She handed it to the man with a satisfied grin and he untied the closure strings and poured the contents carefully into his lap. It was a strange thing, said the seaman. The sack contained what appeared to be pieces of dusty old tesserae, used mosaic tiles, of no particular value. The sight of them had made the man so angry he began acting like a maniac. He hurled the tiles into the sea and stormed off to the stern of the ship where the captain was manning the steering oars during the difficult passage in what were really contrary and strong winds around the rocky promontory.

He shouted at the captain, telling him he had to turn the ship around there and then and sail back to Patara. A ferocious argument ensued followed by a certain amount of pushing and shoving. Suddenly, the seaman said, the man hurled the captain down onto the deck. He seized the steering oars and yanked them furiously in the opposite direction. As the ship lurched violently in response to this untoward movement, a particularly powerful down-draught struck the vessel beam on and forced it backwards against the Cape. The captain recovered his feet, but it was too late. With a terrifying splintering the stern planking was ripped out by the jagged rocks and the ship sank almost immediately. As the foaming waters surged into the vessel no one would have stood a chance, he estimated. As far as he knew, the ship and the others on board were lost. He had banged his head, sending him semi-conscious and it was hours later that he came to, washed up on the shore. He was so badly injured by the tragedy though that he didn't survive more than a day or two, the villagers said. They buried him on the outskirts of their little settlement.

My father seemed particularly satisfied by this account and retold it more than once to anyone who would listen as a cautionary tale of betrayal and retribution, his faithless wife receiving her just desserts. He was rather old fashioned that way, believing in a sort of primitive divine justice, and who was I to contradict him? But he changed for the better in some ways after that. Perhaps it was his release from such a fickle and feckless young wife that did it. Or maybe it was the fact that he had narrowly saved his fortune from the clutches of his deceitful and grasping apprentice, but whatever the reason, he became more circumspect, much more careful in some ways but more adventurous in others.

* * * * *

He'd been toying for some time with the idea of expanding his incense business into a more expensive product – maybe another aromatic, perhaps myrrh bark or even frankincense. In our city there wasn't too much call for frankincense; it was too expensive for most of the establishments that made used of aromatics. But elsewhere he knew it was used in substantial quantities, especially in Rome, where all the major temples burned frankincense as often as they could afford to. It was his old friend and drinking partner Eugenios who tried to swing the balance in favour of branching out into a new line. He'd been in Rome once some years ago and had witnessed first-hand the vast amounts that were used there.

They were sharing a pitcher of red wine in our garden one evening the following summer when Eugenios became quite enthusiastic about it.

"Have you any idea how much of this they buy, Aquila? Tons and tons of it! Do you know that during the reign of the emperor Trajan, the Roman tax collectors became so upset with the amount of money that was being wasted on frankincense they actually got the colonial service to intervene and reroute the traffic from the east to a different route just so that they could collect taxes from it. They actually built an enormous road south from Bostra, the capital city of our Syrian province, just to police its movement. It must have cost them a fortune."

My father was not especially impressed by this. It was too long ago to be relevant. But Eugenios went on.

"And do you know how much they still spend on this frankincense every year? Well, I heard that at the last count it was over a hundred million sesterces. That represents a quarter of the money that Rome spends every year, on anything! It's truly staggering. And that's only in Rome. Imagine if you add all the other cities of the empire!"

"Yes, yes!" replied my father. "But believe me the sale of frankincense is all tightly sewn up. I know it can be hugely profitable, but there are some very well established firms in the market and they control the whole thing. There's a family from the port of Brindisium, Julinianus I think they are called, and they negotiate the lion's share of whatever frankincense is sold anywhere in Italy. And in any case, I heard that the bulk of their cargo doesn't travel by sea. It's transported by land, right across Asia Minor and then from Byzantium along the Via Egnatia through Philippi and Macedonia and over the Illyrian Mountains to Dyrrachium before the family carries it in their own ships to Brindisium. They then carry it on their own carts by road to Rome. We'd never get a look in here in Patara, even if we could find a source for it. We're too far out of the way."

He sighed as he thought back to his own trade that he'd built up with the cheaper local terebinth resin.

"There is a small local market for frankincense. It's all handled by a family in Telmessos up in western Lycia. I met them once and I know they make a good living from it. But again, it's tied up tight. I wouldn't know where to start."

He more or less dismissed the whole idea, before he continued, "It's an interesting thing Eugenios that I don't know exactly where it comes from, this frankincense. It's somewhere very far away, from the other side of the great deserts of Arabia, so people tell me. And the very best quality comes from even further away, somewhere in Africa or even further afield, beyond the edge of the known world. I've never met anyone who has ever seen where it originates. Strange isn't it? I don't even know if it's gathered in the same way as my terebinth resin, from a tree and if so what kind of tree. And how come it grows in the desert? There's so much I don't understand about it."

But Eugenios was in his cups by now and he wouldn't let the matter rest. He took a large quaff of his wine.

"You should go and see the family in Telmessos, Aquila. Why don't you go and ask them where it comes from? They're Lycians like you and me after all and when they know you're in the incense business I'm sure you'll have a lot to talk about. Who knows, they may even open up and let you into a few of their secrets?"

My father gave a shrug and there for the moment the matter rested. But even if Eugenios had not managed to impress my father, he had sown a seed in my mind and I thought a lot about it over the coming years.

* * * * *

My father was considered to be moderately wealthy by now and as I entered my adult life he felt he owed something to the city which had given him his livelihood. So when someone from the Pataran trade association came to him to ask him if he would stand for election to the boulé, the city council, I think he felt it his civic duty to accept. We had a magnificent bouleterion in our city where the council met once or twice a week. It was not too far from the harbour, next to the great theatre, and my father spent many an hour there talking over the neighbourhood's business, everything from town drains to state expenditure. I'm not sure how much he contributed to the more lively debates, but he was very active when it came to port tariffs or import taxes. He drew up long lists of these that the harbour authorities used when trading ships came in from other countries.

I had been drawn into the incense trade since I'd come of age. I remember when I had reached twenty-one, my father had said to me, "You know, Nicholas, you're already in your twenties. It's time you were thinking of a job, something where you can earn your daily bread for a change. You're grown up now and should be preparing for the world. How would you like to join me in the incense trade?"

I said at the time that I wasn't really sure but did he think I would be any good at it? I had become quite bookish of late and enjoyed my studies of the Greek and Latin classics. But it wasn't an enquiry. It was more by way of a demand.

"Yes," he had continued, "you should take yourself off to our warehouse by the harbour and see old Eurymachus there, our storeman. He'll show you the ropes and tell you what's what. You know most of it already; you've been there often enough over the years. I told him the other day to expect you. You could start tomorrow."

So that's how I'd got involved. From then on, day after day, I would go down through the city by the old familiar streets to the sea and the storage building where my father kept all his supplies. He didn't go out into the country much these days, except to inspect the trees and select the best ones. Most of the cutting and harvesting was done by farmers he'd recruited. Every few weeks Eurymachus would organise a cart to do the rounds of the various farms to collect the dried pellets of terebinth resin, which would then be graded and packaged back in our warehouse. It was all very straightforward really. Over the years he had refined the system so it worked mechanically. There was nothing to it, apart from making sure our main clients were regularly supplied – the various temples in the city and some of the bigger villas up at the top of the town who engaged in elaborate rituals for their family gods. And there were the undertakers who needed the incense for their funerals. If it was an expensive ceremony, they would use quite a lot of our resin, both in the house of the deceased and in the necropolis when the body was being interred.

The job that I did turned out to be not particularly taxing, just keeping the books in order and making sure the incense was properly graded and packed. Eurymachus was 'front of house,' as it were, looking after the customers when they came to place their orders. He loved drinking sage tea with the older men who came to the warehouse. They used to sit outside in the sunshine under an awning discussing the world for hours at a time. Now and again my father would come down to the warehouse and after a cursory look around would join Eurymachus and his friends in the shade, watching the general commerce of the harbour and the city pass up and down the quayside. I was paid very little at first, whilst I was 'learning on the job,' though I'm sure my father knew there was very little to learn.

* * * *

Politically, where we were on the south-west coast of Lycia very little really happened. Nominally we came under the Governor of Asia, but he rarely if ever deigned to visit our part of his province. He was mainly interested in the really wealthy cities like Ephesus and Miletus on the west coast. We were rather too far away, or perhaps it was because we were surrounded by high mountains, locked away in our own world. We heard about all kinds of goings on in Rome. We had plenty of ships passing through and sailors being what they were they'd make for the wine shops along the harbour front and after a few cups of the local vintage would soon open up and tell us what was happening in the rest of the empire. We heard endless scare-mongering stories of ordinary soldiers being made emperor by their own legions, taking the imperial purple, only to be assassinated a few months later by their officers, or at least imprisoned by the magistrates and never heard of again.

Our newest emperor had only recently been appointed and was yet another soldier who went by the name of Diocletian. It seems he too had risen through the ranks of the legions like all the others and had finally been proclaimed emperor by his own men. I would have thought it was a fairly risky business, accepting such a position after so many years of uprisings and insurrections, however powerful he might have felt. There had been more than twenty of these so-called emperors in just the last few years. But Diocletian had survived almost ten months already, which was longer than most of the others and he was strengthening his grip on power, that's what everybody who knew the labyrinthine ways of Rome told us.

Interestingly, Diocletian didn't come from Italy. He was a Dalmatian from the city of Salona, the Roman provincial capital on the Adriatic coast, but he knew how to order his soldiers about so I expect that is how he had survived this far. He was 'army' through and through and had made his name in the cavalry, though one or two of the officers who called in at Patara said he wasn't just a good horseman but a very able and imaginative administrator too. He would need to be, with the empire in such disarray. The Persians, as ever, were threatening its borders in the east, along the valley of the Tigris River. This whole region was always one with which Rome had problems. Only recently, just before Diocletian's accession, a previous emperor, Aurelian, had granted a city called Palmyra, located in the middle of the Syrian Desert between the Orontes and the Euphrates, a favoured status with Rome. They were considered to be the most powerful ally the armies had in the east and they had acted as a buffer against the Persians.

Even they had rebelled against Rome and Palmyra's warrior queen Zenobia and her family actually had created their own 'empire' by declaring independence and seizing Egypt and its riches as their own. Aurelian swiftly and brutally dealt with the uprising and with Zenobia, who was captured and ignominiously dragged off the Rome, some said in golden chains. Alas that left the empire's eastern flank directly exposed to the rapacious appetites of Persia again and upon Diocletian's accession it was once more a major problem he had to try to alleviate. There were other rebellions too. Peoples from beyond the Rhine in the west to the Lower Danube on the borders of Dacia and from the Nile Valley in the south to Pontus, north of Asia Minor, were becoming restive, eager to rid themselves of what they considered the dead hand of Roman rule, not to mention wanting to be relieved of the taxes that they were all paying to Rome. You could fully understand their point of view. Tax collectors were forcibly levying dues on people which were ostensibly to pay for the Roman army to protect them, when in point of fact the legions were there to keep them in check in the first place. It must all have been very provoking.

I'm told that it slowly became clear to Diocletian that the essence of the problem was that the empire was too unwieldy for one man to rule. It had been running now for some three hundred years and had grown into a vast hydra, a multi-headed monster. Too many people, too many languages, too many different tribes and far too much taxation! Everybody was ready to complain about that part of the Roman administration. Being a tax collector in one of these outlandish areas can't have been a happy experience, with local people ready to do away with you as soon as they were able. Diocletian's solution to this problem of far flung peoples and restive tribes was incredible in some ways. He decided to divide the empire into two and his way of doing it was to appoint an emperor of the west, someone called Maximian, while he himself remaining emperor of the east. He had thus created what I suppose you could call a diarchy, a rule by two monarchs, in the hope that each side could bring their own sphere of influence into line. It wasn't hard to see the risks inherent in this kind of thinking, namely that the empire could so easily just split in two, or worse, that a civil war would break out and countless innocent people would be caught up in the ensuing catastrophe.

On the other hand, you had to admire Diocletian for trying to stabilize the empire after decades of what most people had come to regard as virtual anarchy. From that perspective, it was a very bold move. And it seemed to work. Maximian for his part took his legions and set off to quell rebellions along the Rhine whilst Diocletian, with only the east to worry about, turned his attention again to the ever present problems of the eastern frontier in Mesopotamia and the preying ambitions of the egregious Persians again.

His military grasp of the problems of ruling such a disparate group of people was without doubt his strong point. Rome had endured the indignity of their so-styled favoured ally, Palmyra, turning coat on the arrangement, declaring independence from Rome and taking control of all the trade routes which crossed the Syrian Desert from the Euphrates River to the Great Sea. Although Aurelian had quashed that ambition and left Palmyra virtually paralyzed, Diocletian could see the sense in re-establishing good relations with Palmyra's desert city dwellers. They were Arabs basically and certainly it seems they had no love of the Persians and their duplicitous subterfuge, so it was not difficult to bring them back under a Roman banner of friendship again.

Palmyra was once described to me as a great city. It was a thriving caravanserai on the road across the desert, but it was also a classical wonder, with long colonnaded streets, theatres and temples. It sat right in the middle of a never-ending, parched plain, but it was built around a large perennial spring surrounded by palm groves. It apparently looked very striking, as you came upon it with your caravan after several days in the aridity and bleakness of the trade route up from Babylonia. Quite suddenly you reached Palmyra's green oasis surrounded by the ultra-sophistication of an eastern Roman metropolis. I've heard people say it's an incredible experience. The people are in no way Romans and nor are they even Greeks. They have eccentric traditions and worship a variety of strange gods. Their chief one is called "Bel" for instance.

Diocletian reopened negotiations with them and re-established political ties with the population there, but to make sure there was no back-sliding or any return to secessionist ambitions, he built a large military camp right on the edge of the city so that the Palmyrenes might feel safe on the one hand and on the other to ensured that there was an army presence embedded among the population so that they couldn't break away again even if they wanted to. It was a clever ploy. The military movements in and around Palmyra also had the effect of intimidating the Persians from trying any under-hand anti-Roman negotiations with the population there.

So, that was where we were by the time I reached my early thirties; the empire had re-stabilized. Rome was in control, though in two halves. Actually, shortly after that Diocletian went one stage further in his reorganisation. He appointed two sub-emperors as understudies to his diarchy, two figures to whom he gave the title "Caesar." In the west, the emperor Maximian was understudied by the Caesar Constantius

Chlorus, Constantius the Pale, whilst in the east, he appointed Galerius as his own Caesar. The result was the tetrarchy, the rule by four. I would have thought this would have been disastrous for the future of the empire, ambition being what it was, but strangely it worked, for a few years anyway.

There was an innate logic in his division. I suppose you could say the western half of the Roman Empire was more Latin in its thinking and the eastern half, where we lived, was more Greek. Patara had always been a Greek city really, although deep down we thought of ourselves as Lycians. The Greek way of life had spread all over the east after Alexander had destroyed Cyrus' and Darius' old Persian empire some six hundred years ago and I imagine you could consider us the remnant of that empire and by now we were Greek in every aspect of our way of life and we were very proud of it too.

And it was into that Greek half of the Roman Empire that a new religion had appeared, one which believed in one God and in the son of God, Jesus. It was a religion based on kindness and comradeship, on love and togetherness and especially on forgiveness and salvation. It was called Christianity and although Diocletian was to try desperately to destroy it and its adherents, in the end it was to change our established world mightily and for ever and no-one was more affected by that change than me.

CHAPTER THREE

GOING TO SEA

My father made a habit of going down to the council meetings at whatever time of day they were held and in whatever weather. He took his civic responsibilities very seriously and hated missing the debates, even though he rarely actually contributed much to the discussion. It was one winter a year or two later that the boulé convened in the afternoon and their session continued until after dark. It was cold that season and a heavy snow had fallen early on the highlands either side of the Xanthos Valley. The winter wind whistled off the mountain peaks gripping Patara with a chilly and lashing rain which made everyone who didn't need to go out to stay huddled indoors over their fires.

My father was hurrying back after the meeting through the sleet which was driving across the agora, our city market place, when he lost his footing on the slippery paving stones and fell heavily on his side. He must have cracked his head too because when the night watchmen found him he was barely conscious. They recognised him and managed to get a stretcher party to bring him back to our house where we put him straight to bed. He was shivering uncontrollably and uttering low groans indicating he was in pain. We piled sheep skins on the bed in an attempt to warm him up and our maid Irene called for a doctor who gave my father a sleeping draught. After that he fell into a fitful sleep and we took it in turns to sit with him through the night. At first his breathing was fairly regular but as dawn broke it became laboured.

When he eventually opened his eyes he looked so piteous in the winter light slanting through the window and he clearly had a fever. He was racked with spasmodic bouts of coughing which caused him to convulse with pain and these fits had worsened by the afternoon. The doctor looked in again in the early evening and stayed with him for some time. When he came out to Irene and me waiting in the next room his face looked grave.

"I'm afraid your father is not at all well Nicholas," he intoned. "He's quite a grand age and his constitution has been getting steadily weaker as the years have gone by. He took a very nasty knock yesterday; I fear he's broken some ribs. He has blood in his spittle from what I suspect is internal bleeding. There's not much I can do except alleviate the pain and I've given him another strong sleeping draught. I think you should prepare yourself for the worst."

Alas he was all too right. Irene and I watched my father go downhill over the next couple of days, slowly losing consciousness in what was a spreading infection. So it was on the evening of the third day that he gradually slipped away from us and by midnight gave up the ghost and died. He had looked so ill just before the final crisis, but after he had passed away he appeared strangely peaceful. The pained expressions on his face and his deeply furrowed forehead gave way to a serene quietness. We had few relatives to inform, just a couple of cousins in one of the outlying villages, so over the next twenty-four hours we made plans to bury him.

Irene was a tower of strength to me at this time and although she must have been equally upset that her master had left us, she kept her composure and arranged all the funerary rituals as well as the actual interment. It was late one afternoon the following week that she suggested she would like to take me to meet a friend of hers. Wrapping up against the biting wind, we walked down to the market place and up into the part of the city which overlooks the sea, the quarter which I didn't know very well where the better-off citizens had their villas. Walking along one of the uppermost streets we came to the gate of what looked to be the residence of a wealthy family. Irene tugged the bell pull and after a minute or two a powerfully built young man came down to see who was there. He peered through the metal railings before smiling and unlocking the gate to let us in.

He led us through the front door of the villa and ushered us into the vestibule. Beyond this was a large internal pillared atrium, made up of a four-sided veranda surrounding a garden where there were shrubs encircling a shallow pool with a small fountain playing. The man indicated we should pass into one of the side rooms of the villa and wait. The room was surprisingly simply decorated and furnished, as I looked around for any signs of who might be the owner. A couple of oil lamps on stands which had recently been lit in the room gave off a soft glow as we waited, but for what or for whom I had no notion. Irene squeezed my hand and smiled comfortingly.

After a few minutes an august gentleman with a flowing beard and dressed in an expensive white toga came into the room. He went over to Irene and kissed her on both cheeks before he turned to me and said, "So this is your master's son, Irene? A fine looking man I must say. Welcome to our home Nicholas. I make you indeed welcome in God's name. Please, take a seat and let's talk a moment."

We sat opposite him as he composed himself.

"I was sorry to hear of your father's demise, Nicholas. Aquila was a fine citizen and he certainly did his duty to this city of ours. My only regret is that I didn't know him better. But he was not one of our number, you see and I'm sure you'll understand that we do have to keep ourselves fairly discreet."

I wondered to what he was alluding, until I noticed on the blank wall behind him there was a small wooden device with the Greek letters Xhi Rho intertwined and realised it was a

Christian symbol, the first two letters of the name 'Christos.' This was a Christian household and this dignified gentleman was obviously someone of considerable importance in their sect.

"Irene," he suggested, "shall we pray now?" Putting his hands together and bowing his head, he waited a moment and then in the stillness of that room he asked God's blessings upon us all.

"Lord Jesus," he began, "have mercy upon us gathered here and we ask a blessing on Aquila, the dear departed. May his immortal soul find eternal peace. And we pray especially for ourselves and for this our brother Nicholas whom Irene has brought here today. May God's love protect and keep him and may he find his calling in this tempestuous world of ours."

Then raising his hand in benediction, he continued, "May the love of God and the grace of our Lord Jesus Christ bless us all and may he keep us in his eye in our hour of need. May we go out into the world in peace, rendering to no one evil for evil, but let us hold fast to those things that are good. Amen."

With that he stood and drawing Irene to him kissed her again and came over to me and kissed me too.

"May God's blessing be upon you wherever you go, Nicholas."

And after a moment, he indicated we should leave. Outside once more, the gate shut behind us and we walked quietly down the street and back to the centre of the city. Irene didn't say a word about what had just happened and it wasn't until we got back to our own house that I plucked up courage.

"Who was that gentleman, Irene?" I asked.

"That was Nicodemus, one of the elders in our church in Patara. I hope I did the right thing taking you to meet him. He is a wonderful inspiration to us. You see, I have been a Christian for some years now and we generally meet in Nicodemus' villa for our eucharist. That's the meal we share to commemorate the death of our Lord Jesus Christ, who was crucified by the Romans over two hundred years ago and who died to save us all. We are small in number, but we are growing every day."

I was impressed that she had kept her counsel about her beliefs for so long without confiding in me or my father.

"They are like a great family to me, you see Nicholas. They are always there to help, never to criticize. They have become my reason to live, my guiding light. And I am sure they will support me now that my job is finished in this house."

"But why, Irene? Why are you thinking of leaving? I am still here and you know how to run the household. Please don't go. Stay with me and look after the house. I haven't got anyone else."

So it was arranged that Irene would stay on as the *mater familias* and minister to me and manage whatever needed doing in the house. I was most grateful to her, being otherwise now all alone in the world.

Sometime later my father's old friend Eugenios came to call, to offer his condolences and to ask me what I intended to do now.

"So, will you continue to run the business down at the harbour? You know that Eurymachus can manage the whole thing on his own, don't you? He doesn't really need you there. I don't know why you don't go travelling, get some experience of the world, try new places and meet new people? You need to broaden your horizons a bit, not stay here bogged down in Patara. Whenever I spoke to your father I told him he should diversify into other trading commodities, get into some other aromatics like frankincense. I know Aquila wasn't too keen on the idea. He could see all the obstacles, trade tariffs and monopolies. Maybe he was too old, too set in his ways. But you're still young. Anyway, why don't you travel a bit and see if you can get any new ideas, maybe from Europe, or even from Africa."

With that, rather conspiratorially he showed me where my father had kept his hoard of gold pieces.

"See Nicholas, you're a wealthy man now, but there is so much you haven't seen yet. It would be a great experience for you. Just take off and get some notion of what the rest of the world is about."

Over the next few days I thought a lot about what Eugenios had said. I'd spent all my life in Patara. I didn't really know the world at all and as he rightly had pointed out, the business was virtually self-sufficient. Eurymachus could manage it single-handedly and Irene was perfectly capable of running the house on her own. Yes, I thought, maybe I should go travelling. I went down to the harbour one morning to talk to Eurymachus. He was deep in conversation with a newly-docked sea captain. They were talking about prices and politics, as usual. Eurymachus introduced me. The captain's name was Polios and he came from the island of Cyprus. He had been in Patara only a couple of nights and was due to set sail again at the weekend for Egypt.

When I showed a lot of interest in where he was going, he rather jokingly asked, "Why, are you thinking of coming with me?"

"Yes," I replied quite suddenly. "Yes, I would rather like to join you on your journey. Do you have any space? How much would it cost? When exactly are you thinking of leaving?"

"Look, you don't need to pay me. Just come for the excitement. I'll be casting off the day after tomorrow soon after dawn. If you can organise yourself by then, you can come with us. How would that be?"

Irene and I talked over dinner that evening and again the following morning. As it became clearer I was going to travel to the east and to the valley of the Nile, she became more and more animated.

"Do you know, you will be travelling near the places our Lord Jesus was when he was alive? I wonder whether you'll visit some of them. Oh, Niko, I would love to see such places, like Bethlehem, where our Lord was born, where he preached and Jerusalem where he was crucified and entombed then rose from the dead. We believe he was crucified and buried and that three days later he rose again and conquered death for our sake. That is how we have been saved from the clutches of the evil one and can attain everlasting life. If you only knew how wonderful this news is for us and all who believe in him! It makes us all into new men and women, in his name."

I didn't really understand the principle of this faith as Irene described it to me, but there was no mistaking her enthusiasm and the light in her eyes. She was almost ecstatic as she described the mystery which she experienced and the love that she so clearly felt in her heart. I was very moved by her sincerity; she was obviously a true believer. It was strange to think that she'd been part of this Christian movement for some years without any of us knowing about it.

But I had heard that the Christians were a somewhat secretive band and I understood that this was because they kept everything hidden to exclude outsiders from being admitted to their religious practices. I didn't appreciate just how vulnerable they all felt in the uncertain political climate of the empire and the upheavals in Rome with its overbearing emphasis on the cult of the divine emperor and the new obsession with the worship of *Sol Invictus*, the invincible sun which currently dominated every town and city. It was such an overpowering craze, but for me it totally lacked any inspiration. It didn't answer the questions that were in most people's minds, questions about life and death, good and evil or fear of the unknown. For me, it was all a bit Roman and as such rather too wooden.

After our mid-day meal the next day, and I had made provision for Irene, I spent the afternoon getting some things together for the journey – clothes, shoes and some gold pieces from my father's hiding place. When I said I was leaving Eurymachus had told me the names of a few traders in Alexandria, our main port of call in Egypt, upon whom I could rely if I needed any help. It was good to know that our family name counted for something even in such a far off and foreign place. I spent my last evening at home looking through the few books Eugenios had lent me to see if I could find out anything about where I was going, otherwise I was about to launch myself into the unknown. It was exciting and daunting and I got little sleep that night turning the whole journey over in my mind, without knowing anything about it.

Just after day-break I bade a sorrowful farewell to Irene, who hugged me and cried as though she was never going to see me again. I tried to comfort her by saying I was only going away for a few months, not for ever, but she was inconsolable. To lose my father and me in the space of only a few weeks must have been very difficult and unsettling for her. But I was eager to be off. If I was going to go, it had to be now. I tore myself away from her and set off down our street, waving at the corner before walking quickly, bag in hand, down to the harbour to meet Captain Polios. I found the ship where it had been moored the previous day. The seamen were getting her ready to sail, but they said I still had about half an hour or so, so I went across the quay to a small stall selling fresh wheat cakes and rather watery tea and for a few coins enjoyed my last breakfast in Patara.

"Going anywhere nice Nicholas?" asked the stall keeper.

"Egypt," I replied, full of a confidence I certainly didn't feel.

"Well, enjoy the experience! I've heard it's very different from here, very Greek in one way, but very foreign and strange in others. You'll come back a totally changed person, I'm sure."

Little did I know just how changed I would be when next I saw my home city. Had I realised just how much I would alter, maybe I would never have started out in the first place. When you are young how can you possibly calculate these things?

Outwardly I felt full of confidence in the future, like all young people. I could do anything, I thought and I mean anything!

I finished my wheat cake and drained the beaker of tea. I walked back to the ship and up the gangplank. I introduced myself to the three crew and a few minutes later the captain arrived with the warping gang and made ready to cast off. The ropes were untied and the gangplank taken inboard, at which point the captain gave the signal to the gang to begin pulling the ship away from the quayside wall. When we had reached the middle of the harbour, the haulage ropes were let go and the crew began to pull the cross spar up the mast until it reached the peak at which point they unfurled the rather patched sail. As Polios gave orders to brail the one side of the sail, the wind caught the other and the little ship started to make way across the harbour towards the mole. It picked up a bit of speed as the captain steered it away and it surged out beyond the harbour wall into the open sea.

As Patara began to fade away into the early morning mist, we sailed around the headland and headed towards the far horizon. My adventure was about to begin and with it, my new life. And what a life that was going to turn out to be.

CHAPTER FOUR

SERVICE IN CYPRUS

For the first two days we sailed close-hauled along the Lycian coast, past the cities of Antiphellos and Myra then across a wide bay as far as Cape Chelidonia where the lofty mountains looked as though they rose almost vertically out of the sea. The winds were kind to us, with none of the katabatic squalls which I'd heard could rip the rigging to pieces and even sink a vessel. From Chelidonia we begán to cross the open sea towards the island of Cyprus. The land gradually receded further and further astern until it finally disappeared altogether and we were alone in a vast expanse of the ocean. I would have been scared witless had I been on my own, but the deck hands seemed to know exactly what was happening and a couple were amusing themselves near the stern playing dice, while another played simple tunes on a pipe he had drawn from his pocket.

That night the sky was clear and a myriad brilliant stars illuminated the heavens until towards dawn a thin moon rose wan and watery from the horizon. The captain explained to me how he navigated by the heavenly bodies, outlining pictures of the signs of the zodiac and a variety of other mythical animals by joining stars together. He pointed out Ursa Major and the North Star, what he called his shepherd star, which enabled him to set a correct course to the west coast of Cyprus. The following afternoon, we could see land ahead in the far distance and the captain confirmed that it was the northwest corner of the island, near an old Phoenician port which had once been a major trading colony centuries ago.

"They were a clever people, the Phoenicians," he said. "They had trading ports all over the Great Sea. But they were odd. They had strange gods and weird beliefs. They disappeared centuries ago after losing their North African capital Carthage to the Romans."

As more of the island became visible, he told me that we would soon be able to see the mountains behind the port of Paphos.

"We'll have to put in there briefly for water. We're running a bit low. And we need some other supplies we won't be able to get once we reach Egypt."

The headlands of the island grew bigger as we approached, green and welcoming in the spring sunshine, until we could finally see the breakwater of the city of Paphos ahead and slightly to the port side. The captain shouted instructions and the little ship veered towards the land and to Paphos itself. It was comforting to know that the captain knew his business, as we cruised around the breakwater and into the secluded waters of the harbour. He ordered the sail to be dropped and then allowed the ship to coast towards the quayside. At the critical moment he directed the stern anchors be thrown over the side and with the ropes slowly paying out he brought the ship to a gentle halt prow-to along the dock wall. A crewman jumped ashore with a rope to make us fast to a bollard on the wharf.

"Did you know that Paphos is the city of Aphrodite?" asked Polios. "The story goes that she came ashore here when she was first born, riding on a wave of foam. There used to be a huge temple to her in the centre of the city. It's gone now, but the idea of the home of the goddess of love still remains. Paphos has some of the best houses of love in the world and many seamen calling in here run off and sample the delights of the local ladies! But Paphos is very much a Christian city too. St Paul, one of the leaders of the early church, came here and is very much revered by the local people. Many pilgrims make the trip to Paphos to see where he stayed. Paul is very important to us Christians", he said.

That was the first time I realised that the captain was an adherent of the Christian faith. I was surprised he was so open about it, but I suppose he felt he knew me and didn't worry too much about keeping it secret.

"I have to go to a house in the middle of the city near the market place. Perhaps you'd like to come with me."

Having nothing better to do I walked down the gangplank after him and we strode purposefully off into the crowds along the quay and down one of the side streets into the city. At first the people of Paphos looked no different to the various nationalities I saw in Patara, but as we walked further into the centre there were some men I'd never seen before, wearing full length dark brown robes and a finely woven head covering held in place by a black head-ring.

"Arabs!" Polios said, seeing me eyeing them with curiosity. "They come from the deserts of the south-east. We'll see a lot more of them in Egypt when we get there."

We turned sharply left into a small alley behind the main market, which I could make out at the end of the street. Pulling me into a doorway Polios knocked quietly on the panelling. After a minute or so the door was opened a crack and an eye appeared, viewing us suspiciously, before it was thrown wide and a huge man stood there beaming at us.

"Polios!" he shouted. "How are you old friend? Come in, come in. You are welcome in Christ's name."

After they had embraced, we were shown into a small shady anteroom opening at the far end onto a small courtyard full of wild flowers growing in pots.

"This is John," said Polios. "He is a very good friend and one of the leaders of our faith here in Cyprus. We have shared many adventures together, both on the island and also in Egypt. This here is my friend Nicholas."

"Have you time to stay for a while?" asked John. "We have a Eucharist service at sundown and we would love you to share it with us."

Seeing my puzzled expression, Polios described what John had meant.

"We share a meal together in our faith, Nicholas, to celebrate the death and resurrection of our Lord. You are very welcome to join us, as an observer. We wouldn't expect you to participate in any way but you would see how sincerely we all believe."

I said I would be pleased to be with them whatever they were doing. We were shown into a large room off the courtyard with benches around the wall and a small table in the middle. After a few minutes more people were admitted, a man and two young women.

"This is Joseph and his two daughters, Esther and Elizabeth," said John. "They live locally and have a stall selling bales of cloth in the market. They have been members of our group for many years. The girls were brought up in the faith."

They acknowledged my presence and greeted Polios warmly, who introduced me as a friend from Patara who was travelling in search of adventure to Egypt. Elizabeth, the elder of the two girls, was a strikingly beautiful woman I supposed to be in her early twenties. She came over and kissed me on both cheeks.

"We make you welcome to our community, Nicholas. The Lord bless and keep you with his protecting hand."

Just then more people arrived, a couple I took to be a man and his wife, as well as two more men in working clothes whom I assumed had come straight from the market. Finally there was a rather distinguished elderly man wearing what looked like an expensive toga, at which point John bade the group to be seated. He signalled to a servant waiting in a side room, who brought in a basket containing a large round loaf of bread and a flask of wine with a beaker. The lad placed them on the table and then sat with everyone else.

John led the prayers which preceded their shared meal. I sat to the side and listened.

"Almighty God, be kindly disposed to we who have done wrong, through deed and word, as we remember the day Jesus called his disciples together in the upper room in Jerusalem on the night before he was tried by Pontius Pilate and then crucified, dying for our sins. He accepted death to give us the hope and blessing for our future."

He paused for a minute or so, head bowed and then he continued, "So Jesus, on the night of the Passover, took bread and broke it before them and handing a portion to each of the twelve he told them that this was his body, broken for them and urged them to take, eat, to remember his death and his passing.

And afterwards, he drank from the cup of wine and passing it to each of them he said that it represented his blood of the new covenant, spilt for them."

With that, John broke the loaf open and gave them all a piece and then sipping from the beaker of wine he had filled from the jug, he passed it around to each of them in turn.

"In as much as we eat of this bread and drink of this wine, we do show the Lord's death till he comes amongst us again."

He went to each person and kissed them on the cheek and then raising his right hand in blessing, he said finally, "Be with us Lord Jesus in our lives, in our waking and in our sleeping. May we bear witness to your goodness to us and prepare us for everlasting life. Amen!"

Then they all bowed their heads in prayer and recited together, "Heavenly father, may your name be sanctified. May your kingdom come and your will be done on earth as in heaven. Give us today our daily bread and release us from our wrong doing, even as we release others who do wrong to us. May we not be tempted today and do not let evil come near to us. For the kingdom is yours."

They all then said "Amen," after which they spent some time in silent reflection. It was very moving in its solemnity and its simplicity and you could feel the uplifting nature of the thoughts that were going through their minds and see on their faces the quietude and calmness that their shared experience had given them. After another minute of contemplative silence, their celebration came to an end. There were a few embraces and hand-shakes before the group began to disburse though the door and back into the city. Elizabeth came over and smiling, spoke to me.

"Well, Nicholas, how did you enjoy that? That is our way of keeping our faith and our beliefs alive. Maybe you would like to join us, if you feel that hunger for the spiritual aspect of your life, that is. Think about it!"

She joined her father and sister and they too went out back into the city, leaving John, Polios and me alone once more.

"May God bless your journey Polios and keep you safe on the sea. I know it's a wild place, but you are used to it I know."

Taking our leave we shook hands with John and walked back to the ship. Polios was deep in thought and I didn't like to disturb him, but I had so many questions about what I had just seen. Why did this disparate group of people feel so much joy together in such a simple ceremony? What was the story of this man Jesus? When had it all happened and why did someone who was crucified have such enormous significance to people in so many cities of the empire, in so many walks of life? I was determined to ask Polios once we had set sail again.

We left at dawn the following morning and sailed into a sprightly breeze which drove us out into the open sea. Polios' navigational skills were outstanding. He determined his course by watching the position of the rising sun and as it climbed the sky he adjusted his bearing accordingly. It was as though the ship was drawn unwaveringly towards its destination, which I already knew was to be the great city of Alexandria, one of the most important and certainly the largest of our Great Sea.

"You will find Alexandria quite over-whelming," warned Polios. "It is so large and cosmopolitan you will come across every species of humanity there. You've got people of every colour and creed you can imagine. And the ideas bound up within the city walls are legion. It's probably the most sophisticated place I've ever been. It has endless teaching colleges, philosophy schools, religious seminaries and commercial buildings and every commodity imaginable is sold there."

"But probably the most outstanding thing," he continued after a pause, "at least for us seamen, is the lighthouse. You've probably heard about it, but until you see it you can have no idea what to expect. It's absolutely huge and will be the landmark we'll aim for. Oh and another thing, Alexandria once had the biggest library in the world. At one time they said it had over half a million scrolls. Imagine that, all the books ever written! That's one book for every two citizens! Yes, Alexandria has almost one million people living in the city and the surrounding towns. It's enormous. You can lose yourself there very easily."

I'd heard some of the stories of Alexandria before but Polios was becoming very animated describing to me his version of the city. I found myself getting goose flesh just listening to him. By his reckoning, we'd see the flame from the lighthouse sometime during the night, certainly before dawn. My first real 'overseas' adventure was about to begin.

"Are there Christians in Alexandria?" I asked somewhat naïvely.

"Of course," replied Polios. "It's one of the main centres of our faith. Many of the people in the old Jewish quarter have converted to Christianity. It's much more obvious there. There are meeting houses and debating schools all over the city; you'll see. I'll take you there if you want."

"Yes," I echoed, "I would like that very much. I must declare that after the meeting yesterday I would really like to learn much more about what you believe in and perhaps even become a part of the movement. You all look so dedicated and so happy when you talk about Jesus and his life and what he has done for mankind through his teachings and through his death. That's right isn't it? He died for us all? Yes, I would like to know so much more."

"Are you sure that isn't just because of the lovely Elizabeth?" he said with a knowing grin. "Sorry, I couldn't resist that! But if you'd really like to know more, there are plenty of elders and teachers among our community who would be very willing to tell you about our whole way of existence. There's probably no better place for it. And it's so cosmopolitan you can really appreciate how its universal message embraces the whole world."

The ship sailed on through the afternoon and I sat in the stern watching the wake bubble up below the transom. My mind was racing at the thought of seeing the magnificent city towards which we were sailing, all its fine buildings and its huge population and especially its Christian community. Polios had given me a small book to read about the life of Jesus. It was called 'The Euangelion of Luke,' what Polios had described as the gospel, the good news I suppose you'd translate it. It was an account of what happened over two hundred and fifty years ago. It was in Greek, not the best Greek I'd ever read, but its descriptions were vivid and the teachings very appealing. Jesus had preached his gospel, his good news, to everyone, not just the wealthy or to any specific class of the population, but to everyone, rich and poor, old and young, whole and infirmed.

He had gathered twelve followers around him to be his disciples, the ones who would carry his message to the world. They were not from any didactic group, nor were they philosophers used to the cut and thrust of debate. They were ordinary men - fishermen, country people, even a tax collector named Matthew. To them he gave the good news of hope and good will, of a life that would transcend destruction and death. That was the crux of the Christian message. However uncertain life may be, however bitter and unfair, however hounded people felt by political upheaval, ill health or any of the other human catastrophes which surround us daily, God was there to care for us. He loved us and would see us through. It was an extraordinary claim, especially in such a troubled world as ours. That I quickly realised was what drew people to believe and to flock to the cause in such numbers and with such faith. That was the "good news."

I read parts of the Gospel of Luke several times that night by the light of an oil lamp. I was fascinated by it! I couldn't wait to meet more of the faith in the great city of Alexandria and to hear more of their way of life that they had all chosen. I wanted to be part of it, to absorb it, to participate in this message of expectation.

"Light ahead!" came the cry of a seaman at the prow of the ship just before dawn. "See, the beam of the great lighthouse."

We all peered through the darkness and sure enough, low on the horizon was an orange flame, appearing and disappearing in the gloom of the night. It got brighter and steadier as we continued and it seemed to climb out of the sea as more of the building came into view. This was where we were heading – Alexandria. We looked fixedly on the growing flame from the top of what was eventually going to be the tallest tower I had ever seen. As we got closer I could see it must be over two hundred and fifty cubits high.

“They keep a furnace burning on the top of the tower twenty-four hours a day,” said Polios. “In the old days there was a temple there to Hephaestos, god of the underworld, who was the protector of the flame. It used to be counted as one of the seven wonders of the world of Alexander the Great. No surprise there eh? We’ll be docked in the Great Harbour before mid-day!”

CHAPTER FIVE

INTO THE LIGHT

As Polios had predicted, we came under the shadow of the massive lighthouse of Alexandria and into the Great Harbour about the middle of the morning. The harbour was absolutely vast, with forests of masts clustering around the quaysides. At some point back in Alexander's time they had connected the mainland to the Pharos Island where the lighthouse now stood by means of a huge mole and this had the effect of dividing the intervening channel into two. Eunostis Harbour was on the other side of this man-made isthmus and was used by naval ships – Roman galleys and transport vessels. The wide bay we found ourselves in on this side was divided yet again by a harbour wall which gave extra protection to an inner basin they called Kibotos and this was where we were now heading. A harbour official was shouting instructions to our ship, waving his hands and pointing further inside to a space where we would be able to draw alongside other ships already moored there. After a tricky set of manoeuvres, Polios managed to set the ship beam-on some three ships out from the quay wall and with the help of the crew from the other vessels we made fast to the gunwale of the outermost. We had arrived.

I was anxious to disembark immediately to visit this magnificent city. I could already see the tall obelisks and statues of exotic Egyptian gods set up in the grand squares that surrounded the harbour. But Polios said there were many things that had to be done first. There was much documentation to be completed with the harbour-master, for the ship, for its cargo, which happened to be baulks of timber from the Taurus Mountains behind Patara, and also for the crew, including me. I hadn't thought of that. It wouldn't be until the afternoon that we would be free to go ashore. There were many small jobs to be done on board too, coiling ropes, cleaning the decks, furling the sails and other tasks associated with a sea-going vessel; actually these took up most of the rest of the day. By the time we'd opened the hatches to the hold so that the sawn wooden beams could be examined by the timber merchant who was going to buy them, the sun was already starting its journey to the horizon.

As evening drew on, Polios suggested we walked along the quayside to find a tavern where we could get something to eat and drink. It was then I realised just how tired I was after two or three days at sea with little sleep. We climbed over the other ships and set off around the harbour. It was at once an amazing experience for me. The dockside was thronged with many different nationalities, speaking many languages and dressed in all kinds of clothing – Syrians from the north, from

Bostra and even from as far as the Euphrates valley; local Egyptians from Alexandria and others clearly from further up the Nile; men from the deserts of Arabia, tanned leathery faces and dark-set eyes shaded with head scarves and black-skinned Africans from across the Sahara. It was like nowhere I'd ever seen before. I could hear all manner of languages too, from Arabic, Nabatean and South Arabian to various African tongues and Greek. Everyone seemed to know some Greek, enough to make themselves understood in the bargaining we saw going on all around us. Latin might be the language of the Roman government, but there was no question that Greek was the lingua franca here.

Finding a small wine shop we ordered what turned out to be a goat stew flavoured with turmeric and ginger, spices that had come all the way from India. There were several different varieties of olives and newly-baked flat bread which was delicious. We drank beakers of a local palm wine and finished with some cakes sweetened with honey and topped with almonds. My eyelids felt heavy with the palm wine and I found myself eager to get back to the ship for a good night's rest. On reaching the little vessel I fell into a dreamless sleep until the sun was already quite high in the sky and I was woken by the cries of the street vendors selling fresh bread rings. After sluicing my face in a bucket on the deck, Polios and I set out to explore the city.

The centre of Alexandria had been built on Alexander's orders. It was laid out with broad boulevards in a criss-crossed grid-iron plan, the principal direction being parallel to the Pharos Island and the sea. We walked south away from the harbour along Sema Street, a wide colonnaded road leading into the middle of the city. It was already busy with shopkeepers bringing their produce out onto the shaded verandas and we had to sidle around the piles of goods – metal containers, carpets, coats, fruit and vegetables, personal ornaments and all manner of household items which were displayed on the pavements. Every kind of cart and conveyance was moving on the road between the colonnades and we had to be careful not to step down from the walking area into the open in case we collided with the moving traffic. The noise and the commotion set up a counterpoint to the cries of the shop-owners drawing attention to their merchandise as we edged our way distractedly through the crowds.

After we'd crossed over a few streets inland from the port we reached the city's main street, Canopic Street, which stretched east to west as far as the eye could see. It was huge, an impressively broad thoroughfare which ran the whole breadth of the city. If Sema Street had been busy, Canopic Street was frenzied, with its large and imposing colonnades running away on either side of the street crammed with shops, offices, street cafes and small workshops. The cacophony from the metal workers beating their bowls and buckets, the furniture makers with their saws and chisels and the shouts of the butchers, the bakers and the other stall holders was deafening.

Right the way down the centre of the street ran a narrow canal which effectively divided it into two separate parallel boulevards and also gave some respite from the clangour and business of the city as well as cooling the already heat-filled air. To the west was the Moon gate. We turned eastwards towards the Sun Gate and the Nile Delta. The double roadway was jammed with carts and wagons, piled high with textiles, timber, building stone, everything imaginable. The drivers were pulling and pushing their mules and horses, their oxen and donkeys, jostling with each other as they careered along the carriageways. There were men bent double with carrying frames on their backs, leather belts tight across their foreheads, piled high with boxes and bales, weaving in and out of the various wheeled transports and there were camels, heads held high in the air, loping along through the middle of it all seemingly indifferent to the uproar, huge burdens roped to their humps. It looked chaotic to me, but everyone seemed to know what they were doing and where they were heading.

A little way along the street, on the left, was what must once have been a truly magnificent Ionic building, but it was now roofless and covered with wooden scaffolding.

"That was the *Biblioteca Alexandrina*," said Polios, "the great royal library of Alexandria I told you about. Can you believe it was built over half a millennium ago by Ptolemy Soter, the first Greek king of Egypt who'd been one of Alexander's generals?"

We stopped to look at the frontage, its empty shell still impressive even gutted by fire as it clearly had been. Polios explained to me what had happened to it.

"Julius Caesar had a hand in damaging it some three hundred years ago during Rome's civil war when he set an opposing Roman fleet alight in the harbour and the flames spread to the library. But by far the worst destruction that you see today happened only a few years ago, when it caught fire during the attack on the city by that fool Aurelian when he was emperor. You may remember he had pursued the Palmyrene queen Zenobia's armies across the Syrian Desert and cornered her forces in Alexandria. She had declared Egypt and some portions of Asia Minor to be a part of her empire and for some reason she'd installed her son Valballathus as the regent here which I suppose must have been like a red rag to a Roman bull. As a result Aurelian rampaged across the Nile Delta and just destroyed everything in sight, irrespective of its importance. It was said he deliberately set fire to the library in retaliation for the Palmyrene insult to Rome. Of course, Aurelian blamed the Greeks for the fire, calling it an act of terrorism, as if they'd do that to their own priceless institution. Anyway, it burnt for three days and nights destroying a major part of the collection."

We stood for a moment in silence staring at the gaunt remains.

"As I said, it was once alleged to have contained half a million books and scrolls," he continued, "all the books ever written in fact. They had purchased all the original manuscripts of the plays written by Sophocles, Euripides and Aeschylus, as well as philosophic works by Aristotle and Plato, from the Athenians. They paid a fortune for them and I suppose they were indeed priceless. They had all manner of scientific treaties as well, works on natural history and a huge medical section with the works of physicians like Galen, the doctor who worked at his centre of healing, the Aesclepion at Pergamon. Most of it went up in smoke, though they did manage to salvage some of the papyri and a few of the parchment books. It was an absolute tragedy. Some scholars say it's the worst thing that has ever happened to our civilization. Anyhow, they've started afresh at the old temple of Serapis. It will never be the same. I'm afraid a lot of the writings were absolutely irreplaceable, but it's something at least. You should go and see it sometime while you're here."

I looked in amazement at the blackened carcase that rose from the broken steps. The bare pillars stood up vertically like accusing fingers raised against the blue morning sky, witnesses to the disaster of human greed and barbarism over culture and intelligence. I couldn't imagine how much human skill and knowledge had been lost, thanks to the vaunting ambition of imperial Rome. Aurelian only lasted a year or two after that, until he was murdered, it was said, by his own staff. Well, he went to his death with this terrible catastrophe to his name.

We carried on up the street, stopping from time to time to admire yet another Greek portico. We were walking eastwards passing some very fine buildings lining the way. There was a magnificent temple to the Muses, the nine goddesses of the arts. The marble pillars in front of the porch shone in the sunlight and beyond it, set back from the street, there was an impressive façade of a Greek gymnasium behind which was a huge palaestra, an exercise hall. Athletic young men mostly younger than me were hurrying in and out through the main entrance.

"We're heading for the Jewish quarter," Polios mentioned. "I have many friends there. Even from the time the city was built the Jews here were very numerous. They were fiercely independent too, both from the authorities in the city and from their own Sanhedrin. They represented the real intelligentsia of their tribe and they even translated their own holy book, the Torah and the Prophets, into Greek, against the wishes of their leaders in Jerusalem. We Christians use their book now as part of our service, Jesus being originally Jewish. We call it our Old Testament."

"So what happened to them?" I asked.

"They were persecuted by Trajan a couple of hundred years ago such that many left of their own accord and went to cities overseas but a large number of them converted to Christianity. We're going to meet a few of them this morning, if you'd like to."

"Yes," I said. "I'd like that very much."

We walked for a while in silence. A patrol of smartly dressed Roman soldiers led by an officer marched down the street towards us, short swords clanking by their sides.

"You might think that they are the hated ones here," said Polios nodding at them. "No army of occupation could ever really be liked or admired, could they? These raw squaddies are not from here. What would they know of the refinements of Alexandria, brought up as they were on the inhospitable banks of the Dacian Danube or in ignorance in the dark forests in Gaul? Yet would you believe it, they're joining our church in growing numbers. It's a really strange thing. They are taught to kill without mercy, yet they want to join our faith which preaches tolerance and passivity. Our way is to love our enemies, to go out to those who hate us, with the idea that it will change their minds, that this approach will make our whole humanity gentler and more caring. And it works! Many legionaries who've joined our ranks spend their free time ministering to the outcasts, to the poor and sick in our community. It's amazing, don't you think? Alas over the years many have become Christian martyrs too, suffering death, often after weeks of torture, rather than go back to a life of confrontation and killing. But we're still winning their hearts. I'm sure you'll meet some of our army converts today Nicholas."

We turned left again down a street leading towards the harbour and stopped before a fairly modest building.

"This was once a synagogue," continued Polios. "It's now used as one of our meeting houses, where we not only pray but the community also provides meals for the needy and the beggars. You wouldn't think so would you, among such wealthy and cultured people, but there are hundreds and hundreds of men and women who don't have jobs or who are in some way incapacitated and who are totally overlooked by the city fathers. It's a shocking disgrace really, but we help anyone who comes to us, with food, clothing and even shelter."

Polios pushed the door open and we went inside. I was amazed. There were scores of poorly dressed men and women sitting at a long table silently eating what appeared to be a thick soup from wooden bowls.

"They come in here off the street," observed Polios. "They've nowhere else to go. Our community feeds them and cares for them and given enough encouragement they can often turn their lives around. See those girls serving there; they were once the very same – street orphans. This is what the love of Christ can do for people. It can transform lives."

When they had all finished what was before them, a man in a white toga raised his hands in blessing, gave thanks to almighty God and wished them all well, after which they all intoned "Amen." Polios led me across the room to the man in white and introduced him to me as Eusebius.

"Eusebius is one of the elders here, but he is much more than that. He's a scholar and a teacher and understands more about our faith than anyone I know. He has studied all the scriptures and the commentaries. He actually comes from Caesarea in Palestine where he was instructed by Dorotheus of Tyre, one of our most important church fathers."

"Whilst what he says is true, Nicholas, don't pay much attention to him! I'm just like anyone else. But I do try to teach people about the kingdom of God when I get the opportunity. Are you of our faith Nicholas?" asked Eusebius.

I was eager to answer him.

"No, but I should like to learn and to become as you all are. What do I have to do?"

Eusebius quickly replied, "I will introduce you to Theodorus our 'Episkopos' here, our bishop. Let's see what he says. I would ask Polios to wait here a moment. Come."

We walked across the room into a small office in the corner where a particularly august old gentleman was seated reading.

"Theodorus," said Eusebius. "This is Nicholas from . . . sorry, which city are you from?"

I told him.

"Nicholas is from Patara on the Lycian coast. He wishes to join our number."

"God is indeed pleased. Welcome Nicholas!" the old man said. "If you have the time, you should spend a month or two with Eusebius, or more if you can afford to, learning about Jesus and his followers and how we seek the kingdom of heaven here on earth. If Eusebius would be so kind as to do that, we will put your name forward for the sacrament of baptism. We have a service in a couple of weeks."

So it was arranged that I should receive instruction from Eusebius on the life and teachings of Jesus. Polios was going to be in Alexandria for some days and I was thus able to go each morning from the ship to find my tutor and so came to learn of the love of God for mankind and the story of our Lord's selfless sacrifice for us, that we may be forgiven our wrongs and cured of the ills of the world. I found it an incredible message, truly the 'good news' of my life. It was so very different from the divisive world of the all-pervading gods of Greece and of Rome with which I had been brought up, or new gods like Sol Invictus, the Invincible Sun, gods whose mien was only too human. These gods were venal and self-centred, peevish and bad tempered and so casual in their supposed relationships with the world and with mankind that we had to wheedle and debase ourselves before their images to try to extract some small blessing or advantage. Christ represented the total opposite of that. As son of God he gave his life that we might live. He sacrificed himself that we may be freed from our sins. He lived his whole life as the picture he wanted us to aspire to, of how life should be lived, how we should behave to one another. He taught love and forgiveness, not hatred, suspicion and anger. This was how I wanted to live own my life, to give myself to Jesus and his message.

Sunday fortnight came around and with Eusebius' help I was now ready for admission into the church of Christ. It was to be the day of my baptism. There were to be three of us given our rite of passage into Christianity that day - myself, a man my own age named Andreas who it seemed was once somehow attached to the Roman army in north Africa, and a pretty, local servant girl called Anna. We were each dressed in a simple white cotton shift and were presented before the bishop, Theodorus, in a baptistery at the back of the old synagogue. Each of us was asked in turn if we wanted to become Christians, to be a member of Christ's flock, to which we said we did. Then one by one we entered a walk-in pool, until we were totally submerged.

Then Theodorus made the sign of the cross with oil on our foreheads and said, "May the God of peace sanctify you in spirit and in soul and in body and make you one with Him, now and ever after, Amen."

The small gathering of people who had stood and witnessed the event sung a short hymn thanking God for all his mercies to us and when they had finished they all shook us warmly by the hand and welcomed us into the church of Christ. I felt incredibly uplifted, as if a heavy weight had just been taken from my back and I was curiously elated to be with all these strangers, though they were strangers to me no more. I was one of them. I had joined the church of Christ. I was now a Christian, something which was to change me so completely it's hard when I look back over my life to remember a time of not being part of this marvellous community of souls. I said a little prayer to myself, thanking God for choosing me to join his flock, for forgiving all my past wrongs and for bringing me into his new light.

The afternoon of my baptism I went back to the ship with Polios and found the crew cleaning out the empty hold. The cargo had finally been unloaded and the hull was clearly riding higher in the water than before.

"We're waiting for a cargo of wheat for Diocletian's armies," he informed me. "We've got a contract to transport it to Brundisium at the heel of Italy. The armies of the Rhine are short of bread and they'll mutiny if they don't get their daily rations. You have to feel sorry for them, don't you, stuck up on the other side of the freezing Alps, although as far as I am concerned, I'd rather not work for the Romans at all. The administrator we're dealing with here is so officious. But we need the money so we have to do it. We sail in a couple of days. What will you do Nicholas?"

"I'm going to stay here a while longer," I replied. "I'm going to learn more about Christianity. At some time, I suppose I should go and see some of my father's old contacts and talk to them, let them know of his passing. After that I have an urge to travel a little, go out into the world."

We ate together that last evening at one of the wine shops on the dock. The following morning, I thanked Polios profusely for the experience he had given me, especially for my introduction to the Christian community in Alexandria whose number I had now joined.

As we said farewell on the quayside, I said, "Truly, Polios, being here has changed my life, and in such a short time. I now have a direction to follow and many new friends to be with. It's the start of a new life for me, thanks to you."

"Go with God," he answered and kissed me on both cheeks. "May the Lord keep you safe, Nicholas."

And with that he turned back to his ship and I walked into the city again. I took a room in one of the less fashionable parts of

Alexandria near the meeting house where I was studying with Eusebius. There was quite a community of believers in that area so I had no difficulty finding a place.

* * * * *

The months seemed to disappear like smoke and my time in Alexandria sped by. In the end I devoted more than two years to studying Christian theology from Eusebius and from other luminaries I met there. It was a life so very different to the aimless existence I had led in Patara. As I immersed myself in study and prayer; I became acquainted with profound ideas about the meaning of our life on earth.

One of the great Christian intellectuals who had lived in Alexandria was the Athenian scholar Clement who was still very much remembered here, almost a hundred years later. He had been very deeply versed in the writings of the ancient Greeks, especially in the 'Iliad' and the 'Odyssey' of Homer, books which I had been forced to read as a child. But he had gone on to compare what he described as 'this pagan literature' with the teachings of our Lord to emphasise the truly revolutionary thinking that Christianity represented. He showed how the steadfast love of God described by Jesus totally triumphed philosophically over the casual relationships even the Homeric heroes endeavoured to have with the manifestly petulant and prejudiced gods of the old world of Mount Olympus. Clement had a mastery of the thinking of the Athenian philosophers as well, especially the stoics, and he drew on these also to highlight the supremacy of the Christian message. Following his example, I applied myself for many thoughtful days in the new library that was being created at the old temple of Serapis, studying copies of the works of the Greek philosophers they had acquired to replace the originals. As Clement had, I compared the thoughts of writers like Plato and Aristotle with Christian ideas.

Another great thinker who had lived and worked in Alexandria was Origen Adamantius, an Egyptian who initially very much followed Clement in the way he interpreted the Christian scriptures. He too knew the works of the Stoic philosophers well and emphasized comparisons between the gospels and the works of Pythagorus and other great thinkers from Athens. Idiosyncratically, Origen taught that to reach God one had to pass through many phases, the last being human. It was not an idea to everyone's taste. But he was very well versed in the Hebrew writings as well and through his wide knowledge he had reworked the Greek version of the holy book of the Jews, the one they call the Septuagint, which had in fact been originally translated in Alexandria soon after Alexander the Great had been here. Alas there were some scholars in Alexandria who thought Origen's writings were bordering on the heretical, especially when he called the idea of the Holy Trinity into question and in the end he had to leave the city under a cloud and he died in Caesarea.

I met many remarkable people among the Christian community living in Alexandria and we spent long hours reading and discussing the gospels together, as well as the epistles of Paul and other writings. Eusebius was a patient tutor and I had a voracious appetite for what he was able to reveal to me. In the end, after all my studies, I felt I was entering a new life, starting afresh. I emerged from the breadth of my studies feeling I had been translated into a different existence.

On the suggestion of Theodorus and after much prayer and soul-searching I took holy orders; I was ordained as a priest. From now on I knew I had a direction to follow, a path to take, to help others and to spread God's word of redemption throughout the world. It was a remarkable feeling but I knew I had a very definite message to deliver, one that I had first sensed on the day of my baptism and as the months went by it was one I was to discern more and more. I knew that God had a mission for me to perform and for the first time in my life I slowly gained the sensation that I was truly needed. I felt ready to go out into the world.

CHAPTER SIX

THE ETERNAL NILE

I had been in Alexandria two years by this time and it was only then that I remembered I should really have tried to find some of the people whom my father had known and with whom he had been trading, if only to let them know he had passed away. Obviously by now I knew the layout of Alexandria very well and so one spare afternoon I walked all the way down Canopic Street and, turning into a narrow alley near the Moon Gate where I had long since discovered all the incense merchants operated, I saw a sign with a name that I thought I recognised, 'Apollodorus Incense and Spices' it read, so I went in. Inside was piled high with sacks full of aromatics of various kinds and heavily perfumed with all the fragrances of the orient. At the back of the shop I found an elderly man with a withered arm whom I supposed to be the eponymous Apollodorus.

"Apollodorus, sir, I am Nicholas, son of Aquila, from Patara. I think you did business with my father, did you not?"

"Aquila, you say?" He looked at me quizzically and after a moment's thought he recalled, "Ah yes, but that was some years ago. I used to buy some of his terebinth resin, as I remember. It was a cheaper product than I normally sell mind you," he continued rather condescendingly, "but there used to be something of a market for it among the lower class households of the city and they did sometimes burn it in some of the temples of the lesser cults and more obscure deities."

"Well," I continued, "I was given your name by our manager Eurymachus as someone with whom I should make contact."

"I don't think I can be of much help to you young man. Your father's partner, Chrolos, was it? No, Chronos, that's it, he came here, well, it must have been two or three years ago and took the last supplies I had, saying they were damaged stock and he would replace them the following day. He never came back. The sacks were worth a tidy sum I can tell you. It left me considerably out of pocket. Have you come to make restitution after all this time, is that what it is?"

For a moment I was thrown into a state of considerable confusion. I was sure Chronos had been drowned in the shipwreck five or six years ago. How was it he'd turned up in Alexandria? Had it really been him? And how did he know about Apollodorus? How did he find out he was a client of my father's? I didn't know what to say.

"You mean," I hesitated, "You actually saw Chronos here, in Alexandria, two years ago?"

"I saw him where you are standing right now, young man, as large as life!"

Then I remembered that Chronos had purloined my father's books with all his contacts listed in them. He had obviously used the information to get his hands on this old man's supplies and presumably sold them again to make money. After all this time I was stunned by his audacity.

"My apologies," I began hesitatingly, "this man stole my father's office books and incidentally his young wife too; he would have stolen his life savings as well had he managed to find them. Alas my father is dead. He died two winters ago. I'm so sorry if you are out of pocket. Is there something I can possibly do to help?"

The old man thought for a while and then stroking his chin he said, "You will no doubt say you don't have the money to pay me directly. But you are young and strong and full of adventure no doubt? Might I ask a favour from you? I need someone to go on a journey for me, a long way from here, into the depths of Arabia in fact. I need someone to go to the Frankincense Mountains of Sheba to buy some of their perfumed gold, as we call it. Would you be prepared to do that for me, to arrange a consignment for me? You must have worked with your father. You know something about qualities and harvest times."

Although I had studied for the priesthood, I wondered if I might not make this short journey before taking a full time position, so I said, "I've never actually been there, but yes, to recompense you I would do it, especially to restore our family's good name. I did work with my father for some years and certainly I do know about the terebinth trade."

"It would be a difficult journey," he continued. "It's a long way to a very wild place. Are you sure you can do it?"

"Yes," I said, thinking what an exciting interlude it would be. "I'll do it for you."

He smiled a wry smile, then coming over and shaking my hand he continued,

"I knew your father well and I respected him as a business man and as a person. It would be a pleasure to work with his son. Is there anything further you need to know that I can explain to you Nicholas?"

I thought a moment then asked, "I know it was some time ago, but tell me, when this man Chronos came here, do you remember if there was a young woman with him, someone he seemed close to?"

"I didn't really pay much attention to be perfectly honest and it was a long time since he was here, but now you come to mention it, I seem to remember there was some young lady hanging about in the background. Maybe that's the woman you're thinking of?"

Could that have been Calista, my father's faithless wife, I wondered? Had she managed to escape from the shipwreck as well? How could that possibly be? For a moment I felt outraged, but then I thought of my new calling, of the message of Jesus to be generous to your enemies, to those who seek occasion against you. I tried to put it to the back of my mind.

"It's of no importance," I said, collecting myself. "So, if I am to make this journey for you what do we have to do next?"

"We have to go to the Temple of Isis to seal the bargain," Apollodorus announced, putting his arm around my shoulder in a fatherly way and, making as if to leave the shop, he confided, "No time like the present, is there?"

He guided me into the street and we walked a couple of blocks to a very colourful Egyptian building decorated with palm columns topped with opening lotus flowers across the façade. The whole lintel above the door was painted with huge outspread wings with a golden sun disk in the middle from which sprang two winged cobras. I'd seen that motif before in one of the Egyptian temples back home. Feeling a little uncomfortable, I walked with him up the steps into the interior where there was a large seated female effigy with a statue of a small boy in her lap. She was wearing on her head another sun disk flanked by two bull's horns. Apollodorus genuflected and sidled swiftly around to the back where a heavily-painted young woman in a diaphanous green and gold robe whom I assume was a cult priestess was standing. She held up her right hand in greeting.

"Welcome Apollodorus. Welcome to the Temple of Isis and Horus. What is your will?"

"Ah, Mother of Wisdom, I need to formalise a contract with this young man here. If you would be so kind as to witness it and deposit it in your archives, I will of course make the usual offering to the goddess."

Saying this, they moved into a small office-like room behind the cult statue, where the priestess drew out a pristine sheet of papyrus and handed it to Apollodorus, pointing to a stylus on the nearby table. He sat and wrote for several minutes in a language I didn't recognise but assumed was demotic Egyptian and then he wrote a brief passage in Greek at the bottom to the effect that I was to act as his agent in a particular incense transaction in Arabia. There was no specific amount of money identified at this stage on Apollodorus' side of the bargain but upon delivery he would pay what he thought fit. He must have expected me to return to claim the money. He re-read the contract, handed the stylus for me to sign too and then gave it to the priestess who added her own very ornate appellation at the bottom and taking a small stamp seal, pressed this onto the centre of the document.

“So is it written,” she intoned, “so shall it be done.”

With that, she raised her arms in blessing. Apollodorus waved me out of the building while he hung back, rummaged in his clothing and gave a few coins to the priestess before joining me in the street. If I had only known at that point what I was letting myself in for, I might not so readily have agreed to make this momentous voyage into the unknown. I naively thought it would be an interesting and exciting journey. Little did I know that this wily old man was well aware of the enormous risks and perils that I would face and that he had deliberately kept those facts from me. I was soon to find out to what extent he had connived in my co-operation.

I walked back along Canopic Street, back through all the maelstrom of traffic to the Jewish Quarter and the old synagogue where I found Andreas, the man who had been baptised with me and with whom I had kept in constant contact. During our time together, he had become a close friend and confidant; he was the same age as me after all. Andreas was an interesting man. He originally came from the ancient Greek city of Ptolemais, one of the Pentapolis in Libya and for some years he'd been loosely attached to the Roman army. He was not a soldier, he had assured me, but had been a junior assistant to one of the *actuarii*, the paymasters, of the III Cyrenaica Legion which had originally been raised from his province. Osmotically he had gained quite an extensive knowledge of the Roman military machine and how it operated. Actually, so that he kept in trim, he had told me, he would from time to time accept an invitation from the soldiers to exercise with them and so he came to know their various eccentricities well. For his own part, to try to improve himself he'd also learnt Latin, as did other Greeks in his city. But with Diocletian's accession the army was 'rationalized', that's what they'd called it. Basically it was a total revision of their administrative system and at the end of it he found himself out of a job, so that's why he'd come to Alexandria.

He was serving soup to a few waifs sitting around the table when I arrived. I was excited to tell him of my forthcoming expedition to south Arabia.

"You've agreed to go where?" he queried incredulously. "Have you any idea how wild that part of the world is, Niko? I don't just mean the country, the desert and the mountains but the people! They're completely lawless, so I've heard. I know a few things about this area. I knew soldiers who had been posted to Arabia Petraea. They told me the people there are beyond our civilized world; like bandits and outlaws, the whole lot of them. They are not amenable to any logic, that's what they said."

I was brought up short by his astonishment at what I'd done. I hadn't thought anything of it when I signed the paper at the temple, but I knew I'd given my word to Apollodorus and I felt I would just have to go through with it. With a sinking heart, I told Andreas of the theft of the old man's stock by Chronos, of my embarrassment for the family name. He was not really encouraged by this, but he nevertheless persisted in his evaluation.

"You know you can't do this on your own, don't you? I wouldn't rate your chances of even getting there very high, let alone coming back, particularly because I have no doubt you'll be carrying some of your gold with you. Even if you're not, they'll assume you are. At the very least you'll be robbed blind in a trice."

He thought for a moment, then said, "I tell you what, I have nothing to do right now. I've been helping out here for months, which is not the most thrilling thing I can think of. Why don't I come with you? At least I know a little bit about the people there and with some military knowledge I can try to keep us both from coming to grief. I can imagine the danger these tribes-people pose. And I suppose anyway I'd like a bit of adventure too. How about it Niko?"

My spirits lifted a little. Andreas had a burly appearance and was clearly not a man to be taken lightly. He'd be a good travelling companion and we were both Christians; what could possibly go wrong? I shook his hand heartily and said I would be very pleased if he would join me. We talked some more about the journey, about the possible excitements and pit-falls, as far as he knew them and we agreed we would set out in a couple of weeks, after I'd said my farewells to Eusebius and been given precise instructions by the devious Apollodorus.

I spent the next two or three days working out how we would get through the first part of the journey. I asked the advice of some of the market traders who dealt in commodities like grain from Upper Egypt and that special red-porphyry stonework they quarried at Swenett on the First Cataract. They told me we'd first have to go to the old city of Memphis at the head of the Delta and then sail all the way up the Nile as far as Koptos, the chief city of the fifth Nome of Harawi, the Two Hawks; they were names that made little sense to me at the time. From there, they said, there was a caravan road running east through the mountains to the Erythraean Sea and down to the port city of Berenike. They were not too sure about anything outside the Nile Valley, but suggested that we should be able to find someone at Berenike who was sailing south down the Erythraean Sea to take us to south Arabia or even India, if that's what we wanted. When I asked how long it would take, they shrugged and said they really didn't know. Weeks, or months maybe? They had no idea, they confessed. Anyway, it was a start.

I went to see Apollodorus a few days later. After making me listen to a carefully rehearsed diatribe on how much he had lost when his terebinth resin was stolen, as he described it, he wished me the blessings of Isis and Horus and sent me on my way. I met up with Andreas again and slowly over the next few evenings we planned our departure. One bright morning a week or so later, having taken our leave of the community, Andreas and I made our way through the eastern city to the Sun Gate towards the road that led along the western edge of the Delta. We were finally leaving Alexandria to begin our journey.

Although the road to Memphis was a good Roman highway it was still going to take us six or seven days to reach that city so we just buckled down and strode on. The journey was reasonably uneventful. We stayed at lodging houses every night and walked as far as we could each day. By the beginning of the following week, we had reached Memphis, which I had learnt had once been the most ancient capital of Pharaonic Egypt. It was now a bit dilapidated, I thought, since it had been totally eclipsed in importance by Alexandria during the last few centuries. It was at Memphis that I saw the main stream of the eternal Nile for the first time. By comparison to the Xanthos River at Patara, it was massive. Broad and slow flowing, it was alive with boats large and small scurrying hither and thither.

The following morning we went down to what looked like the main jetty. All manner of people were thronged together along the river's edge, shouting instructions, selling fruit and vegetables, bread boys weaving in and out of the crowds, farm hands driving animals, dock workers heaving bags on and off transports. It seemed like total chaos. We asked someone where we would find a boat to take us up-river and he pointed his thumb back to a small kiosk away from the bank. We went over and inquired how much it would cost to travel to Koptos. The man in charge pursed his lips and sucked his teeth.

"What do you want to go there for?" he laughed. "Don't we have everything you want here? Anyway, how do you want to do it? Fast private dhow? Wheat transporter? Or do you want a slow ferry? They're all different prices. How many passengers? Two?"

"What's the cheapest way?" I asked.

"Slow ferry," he said. "It'll be a denarius a day. You want that? See that fat man over there. Go and talk to him. He's in charge of the ferries."

We walked over and told him what we wanted.

"There's a ferry leaving in one hour," he replied. "It's going all the way to Koptos. You pay the captain every day, you bring your own food and you sleep on the deck at night. But I warn you, it's slow. It will take over a month to get to Koptos. You might get tired of the whole thing by then."

We told him we'd take it and he pointed to a boat at the water's edge.

"That's it," he motioned. "You'd better get something to eat to take with you."

He indicated some food stalls and we went over and bought some barley cakes and a skin of water. Then we went over to the boat and climbed aboard. It was pandemonium – tall Nilotic headmen, African workers, Arab traders and a number of local farmers with goats tethered with ropes and their wives clutching chickens in baskets. When we asked them each where they were heading, all of them said they were only going short distances, just a day or two upriver. No-one was going to Upper Egypt except us.

The captain took our money and pointed to a pile of reeds on the deck.

"You can sleep there," he said. "We'll be leaving within the half-hour."

And duly we cast off. The crewman raised the cross-spar and the sail filled with light wind and we began to move up-river. Our journey into the unknown had begun.

We stopped at three or four villages that first day. Out on the river, the sun was hot and with the wind it felt like opening an oven door. We tried to rig up some shade with a piece of cloth we found by the reeds on deck which gave us some respite. But nothing could really cool things down. By sundown we were over-heated and thirsty. Our water skin had run dry and our barley cakes were finished. We put in for the night at a small jetty by some fields and women came to sell us bread rings and meat patties. They offered to fill our water-skin free if we bought enough food from them. We had no option. After our simple meal, Andreas quietly recited from Matthew's gospel, the story of the Sermon on the Mount, and we said a short prayer together before falling fast asleep on the reeds.

The next few days were all very like the first. People came and went, goats were pulled off, more pulled on and once a man came with his donkey for an hour or so before getting off at the next village on the opposite bank. Andreas and I were getting very sunburnt.

"I'm not sure about you, Niko, but if this carries on I'll be thoroughly charred by the time we get to Koptos. There must be a faster way."

That night we moored at a larger town of mud-brick houses shaded with date palms surrounding what I was told by one local inhabitant was an old Pharaonic temple. Moored just ahead of us was a much bigger military transport.

"Let me go into town and find out where that ship is bound," offered Andreas, pointing to the boat in front, and with that he sauntered off up the dusty path towards the temple and the town. I stayed behind guarding our meagre possessions and the gold pieces which I had hidden away in our bags.

Andreas was gone almost two hours and he came back stinking of beer. He'd obviously been in one of the ale houses in the town.

"Right," he reported, "that transport belongs to the Legio III Cyrenaica. It's empty at the moment except for a few centurions I've just met who are going to the Roman camp at Koptos to take over command. There was a rebellion there a couple of years ago but Diocletian has reasserted control. These officers are going there to re-organise the whole camp. Now, it so happens the Cyrenaica legion is the very one I worked for as the assistant to the actuarius! I used to know some their centurions too. The long and short of it is I've persuaded them to give us a lift and it won't cost us anything, except beer money. They've even got rations, far more than they need, they tell me. And as you see, they've got large shaded canopies over the stern. And would you believe it, there's even a spare officer's cabin we can use! We can go aboard whenever we like. They are leaving at first light tomorrow."

I was hugely impressed. Clearly Andreas was going to make an extremely useful travelling companion. I gathered our few belongings together and followed him down the jetty to the gangplank of the transport and up onto its high deck.

"What about the captain of the ferry?" I asked.

"Oh never mind about him. If we're not there in the morning, he'll set sail anyway and by that time we'll be way upriver."

We spoke to the soldier of the watch and he pointed to the cabin below. We made ourselves comfortable and I certainly had the best night's sleep I'd had in a week. Just as dawn was breaking, I felt the transport move. I could hear Andreas who was already up on deck talking with a couple of his new friends. I joined them and he introduced me.

"Marcus, Titus, this is Nicholas." I shook hands with them. I looked forward and saw we were already well under way, with both sails full and water foaming around the prow. This was a much superior way to travel up the Nile, I thought and turning I smiled at Andreas. Yes, he'd done us proud. Now I was able to relax a little, with the shade and the guaranteed food, and I settled down to enjoy the cruise.

With no one else on board but the centurions and a couple of sailors, there was enough space and, with the vessel being light and unladen, it positively skimmed over the river. The crewmen knew their business well and they tacked from side to side with very professional manoeuvres. Looking at the deep waters rushing past the side of the ship, I reckoned we were travelling two, maybe three times faster than we had been on the ferry and there were fewer stops. I gave thanks to Almighty God for our good fortune and kept my inherent dislike of imperial Rome to myself.

Apart from buying beer every night for what seemed the ever more thirsty centurions, we were left to our own devices. Andreas spent a lot of time reminiscing about his experiences in Cyrenaica with Marcus and Titus; and me, well I just leaned on the railing and watched the scenery glide by. I'd never seen anything like the banks of this river, wide flat ribbons of intense green on either side from the river's edge right up to the base of the mountains, overlooked in the distance by rocky, pinkish cliffs rising up out of the valley. The margins of the river on each side were fringed with filigree-topped papyrus, beyond which were endless small fields with shining emerald crops looking a picture of abundance – wheat, barley, row after row of beans, cotton and innumerable clumps of stately date palms which added blots of shade in the otherwise strong and shimmering sunlight.

Irrigation furrows ran away from the river and divided some of the fields while in the background bare-legged men worked shadoofs or trod an Archimedes screw to raise water onto the slightly higher ground. Every mile or so there was a cluster of white-plastered mud-brick dwellings with flat roofs, in front of which women could be seen kneeling to grind grain with querns and rubbing stones. Piled up against the house walls were mounds of circular cakes of dried cattle dung which they must be burning to make their cooking fires; and everywhere there were cows, some animals even standing knee deep at the water's edge to drink and cool down.

They were not the only animals we saw. There were herds of goats and a few fat-tailed sheep. Occasionally in the river there were pods of hippos with just the tops of their heads showing above the water, grunting and flicking their ears. I'd never seen them before. Now and again one would yawn and show its cavernous mouth and impressive-looking teeth. Although they looked peaceful enough, one of the sailors said they could be extremely dangerous if disturbed, so we kept well away.

Within six days Koptos hove into view around a bend in the river. It was characterized by three groups of impressive Egyptian temples with a large settlement crowded all around them, itself punctuated with endless palm trees. We had sailed all the way up the Nile and we'd arrived in Upper Egypt. Here we would rest until the next part of our journey began.

CHAPTER SEVEN

THROUGH THE MOUNTAINS

When the military transport was securely moored to the quayside at Koptos we were able to disembark. We said farewell to our Roman hosts who were soon being escorted by a phalanx of armed legionaries up the dusty main street. In fact, everywhere we looked in Koptos there were soldiers carrying weapons. Clearly the Romans were taking no chances with another uprising.

Koptos was an important city and I soon learnt that it had a very long history which went back thousands of years to the time of the earliest Pharaohs, when it had been called Gebtu. A man I spoke to in a shop near the dock said it had always been sacred to Isis and Horus, and especially to the ancient sky god Min. He told me that the temples which we'd seen from the ship were dedicated to these three deities. They'd been rebuilt when the Greeks took over Upper Egypt about six hundred years ago and after that Koptos had begun to replace Thebes in importance, the great Late Pharaonic capital city further up the river. It was all to do with the trading routes, he reckoned.

Andreas had gone off on his own again, leaving me at the dock side. He came back in less than half an hour with information.

“I spoke to some of the legionaries on duty in the city. There is a strong Christian community here based in a building behind the large middle temple, they said. Some of them are in fact Christians themselves and they’ve invited us to a service they’re holding there tonight.”

“That’s great news, Andreas. Why don’t we go there now and see if anyone knows of somewhere we can stay while we’re in the city. At the very least we will find out where they meet, even if there’s no-one there.”

We walked up the street away from the river, making our way between the mud- brick houses towards the middle temple. It was obvious which the temples were because all three towered over the two-storied flat roofs of the houses. We passed in front of one with an especially Egyptian façade decorated in bright colours and found a large, plain building at the back. We knew it must be the one we were looking for because it had a fish painted on the wall outside. It was our cryptic way of denoting a Christian house to one another, derived from the Greek word for ‘fish,’ IXTHUS, whose initials for us spelt out “Iesous Christos, Theou ‘Uios, Soter” – “Jesus Christ, Son of God, Saviour.”

Going in through the open door, we saw it had at one time been a Roman-style villa, with a pillared courtyard, in the middle of which was a small pool although that was currently dry. A young woman was sweeping the mosaic floors around the veranda and she looked up when she heard us.

“Welcome in the Lord’s name,” she said, smiling. “You are strangers to our house, but you are most welcome. Can I do anything to assist you?”

“Good day,” I replied. “I’m Nicholas and this is Andreas.”

She bowed to each of us.

“We’ve come from the church in Alexandria,” I continued, a bit boldly perhaps. “We were invited to join your communion service tonight by some soldiers we met and in the meantime do you know of anywhere we might stay for a few days? We’re hoping in due course to travel to the Erythraean Sea.”

“My name is Esther,” she volunteered. “We actually have a room we use for guests attached to our meeting house here. If there’s space, I’m sure you’d be very welcome to stay with us. Put your packs in the corner there and I’ll see if I can find Father Barnabas; he’s in charge of the building.”

With that she helped us pile what few belongings we had against the wall and led us into a side room where there was an impressively bearded man seated at a desk.

"Father Barnabas, this is Nicholas and Andreas from our church in Alexandria. They're on their way to the Erythraean Sea. Can we put them up for a few days?"

"But of course, Esther. Nicholas, Andreas, I bid you indeed welcome to our church in Jesus' name. Sit down and tell me of your journey and where you're hoping to go. We have a Eucharist this evening and we sincerely hope you will join with us. Esther, bring some herb tea for our guests."

We sat opposite Barnabas on a bench beside a low table.

"We're planning to travel down the Erythraean Sea to South Arabia and the frankincense mountains. I actually come from Patara in Lycia. My late father was an incense trader. We don't know this part of the world at all. Andreas and I joined the church in Alexandria two years ago and I have recently been ordained as a priest but have yet to practise. Everything up here on the Nile is very new to us, so any help you can give us would be extremely useful."

"Ah yes. I see. What you are proposing is not an easy journey. First of all you need to travel through the mountains to Berenike which is the nearest port to Koptos. There are caravans travelling that road all the time, but it's dangerous. You may have already heard that we've suffered a great deal of unrest here on the Upper Nile over the past few years. It's been extremely distressing for us all."

He bowed his head slightly and then continued, "The emperor sent a considerable army only last year to quell what he considered to be a rebellion against Rome. I think it's all quietened down now, at least it has here in the city, and there are some caravans travelling to and from the Erythraean Sea again, but there are constant reports of attacks by bandits on the road. They secrete themselves in the mountains, which are really impenetrable thereabouts, and they attempt to assault traders as they come through the gorges. It's mainly the caravans coming up to the Nile they're after, the ones with the precious foreign cargoes of spices, but they will attack anything and anyone that attempts that route. They're completely outside the law. A small group of them were caught last week and they were all summarily executed by the army without trial. I'm afraid it happens all the time now."

Barnabas looked worried as he told us the story.

"Look, the best thing we can do is to go and talk to some of the caravan drivers in the market. They'll give us the most up-to-date news of what's happening."

We drank the tea Esther had brought in with a few small wheat cakes, a large bowl of fresh dates and a plate of nuts. We talked at length about our experiences in Alexandria, and Barnabas made pointed enquiries about the community there.

"Are they still quarrelling about the matter of the substance of the son of God in Alexandria? You will have known of Origen no doubt. There were lots of arguments about what he had to say. We've heard that one of their young elders, Arius I think his name is, has recently been very vocal on the subject, suggesting that since Jesus is the son of God, he is inferior to him. It has raised a good many eyebrows here, I can tell you."

I said that although I'd studied the works of Origen and I had heard about the Arius controversy, I was constantly amazed by the topics people would haggle over when the subject was something so divine. Barnabas let the matter drop. He then indicated that if we'd finished our tea, we should perhaps walk to the market. We rose and followed him into the street. The sun was hot by this time and wherever we could we walked in the shade of the house walls.

After about ten minutes we came to a large open market absolutely full of people – stall-holders, house slaves buying for their mistresses, donkeys and mules piled high with bales and boxes and crowds simply milling about. Barnabas pushed his way through to the farthest corner where another narrower street led into a much bigger open expanse, less crowded in that there were fewer people but full of camels and their drivers. Most of the camels were lying down chewing lazily, but some were still fully laden and had yet to be unloaded. They had colourfully tasselled bags hanging down their sides clearly full to bursting with trade goods.

Although I'd seen them in Alexandria, I'd never been this close to so many camels before. They were a light, sandy colour, with huge effeminate eyelashes, yet they looked so ungainly - long spindly legs holding their peculiarly-shaped bodies. For the most part they appeared very peaceful, looking haughtily down their noses at us. But occasionally one would snarl with a guttural bark when it was being asked to do something it didn't like. I stood well clear of their huge teeth. The camel drivers were talking to one another, some arguing, others seemingly just passing the time of day. It looked as though a caravan had just arrived and I wondered what exotic commodities they had brought with them.

Barnabas went over to one of the drivers, all of whom were dressed in long dark robes with white headscarves shading their faces. He spoke for a minute or two and then brought the driver over to where we were standing.

"Ahmet here has just come up with a caravan from the coast on the road we talked about. I'll let him tell you what it was like."

"We just came with caravan through mountains," he said, in a very coarse patois which I had difficulty understanding. "The way, she is very difficult, very difficult. Many bad people, you know this? Many people they want steal our silk. Much money, you know this, much money."

"But you've got here, yes?" I observed slowly. "You are here now."

"Yes, yes, but we have soldier. They frighten bad men away. They not attack us this time. But when go Berenike before two month ago, they come in night. Steal one of camels. Is bad, you know this? Can be, how you say, very dangerous. If you go, you must have many people, maybe soldier if you can. This way will be better for you. Worst place is top of wadi, as it comes out of mountains. You must be very careful there, you understand?"

I thanked him for his story. Barnabas turned to me and said, "We must make sure that you travel with a large caravan. There are guest-houses along the route, well, they're more like forts really, where you must stay at night. It's not safe to bivouac. Ahmet here says it will take about seven days to get through the mountains and down the Wadi Hammamat which leads to the coast and then another seven to travel to the port of Berenike itself. It's the mountains you have to worry about. I know there are Roman watch towers at regular intervals, but they're not always manned every day. I know some of the silk traders here. I'll ask them when their next caravan will be going through to the Erythraean Sea. I'll have the answer by tonight. Why don't you go back to the meeting house and get a bit of rest? Let me fix this up for you. Esther will be there. She'll look after you."

Thanking him, Andreas and I walked back to the building behind the big temple. Esther was tending the flowers in the courtyard.

"They need constant watering," she said. "It's probably too hot for some of the more delicate plants, but I love seeing them in the early morning light. They are so beautiful, don't you think? But I am forgetting myself. Let me take you to your room."

She led us along a couple of cool corridors into the rear of the house where there was a large room furnished with three couches, one along each wall, each with colourful coverings and large cushions.

"We sometimes eat here in the evenings," she announced. "But you can sleep in this room for a couple of nights. If you get cold, there are some blankets in the chest over there. Next door there is a small wash room. I'm sure you want to clean up after your long journey."

We acknowledged that we were very grateful to her for her kindness and laid our belongings on one of the couches. It seemed positive luxury after what we had experienced on the Nile, let alone what we were about to face travelling to the coast. I stripped off my dirty clothes and washed myself with water poured from an earthenware pitcher. The water sluiced away down a drain in the corner. It felt really good, particularly because the water was cool. I put on a clean shirt and washed my dirty one in a bowl and hung it up to dry. Andreas followed my example and by late afternoon we were half-way decent and no longer reeking of sweat.

That evening, just after sunset, many people came to the villa, including some legionaries. There was a large room that we hadn't noticed on the other side of the courtyard. Some walls had been removed and replaced by pillars to make the room bigger. The remaining walls had frescoes painted on them which I recognised as stories from Jesus' life – the healing of the man sick of the palsy; the Good Samaritan and the marriage of Cana in Galilee. On the back wall behind a large table was a simple picture of Christ Pantokrator, ruler of the world, hand raised in blessing. The congregation filed into the room until it was packed. Barnabas stood behind the table on which had been placed several loaves of bread, a large flask of wine and a beaker.

After a while, he welcomed everyone, introduced Andreas and me to the others, then held up his right hand for silence before he began, "To you, O Lord most high, our heavenly King and our Saviour, we lift up our hearts and give thanks for our fellowship here tonight. As we celebrate together the ultimate sacrifice made for us, may we too be ever ready to give ourselves to your service."

The Eucharist proceeded as usual with the blessing of the bread and wine and the congregation bowed as they partook of that sacred meal, at the end of which Barnabas raised his right hand again and making the sign of the cross, blessed us all, adjuring us to go out into the world in peace, to witness for Christ and to praise God continually for his many mercies. We all said

"Amen" and after a quiet moment's contemplation everyone shook each other's hand. The short service was over.

I can't begin to tell you what that simple service meant to me, the shared experience, the comradeship of men and women, young and old, people of different cultures, all strangers to me, coming together in one act to remember the supreme sacrifice made for us all, that we might be saved from our own evil, that we might live in peace one with another. It was extremely uplifting. At that moment I felt with such all-embracing spirit that I could face any adversity. And if the camel driver Ahmet was to be believed, there would be hardships aplenty in the days to come. I said a short prayer asking God to guide our way and to keep Andreas and me in his grace. Slowly, the congregation dispersed, one or two hanging back to exchange a word or two with Barnabas. And then we were just the four of us again. We went into a small kitchen area and ate together by the light of a few oil lamps.

"I've arranged a caravan with whom you can travel," announce Barnabas. "It leaves tomorrow soon after sun-up. It's carrying glass to Berenike and some precious metals, gold most probably, for payment for a new delivery of silk that's waiting for them. There will be ten camels and about twelve men in all. They could use an extra couple of pairs of hands and Andreas here looks as if he has some military connections, which is always impressive."

"Well, I was attached to a legion once, though it was some time ago and I wasn't a combatant," said Andreas. "I don't suppose that would help in a real crisis would it?"

"I think you should both get a good night's sleep. I sense tomorrow is going to be a long day in what will probably turn out to be a difficult couple of weeks."

We turned in gratefully, each with our own silent thoughts of what tomorrow might bring. I slept somewhat fitfully at first, worrying about what would happen, until I suddenly realised I could leave the future to God. I smiled to myself and fell into a deep sleep and didn't wake until Andreas shook me at dawn. Today is the day, I thought, when we really venture into the unknown. The two of us crept out of the still sleeping house, and made our way back to the camel market. Barnabas had described to us the man we should contact, somebody called Khalid, who was in charge of the caravan. It took a minute or two to find him, but someone pointed to a large man shouting instructions and we went over and introduced ourselves.

"We've come from Barnabas," I said. "He says we can join your caravan over the mountains. I'm Niko and this is Andreas."

"Peace be with you," said Khalid. "Speak to that driver there and attach yourself to him. His name is Dawud."

We introduced ourselves to Dawud who pointed two fingers to his eyes and then waved them to the left and right, at which point we discovered that Dawud was dumb and had been since birth, but we took his signs to mean we were to be his lookouts. I asked him if that was the case and he nodded furiously. He was tightening the girth on one of the camels and motioned to us to stay by him. He slung our meagre belongings onto the camel's back already laden with full bags and made them fast with a rope, smiling a rather toothless smile as he did so. Around us there were camels being encouraged to rise, levering their legs off the ground back and front with scarcely disguised ill temper, baring their teeth and groaning raucously. I was rather afraid of the beasts, but Dawud seemed totally in control of his camel and casually prodded it upright with a stick. It towered above him and turning its head gave him what looked to me like a disdainful stare.

A few minutes later we moved off in a line. The camels were roped to one another back and front, the foremost camel being led by Khalid. We moved silently in a stately fashion through the deserted streets of Koptos, deep in shadow this early in the morning. After half an hour or so we had cleared the city and begun to walk into the open countryside along what was a well-surfaced Roman road leading towards the distant hills. Very soon the green fields fell behind us as we began to ascend out of the Nile Valley and immediately we were in a wild, rocky landscape punctuated with the occasional scrubby thorn trees. Looking back at the diminishing view of the city and by comparison to the deserted way ahead, it looked a verdant tapestry with its innumerable palm trees and surrounding fields stretched out to either side along the glittering face of the vast river below us.

At first the road was relatively easy, but it soon deteriorated and became more difficult as we negotiated one or two steep turns to get us over the cliffs which flanked the valley, after which we lost sight of the Nile all together, climbing gradually higher and further into the foothills. The little thorny bushes became gradually sparser and the topography more and more barren. After a couple of hours the sun had risen high in the sky and was beating down unforgivingly on our train. Dawud looked at me several times with a puzzled expression before jumping up and pulling a small pannier from the side of his camel as he walked along. He rummaged inside and found two head scarves and head rings, which he gave to Andreas and me, pointing skywards and rolling his eyes to indicate, as I understood it, that if we didn't cover our heads properly we would become maddened by the sun's rays. Andreas and I concurred and soon we had become more or less indistinguishable from the other camel drivers in the party.

The train moved on for several hours in relative silence, broken only by one or two shouts between the drivers as they pointing to something off in the distance. Sometime before mid-day, Khalid called a halt and the drivers pulled their camels to one side of the track and hobbled them, still fully laden. They erected a few sheets on short poles as a shade canopy and the party stretched out under it on the bare ground, ostensibly to sleep for an hour or two. Andreas and I followed suit and soon all that could be heard were a few snores and the buzzing of some adventurous flies that had journeyed with the camels. Not wanting to disturb the group, I sat quietly in the shade and looked at the bleak desert scene now shimmering wildly in the intense heat. I wondered why anyone could have thought of travelling this route in the first place, but this was a very ancient road; for millennia countless people must have passed this way and gazed out at the same view as I was at that moment. I must have dozed off, until after what felt like a couple of hours a water-skin was passed around, the canopy dismantled and we moved off again.

All through the afternoon we climbed slowly higher while in front of us the distant profile of the mountains gradually materialized out of the haze. We passed a couple of watch towers that were deserted, which didn't fill me with a great deal of confidence in the road ahead I have to admit, before in the late afternoon I spotted what looked like a small fort in the distance. Dawud pointed to it and put both hands together on one side of his face. This was where the caravan would spend its first night on the road. We trudged on towards it and finally reached the building which was surrounded by a few scrubby thorn trees. The fort comprised a defensive mud-brick wall with a gate, through which Khalid led our troop. It was nothing complicated, just an enclosed, open square surrounded by simple, wooden-pillared colonnades which provided shade around the inside. The drivers flicked their camels' legs with their sticks and the camels obediently collapsed onto their haunches. They were then unloaded and the packs placed against the wall. Dawud opened out some bed rolls in the shade and another of the drivers poked a group of smoking ashes back to life and put a handful of twigs and couple of cakes of dried camel dung onto them and blew for a moment until flames appeared.

One of the others pulled out a large pan from his pack and filling it with water from a tiny cistern in the centre of the fort emptied a packet of dried beans into it and set it on the fire. Everyone clearly knew what they were doing. One of the other men pulled out a draw-string bag and sprinkled what I took to be herbs and spices into the pan and stirred it with a wooden spoon.

"Is water here," said Khalid, handing me a couple of skins.

He motioned towards the cistern and intimated that I should fill them with water, which I did. I tasted it and it was rather brackish, but it was the only water I'd seen since we left the

Nile. I wondered what Andreas and I should do and fumbled in my pockets for a few coins to pay for the water. Khalid was adamant he wouldn't accept it.

"You guests of Bedouin," he insisted. "We help you, you help us."

And with that he made sure that cushions were arranged in a circle on which we all proceeded to lounge. It was nearly twilight when he motioned to a couple of the other men, who walked over to the entrance gate and with some difficulty shut the huge wooden doors and barred them with a large timber baulk. Clearly if you hadn't reached the fort by sundown you were going to be locked out.

A low table was placed in the middle of the array of cushions and a couple of oil lamps were hung from beams and lit with a spill from the fire. After another half hour or so the bean dish was brought from the fire and placed on the table, wooden spoons were handed round and we all dipped our spoons into the mix and ate. It was really delicious, largely I would think because of the herbs and spices. Of course, it occurred to me, these men knew about spices; after all, they traded in them. We continued eating in total silence until the pot was empty, at which point it was taken off to be washed.

The men sat around in groups in the darkness drinking tea and chatting quietly. Andreas and I moved to one side and he suggested we said the Lord's Prayer together, which we did.

Khalid came over to us and frowning said, “Tomorrow more difficult. We must be prepared.”

And with that we moved over to the bed rolls and fell asleep.

CHAPTER EIGHT

JOURNEY TO BERENIKE

The sky was beginning to lighten as the caravan prepared to leave the fort. The camels had been given water and fodder in the pre-dawn darkness and were clearly ready to continue the journey. The bed rolls had been cleared away and loaded and one thoughtful person had brewed tea, beakers of which were passed to Andreas and me along with some small, dry biscuit-like loaves. Meanwhile the last bags were lashed onto the camels' backs and the drivers proceeded to prod them upright, accompanied by much snarling and baring of teeth. Someone went to open the great doors of the fort and at a given signal Khalid led the string of animals and men out through the gate and onto the road just as the glow of the rising sun was illuminating a cloudless sky behind the mountain peaks far in front of us.

Again we walked in silence for three or four hours, the scenery becoming progressively more rugged as we proceeded higher and further eastward along the road. The sun gradually rose above the skyline and beat down on us; it was going to be another hot day. Large outcrops of rock soon began to punctuate the sides of the track which in turn meandered between them, ever upwards. As the morning wore on I saw a pair of eagles quartering the sky high above us and wondered what could possibly live in this desiccated countryside until Dawud pulled at my sleeve and pointed off to the left. Away in the distance among the rocks, hardly distinguishable from the bleached sandy plains, was a small herd of what looked like white antelope with long scimitar-like horns.

"Oryx," declared Musa, one of the other drivers. "Very good to eat," and then he added ruefully, "but very difficult to catch!"

The landscape extended desolately away on either side of the road all the way to the horizon such that I considered it would have been impossible for anyone to approach our caravan on this part of the journey without being spotted a long way away, but after our mid-day halt the scenery began to change as the mountains in front of us grew nearer and our way steeper and more tortuous. During the afternoon Khalid seemed to be hurrying the train a little until towards sunset we turned a corner and saw the next caravan fort, which was clearly what he had been anxious to reach by sun down. As we turned into the gate we could see there was another camel caravan already ensconced there. They had come up from the Erythraean Sea and must be heading for Koptos and the Nile. Suddenly, there was much shouting and ululating as the two parties recognised each other. Our drivers ran over to the others hugging and shaking their hands. They were clearly all friends and I assumed from the little I'd learnt about these people they were of the same tribe. It turned out I was right. They were all from the Beja Bedouin, Arabs who had lived along the Erythraean Sea coast for centuries and had come to dominate these desert caravan routes to the Nile.

The drivers who were already there had baked bread from flour they'd brought with them and they began to hand freshly-made flat cakes to our own men. As we off-loaded our camels and settled them down for the night, our drivers were exchanging animated conversations with their friends, involving much laughing and gesticulating. A larger fire was made up with some dried scrub and more bread was being baked, along with cans of water being boiled and the ubiquitous bean and spice stew being made. There was clearly going to be a party of some description. It was fascinating to watch the energetic interaction of these normally dour and silent desert people, as they were stimulated and excited by each other's company in this lonely wilderness.

With the encroaching darkness, oil lamps were lit all around the inside of the fort and the atmosphere became very lively. The great gates were closed and barred and full of anticipation the two groups mixed together, to talk, laugh and to eat. When the food was finished, handless cups of very strong, heavily sweetened hot tea were passed around which the men slurped with obvious enjoyment. It was at this point that the music began, one man playing on an oud, plucking ancient melodies on his traditional stringed lute. He was accompanied by another playing a jointed flute, a nay, with a rather haunting air, and another had a daff, a tambourine-like instrument with sistrums set in its frame. This third man picked out the swirling rhythms with the rattles and a complex tintinnabulation on the face, which was covered with tightly-stretched animal skin. Several times the men began to sing along with the tunes in harsh, low strains, often in rhythms which syncopated with the main theme. It was haunting listening to those archaic songs there in the warm night under a vast canopy of stars. At one point two young men entered the circle dressed in what appeared to be colourful skirts. They whirled around holding both hands out and making their skirts billow. The others fell about laughing at these two 'women'. The festivities continued long into the night until, exhausted, the men dropped asleep almost where they sat.

The following morning the fingers of dawn had already crept over the edge of the outer walls of the fort before both caravans made to leave through the gate. We went first amid much cheering and shouts of farewell before we turned towards the ever-climbing sun and the mountains.

“This most difficult days,” Khalid confided to us. “Sami, leader of other caravan, he tell me. He see bad people in mountains, high up. Careful, he say! Bad men there. Danger!”

He grimaced and raised his stubble-laden chin to emphasise the point. We took his word for it and peered upwards at the ever-steepening ascent we had to make. Our way wound uphill and seemed to disappear amid sheer pinnacles of rock. The road surface had deteriorated further, having been partially washed away in a storm some time before and as we lumbered onwards the going got rougher. Andreas in particular kept his eyes open, walking slightly ahead of the caravan, climbing the occasional boulder on the side of the road to get a better vantage point. I couldn’t really understand why anyone would want to steal our cargo of glass, however fine it might be, particularly up here, but then I remembered we were also probably carrying gold. That would be a great incentive to rob the caravan. If anyone in Koptos had found out what we were carrying and passed on the information we would be an easy target.

All through the morning we climbed higher, the camels slowing down considerably on the steep, rocky ground. We passed a couple more watch towers. They too were unoccupied. It was as though security on this route had been totally abandoned, with no Roman presence at all. We didn’t stop at noon as usual, but hurried on through the heat of the day. Khalid was clearly keen to get us off the road and into our overnight stop as soon as he could. Sure enough, in a narrow valley just before the summit of the pass, we found the next fort. It was being guarded by a platoon of Roman soldiers. Although when we spotted them they were lazing about, as we approached they suddenly saw us and smartening themselves up made to stand guard on the walls and at the gate. There must have been ten or more of them, all in full uniform in this temperature. No wonder they'd been a bit slow to come to attention.

They acknowledged Khalid as the leader of our caravan. After we'd unloaded and made tea, Andreas went over and spoke to them; unlike me, he always felt comfortable in soldiers' company. After a while he came back and reported.

"They're pretty fed up in this god-forsaken place, as they describe it. They've been up here for ten days; it's meant as a punishment detail. It seems they'd run amuck in Koptos last month so the commander sent them up here to cool off, if that's the right expression! Some posting! But they're nice chaps. Most of them come from Libya and they're part of the III Cyrenaica again, so we had something to talk about. Two or three of them are Christians. They say that a lot of these Beja running the caravans are Christian too. They were converted many years ago by a priest from Ethiopia, some place way down south near the source of the Nile."

I spoke to Khalid about it. He replied, "Oh yes, many of our tribe believe in uJesu. He very good man. He save us from Satan."

I was amazed. I hadn't realised how far the good news had spread. But remembering what Irene had told me before I left and what I'd learned in Alexandria, Jesus had preached in and around Jerusalem, close to the wilderness of Judaea, where he had also spent forty days and forty nights tempted by the devil. There were nomadic Bedouin, just like Khalid and his tribe, living there. And they had spoken Aramaic, similar to these Arabs here. It all began to make sense and I marvelled at the universal appeal of the message of Christ.

"We not like Rome. Too many gods. All be like human, not like Almighty. Come, eat!"

That night before we turned in I read a passage from Luke's gospel and we sang a psalm of David. Khalid and one or two of the others stood close by and mouthed "Amen" in the appropriate place. If Sami, from the previous evening, was to be believed, tomorrow would be the day we had to fear the most and where we had to be at our most alert. But overnight at least here in the safety of the fort we slept easily, with no apprehensions about being disturbed.

Dawn the next day saw us re-loaded and ready to move again. The gates were already wide and we passed out onto the road again. Julius, one of the legionaries who had opened the gate, told us his group intended to march to the next fort along sometime during that morning, so we'd probably see them later. I wondered if we shouldn't wait for them, but with all our baggage and other gear we would be moving a lot slower than they would.

The scenery became progressively more dramatic as we climbed to the highest point on the road. The mountain peaks soared skywards, huge lances of bare rock set sharply against a cloudless firmament, their upper faces burnished with the reflection of the sun's rays as they rose one behind the other into the far distance. As we went over the pass, the flanks of the mountains closed to form a gorge around us, hemming us in. Andreas, in front again, abruptly stopped, listening. He had heard something and was peering ahead to see if he could see what it was. Suddenly an ibex bolted out of the rocks in front of him and bounded across the road, vanishing into a dark ravine on the other side. Andreas turned, smiling at his own foolishness and as he did so a man suddenly appeared on the road in front of us, as if from nowhere. He was the one who'd disturbed the ibex, not us.

More men materialised without warning on the rocks around and above us, maybe thirty or forty that we could count, just standing in the shimmering heat. We were surrounded. In our nervous state the men looked the epitome of evil and we sensed they were eyeing our camels. We were totally outnumbered. But strangely they didn't make any move to seize us or the camels and we all stood waiting to see what would happen next. If it wasn't so frightening it would have been rather comical, two groups at a stand-off in the middle of these austere mountains miles from anywhere and no-one doing anything.

Slowly the man in front of us walked towards the leading camel and came abreast of Khalid.

"Peace be with you," he said, rather unexpectedly. "You are going to Berenike?"

When Khalid answered in the affirmative, the man leaned on his staff and said,

"My son Harun is sick. He fell in the mountains a few days ago and cut his arm. I fear that if he doesn't see a doctor soon he will die. He is my only son. We are people outside the law here. If I take him near any city, they will arrest me; maybe they will kill me and maybe him too. I don't know how I will get around this problem. Can anyone here help us? Can you take my son to Berenike? We have family near there. They will pay you for your trouble."

Khalid looked around at our group. I could see he didn't want to be caught up in this business. It would be a huge complication. The last thing he wanted was a sick boy who might hold the party back and, to anyone in authority, having one of these bandits in our party might even reflect on our own legitimacy. He was about to say no when I strode forward.

"Wait, Khalid. May I see the boy? How bad is he? Can I have a look at him?"

Khalid motioned me forward and I went up to the man.

"I am Nicholas," I said. "Where is the lad? Is he here?"

The man, whose name turned out to be Nabil, grabbed me by the arm without further ado and led me into the boulders and down a steep gulley to a rock overhang. There in the shadows was a boy of about fourteen years old lying on a makeshift bed. He was ashen white and breathing in short gasps. His left arm was desperately inflamed and the hand was puffed up and very hot to the touch. On the underside of the lower arm was an inflamed weal covered in blood. It had clearly become infected. If nothing was done, he would surely die in a matter of days. I knelt down and smiled at him.

"Don't worry Harun; we'll take care of you. Just give me a moment."

He looked back at me with a mixture of fear and desperation. He was obviously in pain and I sensed he knew he might be dying. I climbed back up the gulley and walked over to Khalid.

"We have to take him with us," I insisted. "If he stays here he will be dead by the end of the week or soon after. He's in great discomfort, but I'll look after him. Andreas and I will be responsible for him. It won't hold us up, I promise you."

Khalid was unimpressed. He'd made up his mind. Then I had a brainwave.

"And if we take him with us, it will mean we won't be attacked. See, he'll be our guarantee of safe passage. That has to be a good thing, doesn't it?"

Khalid massaged his chin for a minute.

"You know, I think you might be right. We no have to worry about outlaws, of attack. Yes, you very clever eh? But is your problem, not mine, right?"

"Very good," I said.

I motioned to Andreas to come with me. We scrambled down to where Harun lay and Andreas took a look at the boy.

"I've seen wounds like this among the soldiers. You're right. Unless something is done, he's a goner. He obviously has a fever. Let's get him up that gulley to the road and see how we can make him comfortable."

With some difficulty we manhandled the boy up the rocky passage and as far as the camels.

"We need two poles," said Andreas decisively, pointing to a couple on the side of one of the camels. "And we need one of your long shirts." He pulled the hem of one of the driver's ankle-length gallabiyahs.

One miraculously appeared. He pushed the poles through the arm holes and down the length of the robe. He signalled to me and we lifted the boy, who was groaning quietly yet fascinated to see what was happening, onto the centre of this new stretcher. Andreas put me at the back of the two poles and he took the front, one in each hand and on Andreas' command we lifted the boy clear of the ground. Andreas indicated we should put him down again and walking over to Nabil he told him that we'd look after Harun. He asked where he was to be delivered when we reached Berenike and Nabil gave him a name. And with a small gesture from Nabil, his gang of outlaws melted away. Nabil stood over his son and after saying a few words of encouragement to him he too disappeared into the rocks. The encounter was over as quickly as it had begun, but we were left with a very sick boy to look after. Khalid raised his hand and the caravan moved forward again over the pass and ever eastwards down into the cavernous wadi which opened up in front of us. We followed behind with the stretcher.

Apart from one of the camels stumbling on the steep, rocky down-slope, there were no more dramas that afternoon and we reached the next fort in good time. My arms were aching dreadfully by the time we got there and it was a great relief to put Harun down in the shade inside the fort. Andreas looked at him and said he thought we should clean the lad up a bit and take a really good look at the wound. The boy was delirious from the infection and from the heat of the sun all afternoon. We'd have to think about what to do about that tomorrow, or he'd die of sunstroke.

Andreas brought over a bowl of water and a cloth and began very gingerly to clean away the blood around Harun's arm. It was heavily caked and took some time, with Harun wincing at every stroke; then he bound the wound with freshly-torn cotton ribbon. Andreas suddenly looked up at me and motioned with his eyes to move away.

"Look Niko, do you know what I think this wound is? He didn't just fall; I'll bet it's from a gladius, a Roman sword. I recognize it. I've seen this type of thing before. Harun must have been trying to defend himself with his left arm when it was slashed like this. I would guess he was probably holding a weapon in his right hand, a knife or a dagger or something. I'd estimate it was about a week ago. Didn't we hear that some outlaws had been captured and executed last week? It's possible he'd been in that party and somehow escaped."

Whilst I considered that, he continued:

"Thinking on, what worries me now is that Julius and the other soldiers we met at last night's fort will be here soon. If they find out about this lad, they'll string him up for sure! We have to keep them away from Harun. They mustn't know he's here. And we must leave at the crack of dawn tomorrow."

We made Harun as comfortable as possible in the far corner of the fort. As we were doing so, Dawud came over and gave us a bag of what appeared to be herbs. He pointed first to Harun then down his throat and raised both arms up in front of him, smiling one of his toothless smiles.

"I think he's indicating that these herbs have restorative powers. Well, we don't have anything else, do we? I'll get a beaker of water."

I mixed the herbs in the water and, kneeling down, lifted Harun's head and put the beaker to his lips. With some reluctance he grimaced and drank the mixture in slow gulps until it was all gone then lay back on the stretcher. I covered him with a blanket and after a few minutes he seemed to fall asleep. After a quick meal of flat bread and dates we weren't far behind him, exhausted after all the carrying we'd done that afternoon. As far as I know the night passed peacefully. Julius and the other legionaries must have arrived at some point because they were all fast asleep in the fort when I woke up. Andreas was already up and about getting our packs ready. He handed me more of last night's flat bread and dates and indicated that he'd already opened the gate of the fort. Careful not to wake the legionaries we lifted Harun up to take him out onto the road and he turned his head and smiled at me, which I took to be a positive sign. Dawud's herbs must have had some effect.

The rest of the caravan followed us out and we began our descent down the yawning wadi. Dawud, ever eagle-eyed, indicated figures of men watching us from vantage points high among the cliffs, Nabil's men presumably, but they made no attempt to come any closer and we continued for a while in the cool of the deep shadow cast by the mountains. The wadi opened out as it descended into a broad valley with secret gorges running like branches of a tree into the hills on either side. There had clearly been a recent spate of flood-water flowing down the centre of the wadi. The road was largely washed away and clumps of spindly grass were growing along the dusty path made by previous caravans. After a mid-day stop and a continuation during the afternoon Khalid announced that we had no need to reach a fort that night. We could camp in the open. He could obviously see now the virtue in having taken Harun with us.

As the sun sank behind the mountains, the camels were unloaded and allowed to wander into the grassy edges of the wadi. Goat hair tents were quickly erected and floored with woollen rugs and a fire was lit in the centre of the camp. A couple of the men were deputed to make bread and the inevitable bean and herb stew was put on to boil with water from full skins. Dawud, alert as usual, pointed to the rock walls of the nearby ravine and Andreas and I walked with him to see what was there. It was truly astonishing. Pictures had been scratched on the flat faces of all the rocks and with them was what I assumed to be some form of writing. I recognised the figures. They represented the divinities of the Nile, with the ancient figure of Min-Amon at their head. He wore a crown supporting a sun disc and two feathers and his chin was adorned with a false beard. I surmised these must be very ancient, maybe two thousand years old, dating back to the time of the first Pharaohs in Egypt. Pecked around them were cartouches, royal names, filled with picture-writing which the people of Alexandria had called hieroglyphics. They showed kneeling figures carrying what looked like a cross symbol with an oval ring on the top, the ankh and others showed reeds and sun disks, hawks and water birds. There were hundreds of pictures here.

I asked Dawud what he thought they meant and he tortuously gestured that they had been made by caravans that had passed this way many hundreds of years ago. We wandered the ravine looking from one to the next until the light began to fail and we returned to the camp. We gave Harun more of Dawud's herbal mixture. It seemed at least to reduce the fever, though the swollen arm and hand were still enlarged. Andreas cleaned the discharge from the gash and re-dressed the wound.

"Do you know, Niko, I think he's going to last until we get to the coast. I didn't think that when we first saw him. I thought he'd only got a couple of days left! But at least he's holding on and in his right mind. We might see if he can walk a bit tomorrow, save us carrying the stretcher, eh?"

We ate the bread and beans under a starlit sky of great beauty, a vast canopy of pin-pricks of light shimmering in the darkness. I thought of the wonders of the heavens and the greatness of creation and I thanked God for our life and our companionship. Sweet tea was passed around and as we stretched out on the rugs we truly relaxed, I think for the first time in the journey.

During the next two days the going became progressively easier. The wadi broadened and sand dunes had drifted against its edges with the wind. After we'd put Harun's left arm in a sling he was persuaded to walk a little, making our journey a lot easier. As we descended, we came across the black tents of other groups of Bedouin who were camped along the valley floor, tending their goats and rather scrawny fat-tailed sheep. They had come up from the coast after the winter to take advantage of the fresh grass. Their flocks were being marshalled by dogs with spiked collars around their necks, I presumed to guard them against attacks by jackals, or maybe wolves. Khalid clearly knew some of the people who were camped here. One night we even joined one of the Bedouin families and enjoyed a goat stew, along with our ubiquitous beans.

As we walked ever closer to the coast, the hills fell behind us and we entered a wide, open plain and began to smell the sea. About mid-morning on the next day it came into view, a glorious shimmering blue which contrasted with the lighter cerulean sky. The waves were breaking gently along a sandy beach making me a bit nostalgic; it reminded me somewhat of the beach at Patara. At this point our caravan turned south, parallel to the shore. The road from now on was flat with slightly undulations and our journey uneventful. During the next six days we walked with the sea on our left and the mountains on our right, the sun reflecting off the intervening glaring white sand being our only inconvenience. From time to time we stopped briefly at some of the many tented encampments to pass the time of day, to fill our skins at the wells and to drink tea. Our drivers knew all the Bedouin from these settlements and I presumed that they must have been related to most of them.

By the middle of the afternoon of the seventh day along the coast, we could see Berenike in the distance, which as we came closer turned out to be a tight cluster of mud-brick houses shaded with innumerable date palms protecting the little fields of the oasis, all set around a small azure bay. Beyond the roofs of the buildings we could just make out the masts of a few boats. We had arrived at one of the ports of the Erythraean Sea. This was an essential link on the spice and silk road and we'd got here safe and sound.

God be praised, I thought.

CHAPTER NINE

A VOICE FROM THE PAST

As we came close to the town, the camels still keeping to their loping, measured pace, baggage tassels swinging from side to side, children ran out from the houses to greet us, shouting and laughing. Did I imagine it or did the drivers quicken their step as they came nearer to what I supposed must for most of them be their home? We were carrying Harun at the time and he raised his head and smiled at us. He would live. We walked on along a street flanked by white-washed mud-brick houses which led into the centre of the town where there was a small square shaded with palm trees. Crowds of chattering people gathered around us as we came to a final stop and the camels were persuaded to lower themselves one last time onto their haunches. Small boys brought leather buckets of water for the camels to drink which they noisily began to do. Young men came over and helped take the camel bags from their backs and pile them to one side. It was clearly a joyous moment for the whole town. We gratefully placed Harun on the ground for the last time.

Khalid pulled himself away from a knot of men he'd been talking to at the side of the square and he came over to me.

“Mr Niko, you have been good for us. You must come to my house. Stay with family until you go Erythaean Sea. You all come. You eat, you sleep, you family now!”

He motioned to Andreas and then Harun and waved a lad over to take our bags, such as they were.

“We get doctor now for Harun,” he announced, “and we let his family know.” So saying he summoned another boy from the crowd and spoke to him, pointing down to Harun. The lad ran off down a side street and Khalid waved us to follow him to the sea front. After a couple of blocks, he ushered us into a large two storied mud-brick house, saying,

“Is my house. Here you stay, all of you. You sleep on roof.”

He pointed to an external staircase running up the side of the building and the lad took our bags up to the top.

“Now first you eat, no?”

We went into the house and he motioned to a large table close to the floor around which were large, flat-weave covered cushions. He waved to the door at the back, at which signal a row of three or four dark-eyed young girls entered carrying trays of dishes which they spread on the table - various bean concoctions in bowls, platters of olives and dried figs, a large bowl of dates, two baskets of freshly baked flat bread and a huge plate piled high with pieces of cooked chicken.

“Come, sit, eat!” he gestured towards the cushions.

We propped Harun up along one side of the table and sat ourselves around the other three sides. Two jugs of palm wine were brought in and a nest of silver cups. One of the girls filled the cups with the wine whilst the others brought even more dishes of nuts, cheese and green vegetables. We needed no further encouragement to help ourselves. We had been on the road for the best part of two weeks, existing on a meagre diet mainly of bean stew and water. This was a feast and we ate with relish. I helped Harun to a variety of the vegetables and pieces of chicken, which he was able to eat with his good hand.

“Come, eat!” commanded Khalid. “The more you eat the more you like me,” he guffawed.

So we did as we were commanded until we had eaten our fill and my head had become muzzy with the palm wine. As we were finishing, a man in a white robe and impressive beard entered and was introduced as the doctor. We helped Harun to one side and set him on one of the cushions facing the room, pointing to his bandaged arm. The doctor nodded to Harun and then lifting his arm, causing Harun to cry out, he untied the bandages and looked very carefully at the wound for a long time.

“It is a bad laceration,” he announced. “If we are to save the arm we must act at once. There is already a risk of morbidity setting in. It needs to be very well cleaned and then disinfected.

I fear the gash has severed some of the muscles, so that he may not get back all the movement in his left hand, but we'll worry about that later. First I will clean it."

And so saying he opened his bag and took out a small box. He lifted the lid and inside there was a writhing mass of white maggots which made us all wince to look at them. Taking a spoon, he ladled out several groups of the maggots and placed them on the wound, quickly covering them with light gauze and then a bandage wrapped around the arm and tied at the wrist.

"We must let this work overnight and then tomorrow we must bathe the arm in sea water for two or three days. I will come again in the morning. By the way, I recognise the boy. Isn't he Harun of the Beni Hasan family? You must inform them he's here. And also, let him take this while I'm away."

He handed me a screw of papyrus with crushed herbs in it and with that, he left. We helped Harun up the stairs on the outside of the house and finding mattresses placed out on the roof, we laid him on one of them.

"Niko, Andreas," he said, the first words he'd really spoken since we found him in the rock shelter, "thank you for all you have done for me. I was very afraid and I feared I was going to die, but thanks to you I am alive. I shall never ever forget the kindness you have shown me."

"My goodness," I replied, "we didn't even know you spoke any Greek. It's wonderful to get you here in one piece. We've prayed for you every night. In a day or two, when you are truly better, we'll arrange for you to be reunited with your mother's family. Now, let me prepare these herbs for you and then you must sleep."

I went back down and finding an empty cup I filled it with wine and mixed in the herbs. I took it back upstairs and gave it to Harun, who drank it in one swallow and then lay back on his mattress. I went downstairs again as the young girls were clearing away the dishes and said our good nights to Khalid and the family, at which point I was so tired with the journey and the palm wine that I crawled back upstairs and fell into a deep slumber until morning.

Next day the doctor appeared again and took off Harun's dressing. The swelling had gone down slightly and when the wound was exposed and the maggots removed, we could see it was very clean. He stitched the wound closed with cotton threads and ordered a small bath of sea water to be brought into which he slowly lowered Harun's arm.

"It must stay like that for one hour, then left to dry for one hour, then placed again in fresh sea water. One hour in, one hour out all day for three days. The salt water will hopefully stop any further infection and the arm will be whole again, more or less anyway. You must dress it each night."

So saying he handed me a stack of fresh cotton dressings and left. We did exactly as bidden and miraculously, within three days, the swelling was much reduced and Harun's fever had left him; he was walking around unaided, looking a great deal better. A messenger had been sent to his family and we hoped to welcome one or more of his relatives in due course.

In the meanwhile, Andreas and I had been asking people about the ships which sailed the Erythraean Sea. All we could see were fishing boats pulled up onto the sand along the beach. We went one morning to the fish market where there were large tuna which had been caught the night before laid out on slabs as well as piles of sardines on mats. We asked a few of the stall holders and they told us they hadn't seen a trading ship for some weeks but they were sure there would be one fairly soon. We had to wait, they said. Sure enough, a couple of days later a sail was sighted out at sea which slowly materialized into a huge trading vessel with two enormous masts and gradually it navigated towards the harbour and finally tied up. There was much excitement in the town. Everyone ran to the quayside to see what would be unloaded. Apparently it had come from India, or maybe even further afield and it was fully laden.

I sat on the dockside with all the other spectators and watched hour after hour as the seamen and dock hands started to unload the vessel. There were any number of bales of silk wrapped tightly in sail cloth, as well as wooden boxes which I was assured contained tea and spices. The unloading took all afternoon. Everyone was so involved in what they were doing I couldn't find anyone to ask when the ship would be returning down the Erythraean Sea to Africa, India or China, if in fact they really went that far; I was so ignorant about their destinations. All I knew is that somewhere on that remote journey was the place where the incense mountains lay, where the frankincense came from.

It was getting towards sunset when I left the harbour and started heading back to Khalid's house. I thought I would take a detour down some of the back alleys behind the warehouses. It was as I was walking down one of these that I heard a woman's voice calling to me from a doorway.

"Show you a good time, mister?"

I stopped dead in my tracks. I thought for a moment. I knew that voice. I'd heard it before, years ago, in Patara.

"Calista?" I questioned incredulously, "Calista, is that you?" I span around.

The woman retreated into the shadows and I went over and led her out into the half-light to get a good look at her. Indeed it was Calista, my father's faithless wife who had run off with Chronos, both of whom I thought had been drowned in Lycia all those years ago. In truth I barely recognised her. She was dishevelled, her hair was matted and she had a livid scar down her left cheek and was wearing what I'm sure was meant to be a suggestive dress but which had lost any attraction it once might have had by being dirty and torn.

"Is that really you, Calista?" I repeated.

"Master Nicholas?" she asked in a startled voice. Then more to herself she continued, "It can't be you, can it? It can't be Aquila's son, surely?" Then after a moment she said more clearly, "Oh, no, it is you isn't it? It is you, Master Nicholas? All the way from Patara?"

She drew a shawl in front of her face as if to hide her humiliation. She was clearly in a highly discomfited, not to mention a very distressed state as she tried once more to draw back into the doorway, as if she wanted the darkness to swallow her up. I drew her out by the hand and looked at her full in the face, mutilated as it was by her wound.

"Calista? Yes, it's me, Nicholas. What are you doing here in this remote place? How do you come to be here? What has happened to you? And where is Chronos? Why are you in this dark alley?"

The questions just tumbled out one after the other. I was in a state of total shock at what I saw. What was she doing acting like a prostitute in this remote town in a foreign country?

"Chronos left me over a year ago, here in this town. He left me with absolutely nothing, no money, no clothes, no pride, nothing." She was clearly very upset. "I've been trying to keep body and soul together for months in this horrible place, trying to get money from the sailors so that I can go back to Lycia, but it's never enough. It's never anywhere near enough . . ."

She broke down at this point and began to weep bitterly, sobbing in huge gulps and holding her face in her hands while the tears flowed between her fingers. I was tremendously moved by her very obvious anguish which I could see was absolutely genuine. She truly was a lost soul drowning in a sea of misery; that much I could totally comprehend.

"Do you have anyone with you?" I asked with some hesitance.

"No," she replied wretchedly, "I'm all alone. I had a baby, a little baby girl last year. Kyra I called her. Chronos didn't want her. It wasn't his, he said. That's why he left me. But she died a couple of months ago. I'm all on my own."

The tears began to flow even faster, streaking her face and making her look even more pitiful.

"Oh, what can I do Master Nicholas? I am near the end. It's all over for me, I know it. I've sunk to the very bottom and there's no way out for me now. I've got nothing, no hope, nothing!"

I looked at her body, wracked with self-pity and despondency and I remembered the stories I had read about Jesus, who had consorted with tax collectors and prostitutes, with sinners and the dregs of humanity, preaching to them the good news of redemption, that God loved them just as much as anyone else and that through him, they could be forgiven, that they could be rehabilitated to a new life through God's grace.

I did something then that I am truly amazed at, even now. I took Calista by the hand, kissed her on her wet cheeks and led her up the alley towards the lighter part of the open square.

"Come," I said encouragingly. "Come with me. We'll get you out of this desperate situation and set you right again. Don't be afraid, Calista; I am a Christian. God will help us. God will forgive you. He will make his face shine upon you; he will give you his peace, he really will. Let's get you among friends, people who will be able to make things better for you."

Wide-eyed and clearly intensely scared she nevertheless followed me, holding my hand tightly with both of her own in case I was a phantom and would vanish as quickly as I had come. She kept saying,

"Master Nicholas, it is really you, isn't it? You do know who I am, don't you? You know what awful things I've done, don't you?" Then after a short silence, weeping bitterly, she pleaded, "Oh, Master Nicholas, you will help me won't you?"

We arrived at Khalid's house and went in. The girls were all sitting around the room laughing and gossiping but as we entered they fell totally silent. They looked goggle-eyed at Calista as though she was an apparition from another world, some malignant spectre that had somehow attached itself to me.

I smiled at them all and said, "This is Calista. She needs our help. She has fallen on very hard times and we need to pick her up. Do you think you can look after her for a few minutes? Show her where to wash? Get her some clean clothes? Make her feel at home? I know it might be a bit unusual, but I know her from another life, you see. She is a friend of mine."

Calista was transfixed and gave me a deeply perplexed look. Clearly she could hardly believe this was happening to her. I made to pass her over to the girls and she became suddenly agitated, reluctant to let go of my hand in case I was about to disappear into the ether. As the girls led her to the next room she kept staring back at me, head craned around, until she'd finally gone through the door. I went to find Khalid to explain what I had done and to ask his forgiveness for the intrusion into the good running of his household.

"Is no problem," he said. "Your friend she is our friend. We help each other, you know this thing? She will stay here with you, no?"

I tried to explain the circumstances more clearly, but I was getting bogged down in rather complex details so I gave up and just agreed. In half of an hour or so, Calista re-appeared in a floor-length cotton shift, her hair newly washed and her face and hands scrubbed. She looked acutely embarrassed and fearful by turns as two of the girls led her over to me.

"I'm not sure I know what's happening to me Master Nicholas. Why is everyone being so kind to me?"

I introduced her to Khalid and then to Andreas and to Harun, who by this time seemed in the peak of health. They shook hands with Calista and Khalid poured out a cup of sweet tea which he handed to her.

"Niko's friend is our friend," said Andreas. "Welcome!"

She sat next to me, clutching at my arm and sipping her tea.

"But Master Nicholas, I've done some very dreadful things. How can anyone ever forgive me my wrong-doing? I am no longer worthy of anyone's affection and help. I don't deserve to live!"

"First, everyone knows me as Niko. That's what you must call me. And as for your past, we are going to leave that for God to deal with. As far as I am concerned, you have done me no wrong at all. I am only too pleased to see you and pleased that I can be of some help in your time of need. You must consider yourself amongst friends, Calista. We will do all we can for you. Everything will be alright, believe me."

We talked for what seemed like hours after that. Her story of her abandoning my father, of leaving Patara, of the shipwreck and of her miraculous escape all lurched out in a rush. It was clearly preying on her mind. She described her year or two's journey around the Great Sea to Alexandria; she couldn't remember exactly how long it had taken. She described how callous Chronos had become, how he frequently got drunk and beat her and how in Alexandria he forced her to give herself to strange men so that he could get money. It was a tale of such desperation it was difficult to credit. They had stolen from innumerable people, including the old incense merchant, then, fearing arrest they had fled the city. They had discovered incidentally that what they had taken from the incense merchant wasn't the right stuff anyway. He'd tricked them and they'd had to throw it away. Eventually, after six or seven months of walking up the Nile Valley they'd reached Koptos. Chronos had some ridiculous idea of getting involved with the frankincense trade. He said he knew all about how it worked.

She continued her story. After some months more, Chronos managed to attach them both to a caravan in return for Calista performing for the men. It was one of them who had slashed her left cheek; she put her hand up to the wound apprehensively. Finally they'd got to Berenike. Calista had then told Chronos about her pregnancy and he became angrier than ever, beating her almost senseless so that she nearly lost her baby. It was born soon after, desperately weak, and the little mite had only lasted a few months before dying in her arms. By that time Chronos had gone;

she didn't know where and quite frankly didn't care. Since then she'd been living as I had found her. Her story ended, she erupted again into uncontrollable tears of desperation and remorse.

"Well, first, you must consider that that way of life you've just told us about is finished and behind you for good, Calista. As I've said, you are among friends here. We will look after you. Let us put our trust in God and he will give us the answer. He will always provide."

She looked open-mouthed at me as though I'd descended from heaven.

"You should know that as I told you, Andreas and I are both Christians and although we haven't talked in detail about it, so I believe are Khalid and his family. It is our way to forgive each other our wrong-doing, not dwell on it and punish people for it. Now, go with Khalid's daughters and have something to eat and get some sleep. Tomorrow we'll talk some more and see what's to be done."

She smiled weakly and biting her lip, allowed herself be led away again by the girls.

Next morning at breakfast time she appeared dressed in a fresh, colourful gallabiyah.

"Master Nich...sorry, Niko. I couldn't be certain you were still here! It all seems so much of a miracle to me. I kept waking in the night and wondering if I hadn't dreamed the whole thing. Oh, what can I say? How can you all be so caring towards me? I've done such awful things to people. I..."

I cut her short at this point.

"As I said last night, from now on you are among friends, Calista. Don't be afraid any more. By the way, the doctor is here. He's been fixing Harun's arm and hand. Why don't you let him take a look at the scar on your cheek?"

It appeared even more raised and livid in the daylight. The doctor walked over to her and looked carefully at the welt.

"Yes," he pronounced, "I think I can make it look much better than that. As I told you Niko, I'd have to recut it and stitch it, but it is more than likely that it would be much improved. What do you think young lady? Would you like me to try?"

She put her hand to her face and frowned.

"You mean you can make it better?" she asked doubtfully.

He answered in the affirmative and sat her down by the window so that the light shone on the left side of her face. He opened his bag and drew out a small scalpel the sight of which made her flinch a little.

"Don't be afraid," he encouraged. "It will all be over very quickly and it won't hurt too much. Can I have a bowl of salt water please?"

Setting her head to one side, he very dexterously cut open the scar, trimmed back the rough tissue, then threading his needle he put in five stiches, delicately drawing the skin together, as he had done with Harun's wound. When he'd finished, he dipped a fresh cotton cloth in the salt water and carefully wiped the small amount of blood that had run from the incision.

"In five days you can take the stiches out and you'll be a new woman!"

I could see her struggling with the notion of a "new woman." Would her soul be as easily corrected, she must have wondered? She eyed me searchingly, as though looking to see if I had an answer. I smiled at her and asked the girls to bring in the breakfast.

It was while we were eating that Harun announced, "I've had news from my relatives in the town about my mother. You know, my father wanted me to go to her if I lived. She's upcountry with another family, north near Myos Hormos. There's far less Roman military activity there and it's so wild in the mountains no one would think of looking for me."

"So, we're going to say goodbye to you Harun. We wish you all the luck in the world. Don't get involved with these military people again, eh!"

"Oh and where's Andreas?" I asked the others, who then told me he'd gone out early to the harbour.

He came back about lunch-time, a bit the worse for wear and reeking of palm wine.

"Right," he said. "I've fixed it! That ship in the harbour is going down the Erythraean Sea starting the day after tomorrow and we have a berth on it for as long as we want. It will cost a bit."

"Have you been drinking with the crew Andreas, at this time in the morning?"

"Look, Niko, you fix the lost souls and the strays, the sick and the wounded and I'll fix how we get to where we want to go! Alright?"

I couldn't argue with that, but hearing that we were making plans to leave, Calista became disturbed again.

"If you are leaving what's going to happen to me? I am all alone here in a strange land. I can't go back to Lycia, even if I had any money, which I don't. My family would reject me. I would be totally ostracised. My life is in ruins. Are you going to abandon me? Please, Niko, help me!" she begged.

"It's not going to be like that at all, Calista; we have no intention of leaving you here! We'll all go to the frankincense mountains together. Why not? It seems the old man in Alexandria tricked me into making this journey in the first place. Well, the least he can do is pay for the expenses! Calista, we're not going to abandon you. You shall come with Andreas and me."

And that was how there came to be three of us on the journey.

CHAPTER TEN

CRUISING THE ERYTHRAEAN SEA

Two days later, as a rose-coloured dawn streaked the sky, we made our way to the jetty; what little luggage we had they'd loaded the night before. We'd said our farewells to Harun and to Khalid and his family and were now preparing for the next part of our journey. Moored alongside the little harbour, the ship we were going to board looked enormous - a dhow specially built for the waters off India, so I was to learn. It had actually been built there, on the Malabar Coast where many of the spices came from, but it turned out it was crewed by Arabs from the coast of Omanna. The Moscha Arabs were the one race of sailors who had worked out the mysteries of the annual shifting winds that made these seas amenable to long distance navigation.

When I had a chance to look carefully at the vessel, it was like no ship I had ever set eyes on before. She was constructed with wide planks stitched very securely together with what looked like leather thongs. Unlike our boats in the Great Sea, they hadn't use pitch to caulk the joints, just the tightly clamping strips of cow hide. Forward the prow rose to a high peak above the heavy bow, presumably to ride the waves and abaft there was a single sternpost to which was fixed the rudder. On the deck above the stern a large covered cabin had been built where the crew and the captain could shelter from the weather. A high main-mast rose from the centre of the deck, anchored at various points with stays to the gunwales. The main spar was set at an angle to raise a large triangular sail and there was a second, slightly smaller sail the same shape above the stern cabin.

Andreas introduced us to the captain, Abdul Hakkim, and to his two crewmen, Ibrahim and Joshua. They looked a bit askance that they were taking a woman on board. Knowing how superstitious seamen can be, perhaps they felt it would bring them ill luck. The captain indicated that we should have a short discussion before we cast off and he asked me for money. He needed to buy the last of his supplies, he said, so I handed him one of my gold pieces and he indicated that was more than enough.

So after one or two more items had come on board, in the light air of the early morning we pushed the beam away from the dock side and Ibrahim and Joshua rapidly hauled up the larger triangular sail, which, when the strengthening wind caught it, pulled us out into the channel. The ship wallowed for a few moments while we changed direction and then she surged forward as Abdul Hakkim worked the rudder to bring the wind behind us causing the sail to fill. The two crewmen then quickly raised the stern sail and we were off down the Erythraean Sea. Calista looked at me smiling and said,"Oh, Niko, I never thought this day would come, leaving this ghastly place. Is this the beginning of my new life?"

The wind caught her hair and she looked happier than I'd seen her at any time since we'd met some days before.

"I want to learn about Christianity," she said. "You have all been kinder to me than anyone has ever been before. And I don't care where we are going. I just want to stay with the two of you. Can I think of you as my family? Will you be that for me?"

I assured her we would always be there by her side if she needed us, whatever may befall and I could see that she was slowly becoming more at peace with herself.

During the course of the day the captain and I spoke together and I asked him where we were bound.

"We're going south down the western side of the Erythraean Sea to what you Greeks call Limen Evangelis. The local Beja Bedouin call it U Suk, 'The Market'. It's the main port for the interior and Nubia. We can get a refill of water there and we may pick up some cargo. They weave textiles in that region which could be of interest to us. We should be arriving in about four days if the wind holds. After that, we'll make our way further south, crossing over to the eastern side of the Sea to the Bay of Mocha, on the coast of the great Kingdom of Saba; I think you call it Sheba. From there we sail through the Bab el Mandeb, the Gate of Sorrow, into the Indian Sea and to the incense coast, about twelve days from now."

We were some distance from the shore at this point, outlined by high ranges of mountains.

"We have to stay well away from the land here. There are coral reefs just below the surface. You can't see any of them until you are right on top of them, by which time it's too late."

He made a grabbing motion with his fist suggesting the hull would be torn apart were this to happen.

The day wore on and in the afternoon Joshua lit a small fire in a bricked-in area of the poop which acted as his kitchen. He mixed and rolled out dough and skilfully baked it on a metal plate set over the coals. As it cooked he added some dried meat and herbs, folded it and gave it to me. It was deliciously savoury. He continued for half an hour or so, poking the fire to keep it hot and handing the cooked cakes round to each of us in turn until we'd had enough. He then made tea in a kettle, sweetened it with sugar and poured six cups and asked us each to take one. The tea had a smoky taste which gave it a wonderful flavour.

The sun set in a fiery pyrotechnic ball over the mountains of the western skyline and we sailed on into the coming darkness until the moon rose on the opposite side of the ship. Large and orange as it appeared over the horizon, then growing in brightness as it rose in the sky, its mazy reflection shimmered on the surface of the sea.

"We are fortunate," Captain Adbul Hakkim said. "We have good weather and can sail by moonlight all night."

Calista, who had been sitting quietly on the deck in deep thought most of the afternoon, came over and quietly put her arms around me and held me in a tight and long embrace.

"You have saved my life, Niko. You are indeed a great man, you know that, a very great man. May you be blessed!"

"We must indeed give thanks to our Lord," I replied. "He is the one who performs these miracles, not me."

* * * * *

We sailed on for the next three days and nights without incident. Ibrahim and Joshua were both of the Christian faith and had been so since birth. Calista began to ask them and Andreas so many questions about their beliefs that they brought out a few leaves of the Testament which they had with them and they read together, parts of the gospels and from the letters of St Paul, the apostle who had travelled around the Great Sea spreading the good news about Jesus Christ and of the forgiveness of sins. Calista was especially moved by the stories about Mary of Magdala, with whom she clearly identified.

I overheard her saying, "And you mean to say that Jesus forgave her all the bad things she had done? He made friends with her even after all that? Wasn't he afraid of what other people would say? That he was consorting with the lowest of the low? Oh, Ibrahim, I was like that. I have done dreadful things too. I was possessed with devils, just like Mary. Niko brought me out of my deep well of despair."

She came to me and repeated the stories about Mary Magdalene, about how Jesus had befriended her and how she had become, in effect, one of his closest followers. This message had moved Calista to tears, but I sensed they were tears of joy.

"Do you think Jesus would love me too, after all that?"

"Of course he will. His love is for everyone, rich and poor, man and woman, saint and sinner. If you turn from your wrong-doing and truly repent what you have done, he will give you his forgiveness and his love. You will be made whole once more, acquitted of all charges against you, as you had been when you were a little girl, innocent of the world's evils."

"I do so want to do this, Niko. I want to become one of his followers. I want to be whole again. Do you think I can do that? Can even I become a Christian?"

"Certainly you can," I told her encouragingly. "Read with Andreas, Ibrahim and Joshua, listen to the stories of our Lord, of his love for us and the sacrifice he made to make us whole. In a few days we shall be at Eudaemon on the coast of South Arabia. When we were in Berenike I was told there is a large

Christian community in Eudaemon. If you want, you can be baptised there."

"Oh, Niko, I think I should like that more than anything in the world, to have the burden of guilt lifted from me, the wrongs I did your father and you and everything else I have done. I can't believe it's possible, but if you say it can happen, I must trust you."

"Calista, you will be healed just like your wounded cheek. By the way, it's time to take out those stitches and you'll see it is so much better. Why don't we do that right away?"

And so one by one I carefully removed the stitches the doctor had put in at Khalid's house. Cleaning the dried blood from around the cut, I called Adbul Hakkim for a bucket of water and Ibrahim drew one from the sea and placed it on the deck. When it had settled to a mirror finish, Calista was at first reluctant to inspect herself, fearful of what she would see, but she finally glanced sideways into the dark water and looked at the reflection of her new face. The lesion was not totally healed yet, but the livid gash had gone. Her face was almost restored to its former appearance. Her broadening smile said it all.

"In Alexandria," I said, "Eusebius taught me that in the Bible it is written: 'Though your sins be as scarlet, they shall be as white as snow; though they are red as crimson, they shall be like new wool.' So it shall be with you, Calista. Just like your face, so will be your soul, your life."

An hour or so later Abdul Hakkim called out some instructions to Ibrahim and Joshua who dropped the main sail and re-set the sail at the stern as he put over the tiller and we began to drift towards what looked to me like a blank shore.

"U Suk!" he said, pointing to the east.

We gradually ran on towards the sea coast, Ibrahim leaning over the prow and shouting directions every few minutes. He was looking for a navigable passage between the shoals of coral. Ibrahim's shouts and Abdul Hakkim's corrections were constant for a full hour whilst Joshua manipulated the little sail. Slowly the land materialised and I could see a narrow channel, an inlet into which we eventually and very slowly cruised. The featureless shore ran away on either side for some considerable distance as we cruised slowly down the channel until a scattering of fishing boats and a stone-built town appeared, seemingly constructed on an island at the inner end of the inlet. The sail was lowered and we glided to a halt beside a rather dilapidated harbour while ropes were thrown to men on the quayside who pulled our ship in against the mud wharf.

"Limen Evangelis," beamed Abdul Hakkim, pleased to have avoided an encounter with the coral reefs. "'The Port of Good Hope', I think your Greek king Ptolemy called it. We've arrived. Wonderful, eh?"

Ibrahim had jumped down and was securing the ropes to the ends of palm trunks set in the ground, whilst traders in striped gallabiyahs and round hats rushed from the shade of the buildings up to the side of the ship calling out their wares to the captain, everything from fresh dates to trinkets made of coral and shells. I looked at the town beyond the narrow earth-ramped quayside. It was extraordinary. Set among majestic clumps of date palms it seemed the whole town was made of blocks of coral, a coarse, pinkish-white stone obviously quarried from the nearby reefs. The houses each had elaborate wooden balconies at the upper windows and every building had a heavily-carved wooden entrance door. On one side of the harbour there appeared to be a small daily market where awnings had been set up over a number of stalls and where we could see people strolling about.

"We'll be here for the rest of the day and we leave in the morning," announced Abdul Hakkim. "We have to take on water and other essentials and maybe some of their trade goods – they have excellent cotton cloth here. We'll see. By the way, there's an ancient caravan route which links U Suk to the interior. You can travel all the way across the desert and through the mountains right up to Meroë on the Upper Nile. Centuries ago it was the major trade route into North Africa."

U Suk might be less busy than it once was but there were still lots of people going about their daily business, to and from the market and in and out of the houses on the harbour front. The three of us walked over to the street market. There were piles of strange cereals like sorghum, millet and a fine grass they call teff, as well as many varieties of beans and the ever-present dates. On their stalls the date sellers displayed huge bunches of fresh dates, but they also had baskets of dried dates, bowls of dates mixed with honey and one or two even sold flour made from ground date stones. Little children tried to sell us necklaces made from date pips or carvings of animals made from date wood. And there were stalls selling date-palm wine too.

Looking into the faces of the people buying and selling, they exhibited such a variety of origins, from the typical coastal Beja Bedouin we had encountered further north, to dark-skinned Nilotic men and women with fine noses and ringleted hair and others with strong, black African features, people from deep in the interior. Although most could speak some Greek, they spoke to each other in a peculiar guttural language which I discovered was Kushite. Far inland lay what was once the ancient Kingdom of Kush, a domain whose history stretched back thousands of years.

On the side of the market nearest the boats there were the stalls selling fish, some dried and salted, but most of them were selling gleaming silvery fish that had been caught that morning. There were huge yellowfin tuna laid out on the sand in the shade and we ventured to think that Ibrahim would be making a fish dinner for us that night. Having sampled the market we made our way through the town among the streets of coral houses and found workshops where men were busily making metal tools and other utensils. There was one workshop with a forge where two small boys with soot-blackened faces were working pairs of bellows to keep the fire bright while the blacksmiths were hammering iron into hoes and mattocks and we even saw spear points at the back of one shop. As we walked I glanced upwards and saw dark eyes peering out from the balconies where the women of the town were watching us from the shadows.

Around the corner were open-fronted shops displaying bales of finely woven cotton fabrics as well as some made up into gallabiyahs hanging from hooks. The predominant colour was white, but there were some with yellow, black and deep red stripes too. From the rooms at the back we could hear the clatter of looms being worked, shuttles being run back and forth and cross beams pushed and pulled as the threads were woven together. I wondered if Calista would appreciate one of these gallabiyahs; she was still wearing the one she'd been given by the girls at Khalid's house. Against her protestations that she didn't have any money and that they would be too expensive I bought her a white and a coloured one and thrust them into her hands.

"Oh Niko, they're so beautiful," she whispered, full of sincerity. "Thank you! Thank you! I have never been with anyone who's been so kind to me."

After that we walked back to the ship and found Ibrahim cutting a large piece of tuna into thin slices which he was going to cook for us all.

The following morning two local men came with camels weighed down with cotton bales. They off-loaded their bundles and man-handled them onto the ship, where Ibrahim and Joshua carefully stored them in the hold.

"In India the women love this fabric," volunteered Ibrahim. "They grow cotton there themselves, but they don't weave it anything like as skilfully. They'll pay a lot of money for this fine cloth down on the Coromandel Coast."

Once the hatches over the hold had been closed and we'd let go the ropes from the bollards, two small rowing boats pulled our ship into the channel until we could raise the stern sail and make a bit of way on our own in the light air. Slowly we wove our way back down the channel and reached open water where Abdul Hakkim ordered the main sail to be raised. The off-shore wind caught it and we began to sail away from the coast of Africa. We were finally on our way to the frankincense mountains.

"We are very lucky, Niko," Abdul Hakkim announced, "the wind is from the north-west, directly behind us. If it stays that way we'll be in the Bay of Mocha in less than four days. It's not much of a place, but they have salt there which I can sell along the Malabar Coast."

We sailed without a break, the swell surging behind us, lifting the ship forward with each wave and speeding our passage. Calista and Andreas spent their days listening and talking to Ibrahim and Joshua as they read from the pages they had brought with them and they also learnt prayers and to sing hymns together. I too joined their devotions from time to time. Otherwise I spoke with the Captain and found out about the secrets of sailing in the Indian Sea.

"We have two sailing seasons during the year," he explained. "These are determined by two winds blowing from opposite directions. This time of the year, from the middle of the cool season to the beginning of summer we have winds which always blow from the north-west, like now; actually they're just finishing. This means we can easily sail south, down the coast of Africa, or along the coast of India, even as far as China if we wanted to. Then the other time of the year the winds blow in the opposite direction and allow us to sail north again. I learned this from my father as he did from his father. We will spend this summer in Omanna with our families and wait for the north-west winds again next winter and then we'll sail along the Coromandel and Malabar coasts where we will sell our goods and from there we shall bring back the silk and spices the following summer. Our families have been doing this for generations."

It was a mystery to me. Winds off the Lycian coast were either balmy breezes or stormy; there didn't seem to be an in-between, though truthfully I had never paid too much attention to them.

On another occasion I asked him why his ship was called 'Hatshepsut,' the name I'd seen painted on the prow.

"It's the name of an ancient Egyptian queen, a long time ago," he recounted. "The story goes that she sent a fleet of ships down this very coast, the one we are sailing right now, to find out where the incense they were using came from. No one seemed to know, so she sent sailors and soldiers all the way to Sheba and to the Land of Punt on the coast of East Africa to find out and to bring back live trees for her palace on the Nile. They say that she carved pictures of the whole journey on the walls of her mortuary temple across the Nile from her city at Thebes. I'm told you can still see them today."

We sailed for two nights and three days, most of that time out of sight of land. Towards the end of the third day Ibrahim shouted that he could make out land on the horizon off to the south-east and an hour or so later high mountains could be seen fringing the coast.

"That's the coast of Saba. Way over those mountains is where the frankincense grows. We'll call in briefly at the Bay of Mocha before going on through the Gate of Sorrow to Eudaemon."

Just at dusk we sailed between two broadly separated headlands ringed by rugged highlands. Abdul Hakkim drove the ship towards the Mocha shore. There was no harbour here so we dropped the anchors a short distance away from a small village and spent the night on board. When we woke next morning there were fishing boats all round us and the fishermen were calling to us and holding up huge kingfish and handfuls of squid. We bought one of the kingfish and Ibrahim handed down a bowl for some squid. When the captain asked about salt, someone in one of the boats said they would bring him some sacks later that morning.

"I went ashore here once," said the captain. "In the little village over there they make a drink from the ground-up roasted beans of a plant that grows on the mountainside. They mix it with boiling water and leave it to sit for a while and it makes a dark brown infusion which they use as a cure for various ailments and as a pick-me-up. They call it *qahwah*, as I seem to remember. It has an interesting but slightly bitter taste. The local people swear by it, but I can't really see it becoming popular myself. It's a bit too astringent. But I suppose you never can tell with these things can you? Look what happened to tea."

By the time the sun had passed its zenith, the sacks of salt had been carefully stowed in the driest part of the hold and the hatches had been battened down again. We weighed anchor and sailed away from the coast.

"By dawn tomorrow," said Abdul Hakkim, "we'll be approaching the Bab el Mandeb. We need to pass through there in daylight so that we don't become ship-wrecked. I think that's why it has been given the name, 'Gate of Sorrow'; so many people have drowned there."

I was glad he knew what he was doing, but said a silent prayer anyway for God to protect us. The air that night became noticeably balmier as we were approaching the warm waters of the Indian Sea beyond the narrows and at dawn we could see land on both side of the ship. The captain steered to the western side of the channel, towards Africa where, he said, there was a current flowing into the Indian Sea which would help us through. He also told me that it was across these narrows that Christians had first migrated from Arabia into Ethiopia, a huge mountainous country inland from the coast hereabouts.

By the afternoon we were through the 'Gate of Sorrow' without mishap and heading east along the coast to Eudaemon, the main port of Saba, the ancient kingdom of Sheba. The sea was more active here, at least just the other side of the straights. All being well, by tomorrow morning we would be nearing our goal, the frankincense coast of south Arabia. I slept soundly that night and woke to find that we were in a calm sea, barely moving.

"The wind died overnight I'm afraid," said the captain. "It happens at this time of the year, as the season for the north-west wind comes to an end, but we could get a bit of wind by the afternoon. Let's hope so anyway."

Sure enough the wind picked up during the day and blew strongly along the coast. We changed the set of our sail on the main mast and carried on into the night. Soon after dawn the next day we were off the port of Eudaemon. This was one of the frankincense ports, though we would have to sail a little further eastwards to the port of Qana, inland of which is where it actually came from. I thought of the story about the birth of our Lord. When Jesus was born in that stable in Bethlehem, the gospels tell us that wise men came from the east, may be it was from here. One of them had brought a present of frankincense, a gift fit for a king. It was so expensive then – more expensive than gold in those days, so I read in the 'Natural Histories' of the Roman author Pliny the Elder. That was one of the texts my tutor had forced me to read when I was a boy. Well, I suppose my lessons did have some use after all, I thought.

By sun-set we had navigated into the well-sheltered haven of Eudaemon, behind the remains of an ancient offshore volcano which had been joined to the mainland to create the harbour. The backdrop of the city was magnificent, with high peaks running up from the shore in serried ranks, one above the other. I looked at Calista and Andreas who had been deep in conversation together all afternoon and we smiled at one another. Hopefully this is where we'd find the Christian community which would allow Calista to be baptised.

CHAPTER ELEVEN

INTO THE FRANKINCENSE MOUNTAINS

The following morning the three of us went ashore with Ibrahim and Joshua. The two crewmen knew where the Christian meeting house was and after a short walk we arrived there. Inside we met one of the elders, Brother Paul, and spoke to him about Calista wanting to be baptized.

"All are welcome," he said expansively. "I would guess you're not in Eudaemon for very long. Would you like me to perform the sacrament this afternoon? We have a baptistery at the back of our building."

We went back to the ship and Calista changed into the white cotton gallabiyah I'd bought for her in U Suk. We returned to the meeting house at the appointed time. Brother Paul welcomed us and took us to the baptistery where he explained to Calista what baptism meant. When we had recited a couple of opening prayers, he read the story of Jesus being baptized in the Jordan River by John and of the dove descending from heaven.

Then he reached over to Calista, who was frowning with concentration, and taking her by the hand he asked her to step into the pool and immersed her in the water, saying, "I baptize you in the name of the Father, the Son and the Holy Spirit. May God absolve you from all your wrong-doing this day and wash away your sins. I bathe you with water, but he will bathe you with his love and forgiveness. Arise, Calista, to your new life in Jesus."

Paul reached for a phial of oil and made the sign of the cross on her forehead, at which Calista rose from the pool looking completely radiant. We said the Lord's Prayer together and then we all shook Calista's hand.

"What a fantastic transformation for you; I'm so pleased you've done it," Andreas murmured encouragingly.

I noticed Calista looked slightly askance at him, smiling coyly. Later she told me, "Oh, Niko, that was the most wonderful thing I have ever done. I felt all my past wrongs sliding away from me, like a lead weight being lifted from my shoulders and I feel I am a new person. I never knew that could ever happen."

As we got back to the ship, Abdul Hakkim was already completing the preparations to leave.

"If you want to get to the frankincense country we have to sail a bit further on, as far as Cana. From there you will be able to find someone who will know about its source in the mountains. It will take us about three more days sailing, depending on the wind."

We climbed aboard and with deft maneuvering the captain took 'Hatshepsut' out to sea again. Sails set, we began to navigate further east along the coast and indeed it did take us three days and nights before we rounded a windswept island and a promontory where Abdul Hakkim pointed to a small town on the beach of the mainland which he said was Cana.

"In ancient times, this used to be the main port for the incense traffic. The camel trains used to bring it all down here from the interior and it was transported by sea up to Egypt. But for the last few hundred years, the Arab caravans have dominated the trade and it now goes by land through Arabia Felix and Arabia Deserta to the Great Sea at Gaza, though even that changed a few years ago and much of it now goes up to Mesopotamia by sea from Omanna and then across the Syrian desert to Palmyra. Everyone wants to make money out of it! My great grandfather used to take it from Cana here to Barygaza on the coast of India as well as up the Erythraean Sea to Berenike or even as far north as Myos."

The ship hove to. When he'd brought the vessel more or less to a stop, Abdul Hakkim announced, "Niko, we're not going to moor here. We'll just let the three of you off. I sure you will understand that we have a few more days sailing to get home to Moscha, which we are all anxious to do, so we'll bid you farewell now. I hope all goes well for you."

When we had been spotted by people in the town a few came out towards us in little rowing boats to sell things to the crew. The captain shouted down to them to tell them what he wanted and a couple of them came up to the side of the ship. Bidding God's speed to the crew, we climbed over the gunwale and down a rope ladder into the boats and the crew let their ropes free. 'Hatshepsut' swung around ahead of the breaking waves and resetting the mainsail began to make way again out to sea. We waved and waved as she slowly moved away, then we settled down for the short ride through the surf to the beach in front of the settlement. As we grounded I jumped out of the leading boat onto the sand. We were finally setting foot in frankincense country.

Although the local coastal traders had learnt some Greek, mainly absorbing it from sailors that had called in there over the years, many of the people in the town and outside in the surrounding countryside spoke only Sabean, the ancient tongue of the region and still really the only one spoken in the uplands. So in a mixture of fairly simple Greek, a few Arabic phrases that Calista had learnt during her time in Egypt and some vigorous sign language we endeavored to make ourselves understood.

Everywhere we walked along the streets there were the fumes of burning incense; every shop and every stall had a smoking brazier in front of it. It was overpowering. I soon found the incense dealer in the town whom Abu Hakkim had recommended, a man named Bin Samer, who spoke in heavily accented but passable Greek and he told us that times were hard. Ships very rarely bought frankincense from Cana these days. It was all going by land, by caravan through Arabia or east to the ports in Omanna. I asked him that should I buy frankincense from him, could he organize for it to be shipped and delivered to a particular address in Alexandria. He said he could do that. Afterwards, to more of my questions, he described a little bit about how the incense was gathered.

"There are many different qualities, depending on how clean the droplets are – we call them the 'tears'- and especially what time of the year they're gathered. The resin comes from trees that grow in really harsh conditions in the Hadhramaut Valley, way over the mountains from here. The people cut the bark and the resin oozes out and they let it dry. That's what you see here."

He ran his fingers through a sack of variously-sized little whitish fragments.

"You say you'd like to go and pay a visit to the place where this comes from. I should warn you that until recently they've let no-one foreign anywhere near their valley. They guarded their secret very jealously, to the death I might add. But in the last few years they have eased off a little, I think because the demand for the tears just isn't what it used to be. Strangely enough, there was another foreign gentleman here about a year ago who went up there. He was a Greek too. The odd thing is he spoke just like you, the same accent, but he wasn't a particularly savory individual; he was quite unpleasant actually. What was his name now? Something to do with time, I seem to remember; I forget exactly now. I don't know what became of him."

"His name wouldn't have been Chronos, by any chance?" I interrupted.

"Yes, yes that's it, Chronos. That's the man. Did you know him? He really wasn't a nice character at all. He told us he knew all about the incense trade – said he was going to buy a large consignment of the stuff. But we all got the impression he was not at all trustworthy. Spoke as though he owned the place, but he had no belongings, nothing. You can always tell with some people, can't you?"

I could see Calista was becoming agitated hearing the news of her nemesis. She was frowning and looking anxiously at Andreas, but he smiled at her as if to tell her not to worry. I quickly changed the subject and asked Bin Samer if he knew how we might get to this mysterious Hadhramaut Valley and he replied that he was himself due to be going there in a few days' time for the first of the new harvest. He could bring his visit forward if we liked; we could go up together. It would take us about five days travelling, he told us. We readily agreed.

I then asked him which quality of incense I should buy for Apollodorus, the dishonest merchant in Alexandria and he pointed to a couple of small sacks and said, "I'll give you these two at a special price; it's actually old stock and less than half the normal tariff. I need to sell it to clear it out of the shop."

He named a figure and added a shipping cost and after fumbling under my shirt behind a pile of bags I parted with one or two of my gold pieces. I gave him Apollodorus' name and told him his store was in the Street of the Incense Sellers near the Moon Gate in Alexandria, which seemed to be enough for Bin Samer. I had discharged my obligation to my father's name.

"I'll get them there for you; and I tell you, whoever he is, he's getting an absolute bargain! You must like this chap a lot."

I didn't tell him the man was not to be trusted at all and that I was only buying the sacks to keep my part of a thoroughly bad bargain.

Bin Samer went on, "I suggest you stay at the guest house by the harbour tonight. We'll set off in the morning. Will that suit you?"

We did as he suggested. Calista was still a bit restive after hearing Chronos' name spoken in this remote region but Andreas managed to calm her down and eventually we all had a good night's sleep, on dry land for a change.

* * * * *

By the time we'd had an early breakfast Bin Samer was already outside with a string of camels loaded for the journey. With him were about twenty mounted Bedouin, all of them alarmingly armed to the teeth with spears and all manner of sabers and knives hanging from their belts. They looked quite terrifying.

"Perhaps I should tell you, Mr. Niko," admitted Bin Samer, looking rather awkward, "that to get to Shabwah, that's the place in the Hadhramaut to which we are heading, we are going to have to travel through very lawless country. You should know that there are well over a thousand different tribes in the interior all of whom have been constantly at war with each other for hundreds of years. I suppose it's caused by a couple of things – extreme drought at some times of the year leading to fights over water rights, and very, very long-standing blood feuds between families. It's been marginally better since the Ḥimyar Kingdom conquered the Kingdom of Shabwah a few years ago, but in some of the more remote areas and around any unprotected springs there is always trouble. They just don't forget their grievances these tribes. People are killed here all the time. Are you sure you still want to go?"

I looked at the other two whom I must say looked rather cowed by Bin Samer's description of such widespread mayhem, Calista in particular and for a moment I thought they would decide against it. Then Andreas spoke up, "Oh come on Niko, it can't be all that bad. Let's do it. We've come all this way. It would be a pity not to get to the heart of the frankincense country after all we've already been through."

So, saying a silent prayer, I affirmed with Bin Samer that we would indeed go with him. In fact, it quickly dawned on me that we couldn't have done it on our own anyway without a party like this. They knew the country and its peoples and I presumed they'd made this journey many times before and faced the same hazards, but clearly they'd survived, so, with some trepidation, I said we'd go with them.

It was then that the really challenging aspect of the journey became apparent. Bin Samer assumed we would travel by camel and he had brought three extra riding camels ready-saddled for us. I had to tell him the three of us were novices as far as camels were concerned; Andreas and I had walked with them in Egypt, but none of us had ever ridden one. Bin Samer was very patient and demonstrated how to get on and off, how to start and stop and how to lean at the right moments.

"You must remember, your camel will travel in her own way and at her own pace. You just have to relax on its back. Climb onto the saddle and we'll do all the rest for you. Just remember to lean back as the camel gets up. Camels stand up with their back legs first. If you're not careful, they'll throw you face-first into their neck and you can topple off. Hold onto the saddle and lean back as she rises."

After one or two abortive attempts to clamber on, the three of us were finally seated and the animals rose from the ground with us sitting high on our camels' backs. Once we were all mounted we set off. Actually when we got used to the motion it was quite a pleasant experience, gently rocking with the camel's slow sway. I began to understand why they were called the "ships of the desert."

At first we easily negotiated the narrow coastal plain, but we could already see the stark and imposing escarpments of the mountainous interior and after no more than an hour or so we began to climb into the hostile territory Bin Samer had described. The sea-facing sides of the foothills were still green after recent rains, but once over the passes of the first range the country became drier and drier and progressively wilder. It was difficult to credit that anyone would ever want to live up here in such a harsh environment, let alone fight to the death over this barren land, I thought.

After a strenuous climb all day through the highlands we dismounted and stopped for the night by the side of a huge rock outcrop. Goat-hair tents were quickly unloaded, erected and floored with rugs whilst the bed rolls were laid out at the back of the tents.

"You have to take great care in these mountains, I can tell you, Mr. Niko," declared Bin Samer. "We're high up here and it can get really cold, even at this time of the year. During the winter people have been known to die in the frost if they weren't prepared for it. It can be bright and sunny in Cana, but up here can still be perishing, especially after dark."

As we built up the fire and he set sentries round the camp for the night I wondered what other dangers we were facing that Bin Samer had yet to mention.

"In the old days they used to bring ivory and myrrh from east Africa and spices and silk from India and beyond along this road to Shabwah. I haven't seen that happen for years I'm afraid. Maybe the traders were eventually frightened off by the constant warring here. Well, all I can say is that we've got this far at least – so far so good, eh?"

The next two days were much the same, the unrelenting emptiness of the mountains, searing sun by day and shivering nights in camp. We saw almost nobody except one or two goat-herds by the side of the track. On the fourth day, soon after noon, we began to descend into a massive inland plateau intersected by dry stream beds. Now, every so often, a mud-brick village appeared crudely defended by a wall of rough stones. Some of the walls had been recently broken down, evidence of the war between the villagers and the Ḥimyar people, or so Bin Samer said. We stopped at one such village for the night. Its walls were still intact I noticed. I wondered if Bin Samer had chosen it for that reason.

"Mr. Niko, these people know me," he confided, after he had spoken to someone I took to be the headman. "My wife belongs to this tribe, so we'll be alright, at least for tonight. The sheikh here says there's been a lot of trouble in the past few months – tribes not happy with the Ḥimyar. They really are very war-like, I must warn you. I remember some years ago when I made this same journey tribesmen tried to carry off two of our womenfolk who'd come with us."

Eyeing Calista, he continued, "You can't be too careful."

As we were arranging our camp for the night, Andreas was trying to talk to a gaggle of children huddled by the side of a wall who'd come to gawp at the 'foreigners' that had just arrived in their midst.

"It's really difficult, this Sabean language. It's a sort of Arabic, but like nothing I've ever come across before. Using mostly sign language I think they were saying that war's exciting and lots of their brothers have gone off to fight, exactly where or against whom I couldn't quite make out."

At which point four women from the village appeared and shooed the children away. They brought trays of food for our party – fresh bread, dates, bean dishes and even fresh green onions. It was all gratefully received by Bin Samer. I presumed that these must be his wife's relatives. They chatted for a bit before spreading their meal on a cloth for us in the middle of one of the tents. We began to eat and soon finished it all, after which strong, sweet tea was handed round. That night we slept well, with no sentries posted.

The following day we came upon the Hadhramaut Valley, a huge gash in the otherwise austere countryside stretching way into the distance, with vividly green cultivated fields clustered around a dry water course, on the far bank of which there were austere cliffs leading up to the mountains. Bin Samer said that at this point we were only an hour or two from Shabwah, but that we should not relax our vigilance.

"And we can't take the easy track down in the wadi, Mr. Niko. They get terrible floods here, even at this time of the year. It rains heavily somewhere else, well away from here and a deluge comes racing down the water course. People are drowned in the wadi all the time!"

It was a wonder to me that there was anyone still alive in a place bristling with such manifest catastrophes. But with no further problems, in an hour or so we saw the oasis of Shabwah in the distance. We hadn't been killed by bandits, or frozen to death by the cold, or sluiced away and drowned by unexpected floods. We were still here. As we approached the oasis I could see that it was a large settlement built on a slight rise in the ground by the side of the wadi. White-painted three and four story mud-brick towers were surrounded by a very solid stone wall topped with mud-brick defenses. All around it were groves of date palms and coconut trees. This was the epi-centre of the world of the frankincense trade, I thought. Here was what we'd come to see – and, God be praised, by some miracle we were still alive to enjoy it!

Our caravan made its way slowly towards the gatehouse which I could clearly make out on this side of the settlement. Before we had reached the walls we were challenged by men on top of the entrance and Bin Samer went forward to explain who we were. It seems they knew him and let us pass unhindered through the gate and we made our way into the centre of the town where there were many other camel drivers and merchants milling about.

"Mr. Niko, I'll take you to one of the leading incense traders in Shabwah," offered Bin Samer. "He'll look after your party and hopefully let you see what you want."

With that he led us between the tall buildings. As we rode through the streets he pointed out a temple dedicated to the main Sheban goddess, Sian Dhu Aleen and another complex which he said had been the palace of the one-time rulers of ancient Shabwah, now deserted. Finally we arrived at a warehouse nestling against the inside of the defending wall where we all dismounted. He went inside and called out to the men hauling sacks at the back of the store.

"Where is Bin Habib? I've come from Cana to buy his frankincense. Where is he?"

Out of the shadows at the rear appeared a very large man dressed in a finely embroidered gallabiyah.

"Is that Bin Samer I hear? Welcome, welcome my old friend. You are indeed welcome to my emporium. Blessings be upon you!"

Bin Samer embraced his old partner and pointing to us, said, "This is Mr. Niko and his friends Miss Calista and Mr. Andreas. They're here to see the frankincense harvesting. They've come all the way from the Great Sea. I should add that Mr. Niko is a very good customer of mine. I want you to look after them, you know, extending your legendary Hadhramauti hospitality to them and see that they come to no harm. Do you think you can do that, you old rogue?"

"To hear is to obey!" responded Bin Habib loudly and after exchanging a few more pleasantries, Bin Samer wished us well and telling Bin Habib he would see him in a day or two, left us with the great man.

"Come, first we must feast, then tomorrow we will look at the trees of gold", Bin Habib said expansively. "Come with me to my home. My family is your family. My house is your house. You are under my protection. Do not be afraid of anything in the Hadhramaut. Let it be known that to harm you is to harm me! Come, follow me."

Bin Habib led us out into the street where it immediately became abundantly obvious that he was someone to be reckoned with in this city. Everyone we passed acknowledged him, bowing low as he walked and he returned their every greeting with an ostentatious flourish. We went in the same manner along a variety of streets until he turned abruptly into a doorway of a particularly elegant property where smartly-dressed staff opened the doors as he approached.

"Welcome to my home," he announced. "Your baggage will be taken to your rooms and in one hour we shall eat."

So saying he spoke to a group of his retainers who rushed to do his bidding. Duly, at the appointed time we presented ourselves in the entrance hall and were led into a lavish dining room and invited to lounge on couches around the wall. With a deft clap of his hands Bin Habib signaled for the banquet to be brought in and we feasted on roast lamb heaped on a bed of carefully spiced rice with an added flavoring of soured milk, together with a vast number of accompanying dishes, the whole followed by honeyed pastries and endless amounts of sweet tea.

"In the morning," he proclaimed, "it will be my pleasure to show you our aromatic harvest. You will see how we gather our precious tears from nature's bounty!"

Equally abruptly the feasting ended and wonderfully satisfied we retired to our rooms for the night. In the morning we were marshalled through the streets by a constant stream of servants, many of them armed. We were told that Bin Habib was already at the frankincense groves supervising the gathering of the 'tears of gold'. We walked out of the city with his entourage and up onto a steeply-angled, rock-strewn slope on the opposite side of the wadi where a forest of scrubby trees was growing out of the otherwise unyielding earth. Despite the fact that they grew seemingly straight out of the bare ground, against this rocky, bleak backdrop they looked amazingly healthy, with clusters of robust green leaves along the branches. Amid the foliage many displayed delicate rows of tiny yellowish-white blooms with red centres; this was the spring, the flowering time, the beginning of the season when the sap was starting to rise. Among the trees there were many workers lying underneath them scuffing the greenish outer surface with chisels and in some cases we could see the milky latex slowly oozing out in droplets from the incisions onto the undamaged papery bark.

"It will take two weeks to dry properly," revealed a foreman nearby in halting Greek, at which point Bin Habib came striding over.

"My friends, welcome! The trees over on that side," he waved his hand towards the west, "have already been tapped. These ones this side we shall collect in about two weeks. This is the first harvest of the season and is the most prolific. It is also the cheapest, if anything to do with frankincense can be said to be cheap!"

He laughed loudly then pointing he continued, "See! The droplets flow freely and the dried 'tears' are clear and hence the least aromatic. The next cutting will be in mid-summer, slower to flow but with greater pungency. But then, we achieve the real alchemy. There is a third harvest at the end of the summer, as the leaves begin to drop. That, my friends, is where the true value lies. The 'tears' will be opaque and slightly silvery and when burnt they impart the finest perfume, the 'breath of the gods,' we call it; pure divinity!"

We watched as laborers over on the other side of the slope were filling saddle-bags from baskets in which they'd gathered the dried "tears." As each bag was filled, they hoisted it onto the sides of one of the camels kneeling patiently in a patch of open ground, waiting their turn and chewing from nose-bags of fodder. It reminded me very slightly of my old life in the terebinth trade, though I knew that each of the filled saddle-bags here would bring many, many times more income than anything we gathered from around the shores of the Great Sea.

After an hour or two walking among the trees, Bin Habib signaled that we should return to the city, so we went back across the wadi into Shabwah and back to his warehouse. As we walked, I asked him casually if he had seen anyone like us in the last year or two, a foreigner, someone who spoke like us, a man perhaps?

"Ah, why yes. Some character did make it up here, which in itself was a rarity. He was alone, as far as we could tell. Loud-mouthed chap, very unpleasant; said he knew all about our trade, but we didn't show him anything."

"So what happened to him?" I asked innocently.

"Well, as far as I know he fell in with a particularly rough crowd from a village in the mountains way west of here. Last I heard, they'd killed him, stabbed him through the heart. He'd said he could do something for them, buy some of their 'tears'. But then they found he that he couldn't as he had no money and what he was actually trying to do was to steal from them. They didn't like that, naturally, so they got rid of him. Lawless lot some of the tribes-people hereabouts," he finished dismissively. "They're always doing away with people up there."

I said nothing, but looking across at Calista to see if she'd heard, I noticed her visibly relax. She looked pointedly at Andreas and smiled. The menace that had haunted her for years had been lifted, albeit rather brutally. As we walked in silence towards the warehouse, she came over to me and squeezed my hand and then walked on with Andreas as if nothing had happened.

"Now, you've seen our magic crop," Bin Habib boomed, "what is your wish? Will you go back with Bin Samer to Cana? Or would you like travel with one of the caravans up through the deserts of Arabia back to the Great Sea. There should be one leaving in a week or so. They will be glad to escort you. It will take two or three months at least and you'll have to walk, but it might be interesting for you."

I thought for a moment.

"I think we'd rather like the experience of travelling with the frankincense caravan to the Great Sea, if that can be arranged."

Bin Habib said he'd see what he could do.

CHAPTER TWELVE

THROUGH THE DESERTS OF ARABIA

Whilst waiting for news of the caravan, we spent the next few days wandering around Shabwah on our own, though I noticed we were always shadowed by a couple of Bin Habib's retainers, each armed with a scimitar in case of trouble. I don't know quite why, because as far as we knew we didn't meet with any antagonism and at no point were we ever challenged. Calista and Andreas haggled with a few of the shopkeepers over a few items they wanted to buy as a memory of this extraordinary place and for reasons of my own, I managed to purchase a very small amount of frankincense which I kept among my other few possessions. I had an idea for this at the back of my mind in relation to where we were likely to be travelling.

It was at the beginning of the following week that Bin Habib told us a caravan was preparing to set off for Arabia and would leave the next morning.

"I should tell you Mr. Nicholas that these are a dour people," declared Bin Habib, a little derogatively. "They are Nabateans, desert Arabs, from the real thirst lands of the interior. Unlike us here who have an abundance of rain, they often have to go without food and water for long periods. It must be very grueling for them I should imagine, a life full of adversity and privation. It's no wonder they're so surly. But you will just have to put up with them I suppose and with their camels too, which are always so unpredictable."

Having experienced Bin Habib's parched country first-hand I wondered what it was that could possibly have persuaded him that his own land had water aplenty. From my own observation every single drop was patently so very precious to the local tribespeople that everyone in the vicinity fought to the very death over the use of what few waterholes there were. But I conjectured perhaps that there might be a touch of envy in his portrayal of the implied hardships of these wilderness travelers. In the end, as I suspected and later indeed I discovered, by traversing the whole of Arabia the Nabateans made much more money than he ever did out of his "tears."

When we were finally introduced to the leader of the caravan, Rabbel, the following day I was rather surprised when he greeted me in Greek, Arabic and in Latin. For an uncouth desert Arab, I thought, that was remarkably civilized and it rather gave the lie to Bin Habib's description of them. As it turned out, the rest of his party were equally accomplished; they all exhibited rather more sophistication and less bluster than our current host. Was it perhaps the extra-severe conditions they were used to that had bestowed on them what I discovered to be their singularly quiet and contemplative demeanour, I wondered? I took to them immediately and they turned out without exception to be a splendid group of men. As he left us Bin Habib wished us an exciting expedition. Once we were on our own, Rabbel described the journey to us in more measured tones and gave us his assessment of the people we would be confronting on the way.

"Bin Habib has no doubt told you that it will take us about sixty days to complete the main part of our journey, that's provided all goes well with our camels. Now, once we're passed Ma'rib in a few days' time, for two thirds of the rest of the journey we shall be travelling in challenging conditions among disparate bands of Sabean tribesmen. These people have been constantly warring with one another since time immemorial. That is especially true when we're in the mountains. We find that allegiances shift between tribes from one year to the next and we're never quite sure who is doing what to whom when it comes to family insults or gains and losses."

He shook his head, before continuing, "But although they are constantly fighting one another, they grudgingly respect our right to cross their territories, provided that we recompense them in full for their hospitality and by hospitality that actually means alas no more than allowing us access to their water. Which clans control what wells seems to be their sole preoccupation. It is their constant obsession."

Rabbel paused to listen to one of his men, before resuming, "So, my advice to you throughout the journey is to stay close to the caravan, don't wander off and don't talk to anyone outside our group. These people are highly suspicious and they really don't like outsiders at all and anyone who isn't directly related to them is considered foreign. They just about tolerate us Nabateans because their lust for our gold is even greater than their mistrust of strangers! Mercifully, it's that venality which enables us to pass unhindered. You understand?"

We were then introduced to the other six men in our party. They all appeared lean and weather-beaten from their outdoor travels as they stood quietly waiting for the command to move off. They were looking after twelve fully grown camels belonging to the caravan, six loaded with goods from Shabwah and the other six with supplies and equipment for the journey, especially fodder for the animals. In addition they led two young ones not yet able to carry loads. So, about mid-morning we set off towards Ma'rib, the ancient capital of Sheba. It would take us three days to reach there, traversing a series of huge elongated sand dunes by skirting around each one into the next sandy depression, then along that dune and round again to the next and so on. This was the driest country I had ever experienced; it all looked the same to me and I wondered how these nomadic people, far from home in a strange country, found their way amid this unutterable emptiness and in the extreme heat.

But with unfailing accuracy we eventually walked clear of the last of the dunes and to my complete astonishment found ourselves in a wide valley inexplicably green with fields of cereal crops and vegetables, not to mention large groves of date palms and other fruit trees. The mountains rose abruptly on either side, stark and unforgivingly desolate, but here the valley floor was one vast oasis of fertility, stretching far into the distance.

I was totally bewildered until Rabbel came over and said, "It's the dam. They have built a long earth and rock wall across the wadi upstream of the city. It rains quite heavily here in the middle of the summer with monsoons coming from the Indian Sea and they've learnt to capture the resulting run-off behind a massive wall. They then let the water out along channels to irrigate this huge area That's why Ma'rib is here. Hundreds of years ago it was a place of unimaginable riches, truly beyond belief. Look, you can see the sunlight glinting off the canals. They have made the desert bloom like a garden."

We walked along the edge of the fields until we crossed a small bridge into the city. It was built like Shabwah, but without the defenses and everywhere was a picture of emerald abundance. After the camels had been watered and made comfortable Rabbel and I walked for a few minutes west of the city onto a long, high bank and there behind it, held by the earth, was what looked like an inland sea, with a surface of tiny wavelets sparkling in the sunshine, a sight made even more dramatic by the starkly arid mountains surrounding it.

"This was once the centre of the ancient Kingdom of Sheba which flourished here maybe one thousand, maybe even as long as fifteen hundred years ago. This dam was their secret. You see that building there, that is the Mahram Bilqis, their temple to the Moon God and down there," he pointed, "you can see the sluices and spillways with which they control the run-off. Brilliant isn't it? Nowadays it's not what it used to be, but it's still impressive and the only system like it that I know of anywhere in Arabia."

As we stood there gazing, huge flocks of sand grouse flew down to the edge of the lake to drink. We watched them for a while before walking back to rejoin the caravan in the city, the largest settlement we would see for many days. Rabbel left, saying he had to visit the headman to pay our dues for watering the camels. He led us to believe that here this would be fairly straightforward, but it was something which was going become progressively more difficult in the days to come.

"We have to cross al-Harith country; these are an impossibly stiff-necked people. They will want everything. It will take time to negotiate with them. But we'll manage."

The following morning soon after daybreak we were on the move again. Andreas and I were dressed as Arabs and Calista had been lent clothes and a head-dress to make her too look like another of the men. I suppose if you really paid attention you could see she was far too glamorous, certainly to be a desert Arab, but to a casual observer she could blend in with the group. Dressed like this we drew far less attention to ourselves as we left for the mountains and the north, the great journey along the west side of the Nefud, the great desert of Arabia.

For the first two days after leaving Ma'rib the scenery became if possible even more parched, with ridge upon ridge of remorseless rock faces. Rabbel spoke frequently with Malichus, the man was leading the front of the camel train. Of them all he was the one who understood best the precise direction we should travel and which tracks to take and which to avoid. It was made clear to me that a mistake in this remote and uninhabited wilderness could easily prove fatal. So we followed wherever Malichus led, with no-one becoming irritable even in the heat of the day. I could see the going at times was proving taxing for Calista. But Andreas always walked with her and helped her over any rough ground and to her credit she didn't complain once and kept on walking with the rest of us.

Without warning, on the third day two fearsome-looking, heavily-armed camel riders suddenly appeared in front of us from behind a spur of rock. They sauntered towards us and Malichus whispered to us a commentary of what was being said.

"Peace to you Malichus and to you Rabbel and to your party. We hope you fare well in al-Harith territory. Have you paid us your dues yet?"

"Obviously not, Ibn Hasan!" replied Rabbel. "How could we do that when, as you see, we have only just arrived in your accursed country?"

"Then perhaps you should draw aside so that we may discuss the matter before you reach Dammaj."

This was not so much a suggestion but more by way of a command. We halted the caravan, haltered the camels and erected a shaded, open-sided tent where the negotiations would take place. Tea was brewed and everyone sat cross-legged on mats laid over the sand.

After a few other cursory formalities, Ibn Hasan began, "You must understand that the price for your caravan to cross al-Harith lands has gone up since the last time you were here. Alas, water is scarce for us; it is becoming more and more precious. Shall we say…"

And he named a price in gold pieces.

"Ibn Hasan, you know that price is totally outrageous!" Rabbel countered. "You are aware I'm sure that it's more than double the amount we paid you only a few short weeks ago. How can you possibly justify this increase?"

“Well, Rabbel, times are hard for us as you see,” he wheedled, grimacing and spreading his arms out, with his palms upwards. “We have to feed our children; we have to water our herds. Our resources are disappearing fast. Our wells are drying up and maybe this time it will be forever.”

“But in two months you will have rain!”

“Ah yes, in the past this has been so, but what if the rains don’t come this year? Have you thought of that? We shall lose our animals. We shall all of us die of thirst. As a people we shall be eradicated, erased from human memory!”

“What you say is absolute nonsense as you well know, Ibn Hasan! Of course they will come. They have done so every year you have ever known, every year of your miserable existence! For shame on you! You bring disgrace upon your father’s name with your grasping suggestions. We’re not going to pay you a single obol more than we paid you four weeks ago.”

I was told later that his father, who had died a couple of years earlier, had he still been alive would have attempted exactly the same bargaining tactics as his son was now employing.

Ibn Hassan continued, “Ah yes, but see, your young camels have grown bigger. They will drink so much more water now and it has not escaped our notice you have more people travelling with you. If you were to ask me, I’d say they looked particularly thirsty individuals. Shall we say then one and a half times more than last time?"

"I know you, Ibn Hassan. You will pocket the difference before we even get to Dammaj and deny to everyone there that we ever paid you any more than we did a month ago. You are a grasping scoundrel, Ibn Hassan. You would steal from your own mother if you could; don't forget, I know you only too well!"

"Ah Rabbel, you are a very wealthy man, but you will bring my people here to the very edge of ruin with your callousness." He paused and then continued, "But alright, because we are old friends and because I want to help you, with great reluctance we will keep the price for you the same this time, but give me one of your cotton gallabiyahs, for it gets colder these nights."

"Very well, but as you are only too well aware the nights are becoming progressively warmer at this time of the year. You are an unconscionable brigand, Ibn Hassan. But let us shake on it."

Which they did! Apparently, Malichus told me, Rabbel had to go through the same unconstructive conversation, the same specious arguments, every time they met. It was always like this and it would be the same with each of the clans we would encounter all the way through the interior. It was as though it was part of a ritual, a game they indulged in for want of anything better to do.

"Wait until we get to Paran," Malichus volunteered. "The elders there argue the most vehemently of them all and it takes so much more time to bring them around to the right way of thinking."

After finishing our tea we packed up and continued around the corner of the mountain into a dry, shallow valley with a few small fields of barley stubble and one or two stunted date palms set around a tiny oasis of mud-brick houses. The caravan aimed for the stone-walled wells in the centre of the settlement where water was drawn up in leather buckets and poured into wooden troughs. Having been offloaded, the released camels all rushed forward at once and nearly overturned the troughs in their eagerness, but they then settled in for a long drink. We set up our tents close by and made ready for the night.

That evening, seeing that I had been puzzled by the encounter with Ibn Hasan, Rabbel explained more to me about his experiences on the journey.

"You have to understand, Niko, now we have left Sheba the Arabs we shall meet along the way are all like this. They have never acknowledged any central authority over them at all, neither king nor paramount chief, no-one other than the sheikh of their own clan. For that reason they are totally lawless and are all completely and separately autocratic. They have lived like this for generations, no, maybe more like for centuries, with no administration of any kind. It has always seemed to us that disputes or wars between the tribes are more a kind of diversion for them; you could say that warring is more a dangerous sport. I suppose in some perverse way it provides an escape from the monotony of their life in the desert. Half the time, they argue for the sake of arguing, or just fight for the sake of fighting, whether or not there is an actual reason behind it. It's so senseless!"

"But, I see what you're thinking," he continued. "Why don't they just steal all our possessions, do away with us altogether and have done with it? Well, traditionally they won't do that. Many generations ago the incense and spice trade used only to go up the Erythraean Sea by ship. These clans got nothing. It was we Nabateans who established the land route from Shabwah to the Great Sea at Gaza. As far as these tribes are concerned, all the traffic is now supposed to come this way, as a result of which they all get paid. I suppose you could imagine it more as an annual tax on each of our caravans. But most importantly, it represents their only real source of income. So as long as we always abide by their rules and all come the same way and pay our dues, they will allow us pass unhindered. That's the reason."

And so it was to be, as we travelled ever northwards. Although we had to negotiate afresh with every new tribe as we went deeper and deeper into the seemingly impenetrable mountains of western Arabia, I began to realise that we were never actually in any danger. With the Kath'an, the Midhal, al Azd and the Daws, each family tried to drive a harder bargain, citing all manner of imagined forthcoming catastrophes and potentially life-threatening tragedies to increase their share of the tithe on the caravan's goods, only in the end to settle on the pre-ordained amount. It was as we were getting into Hawazan territory that we finally came across the tribe that controlled the spring at Paran, the Quraysh.

"Now this spring has always been important," announced Rabbel. "They call it Zamzam and there has seemingly been a shrine here forever dedicated to the thousand gods of the Quraysh people. They always try to drive a very hard bargain, harder than anyone else, which is curious really because their water is by no means the best quality, but alas we need to use it."

Rabbel spent a good two hours that afternoon in a tight argument with their representatives and the discussion covered a whole variety of subjects before they finally reached a conclusion and we were able to draw water for the camels from their wells.

The next two weeks we laboured onwards, through ever more mountainous scenery and, if it was possible, meeting ever more truculent desert tribesmen. We treated with each of the various clans one by one, the Khuza'ah, the Ghatafan and the Khazraj at Yathrib. Each time we were met by the same nerve-wracking arguments and faced the same recalcitrance and apparent obstinacy. The people who greeted us were always conspicuously armed, but although they looked threatening they never did us any harm and eventually at the end of each protracted dispute we ended up paying the exact sum that Rabbel had set aside for them in the first place. It was only after another ten days or so beyond Yathrib that Rabbel turned to me and said,

"Thanks be to God we are coming into the territory which is controlled by our people, the Nabateans."

The scenery had changed too. It was no longer the interminably severe mountain ranges of the Hejaz, the region through which we'd been travelling for week after grueling week. Now the landscape was broken into a series of fantastical and impressive colossal rock towers and stone pillars made of dark red sandstone, like gigantic hands and fingers rising vertically in front and beside us and through which our route lay along constrained sandy valleys. Though it was just as dry, somehow the contrasting colours of the uplands and the flat valley floor, together with the more broken nature of the panorama ahead allowing as it did a glimpse of a far horizon, gave us a focus, an added objective for our journey instead of the endless glowering highlands we'd been experiencing day after day until now. And there was another advantage.

"From now on we are amongst friends," Rabbel resumed. "We still have two weeks to go, but our route has just become a lot easier as we approach this town up ahead, Hegra."

As we came into Hegra I could immediately detect numerous indications of a much more advanced history. Primarily, the first thing I noticed was that some of the red sandstone rock faces that surrounded the town had been dressed back and carved into huge, formal, pillared façades, which I later learnt were ancient Nabatean tombs. Stone masons had clearly chiseled the rock faces and they had been vertically finished as though they were ancient temples or civic buildings and the architraves above the tombs had been cut into a series of ascending, antithetic stepped decorations. This was the first monumental architecture that we'd observed since we'd left the Nile all those months before. Having been brought up with city scenes like this at Patara, although the red colour and the somewhat austere character of these tombs were rather alien to me, I recognized a familiarity in its overall concept which I for one certainly found reassuring.

"I should tell you, Niko," Rabbel offered, seeing me gazing at these tombs, "once upon a time, a couple of hundred years or so ago, we Nabateans ruled a great Kingdom, from Hegra here in the south all the way as far as what is now the Roman province of Syria in the north. My great grandfather told me that we once even controlled Bostra, the present Roman provincial capital there." He sighed.

"But the Romans systematically dismembered our Kingdom," he continued, "first Syria, then our lands along the Great Sea coast and finally our very heartlands, here in this Arabian part of our Kingdom. The emperor Trajan even constructed a military road, from Bostra in the north to Aila at the tip of the gulf leading to the Erythraean Sea and there is no doubt that he intended it deliberately to divide our Kingdom and break it in two. 'Trajan's New Road' they called it. He had it built at what one can only assume to have been huge expense just to move his legions up and down and prevent us 'getting out of hand', as he put it. It nearly destroyed our incense trade, I can tell you. I think secretly that's what Trajan wanted, so that his financial controllers in Rome could decrease the vast amounts the inhabitants of their city were spending importing our aromatics and other luxury goods or also more acquisitively so that they could tax them. After that most of the incense and other expensive imports moved and went up the Euphrates Valley route and across the Syrian Desert through Palmyra, which they controlled. We lost our lucrative monopoly. It's marginally better in recent days, but nothing like it used to be."

I sympathized with him as best I could. Everyone for one reason or another had felt the dead hand of Roman government; they seemed to want to control everything and everyone. In fact it was while we were halted in Hegra that we first heard vague rumours about the latest of their irrational and domineering excesses – Diocletian's attempt at the rooting out of Christians in his army. It was Andreas with his military antennae that had picked up the news first and as he explained, the process had begun some months before somewhere in northern Syria, possibly in the city of Antioch. Diocletian was there making sacrifices to his god Jupiter to try to read the omens regarding his future, when the priests who were conducting the divination ceremonies associated with it complained that after numerous attempts they had been unable to get a clear answer as to what was going to happen. They blamed what they called 'religiously incompatible elements' present in the army and cited the incidence of large numbers of Christians among the rank and file of the legions, especially among the officers.

"As a result, Niko, they were suggesting that any Christian centurions should be demoted, either sent back to the ranks, or better still, dishonorably discharged from the army all together if they didn't offer sacrifice to the imperial gods and thus denounce Christianity. As far as the soldiers were concerned, if they were summarily removed that would mean they would not only lose their salaries, but also much more importantly their aerarium militare, their imperial pension. That would be disastrous for them, absolutely devastating. I know. I used to handle these pensions for the legion I worked for. Some of them would have been in the army for twenty years or more and were nearing the end of their career. They'd be relying on that pension."

"But how many men would that affect?" I asked.

"From my experience, certainly among the legions of the east, it could be twenty to thirty percent of the army, or possibly more. What does Diocletian think he's playing at? We don't want to go back to the useless gods of ancient Rome. Reading between the lines, what I think he's doing is trying to re-establish the traditional forms of religion to secure his own position, both his, Maximian's and those of the two caesars. He's obviously scared the people are turning against the whole senseless notion of divine emperorship and that somehow he'll be swept away in the process."

We prayed about it that night, asking for reason and clemency to prevail. During the two weeks we still had to travel, we heard nothing further about the harassment of Christians by Rome. However, we were going to find out a lot more about it shortly and particularly the greatly increased excesses of Diocletian and his agents against believers in the one true God when we were finally to reach our destination, the wonderful rock city of Reqem, capital of the Nabateans, the place the Greeks called "Petra." This delightful city was awaiting us at the very western edge of the Arabian Desert.

CHAPTER THIRTEEN

THE ROCK CITY OF REQEM

We continued through the same magnificent scenery for the next few days, a fluctuating vista of dramatic red sandstone massifs and perpendicular cliffs. The camels kept up their usual constant unhurried pace, the men walking beside them with the same rapt attention. It could have become soporific watching our progress were it not for the reality of the sun beating down the whole time, reflecting off the glowering rock faces. We saw few if any living things as we passed - a couple of goat herds in the distance, a few ibex on the edge of the stony shadows - otherwise we were quite alone. Malichus led as always with the same steadfast purpose; he was our spearhead, a pioneering figure confidently striding out in front, reading the landscape as he went. As for the rest of us, we quietly followed his lead, speaking little to one another during the journey, each of us perhaps preferring our own thoughts and imaginings.

For myself I was contemplating the place to which we were heading, Reqem, the rock-cut city of Petra. From the few descriptions I had been given of this capital of the Nabateans it sounded like an outstanding place, much of it carved out of the solid sandstone like the tombs we had seen at Hegra. Our companions had been enthusiastically recounting Reqem's history, telling us that their forefathers had developed a sophisticated irrigation system which brought much needed water to the fields they had created around its periphery, as well as tunnels bringing the water right into the very centre of the city. Evidently, higher up the wadi above Petra there was a vigorous perennial spring; Ain Musa they called it, the Spring of Moses. The name related to a story which the Jews told of their prophet Moses leading his people out of Egypt and smiting a rock somewhere in the desert and making water flow. This was supposed to be the place. Whatever the truth may have been, it was now firmly the source from which the heart of what had been the Nabatean Kingdom obtained its life-blood.

We passed through Tabouk and one or two other smaller villages until we came to the spectacular scenery of Wadi Ramm, the Valley of the Moon, a long straight defile with lofty, vertical rock walls on either side, still in the same dull red sandstone with a wide sandy valley running between them. One evening we stopped in the shade of a cliff in the wadi and walking off to explore a little I found the rock faces covered in roughly-hewn yet fantastic petroglyphs of etiolated human figures and running animals. When I got back to camp Malichus told me they had been made by people many thousands of years ago, people who had lived here long before the Nabateans, before there were any towns or cities, before even history itself. I marvelled about what manner of people they might have been.

In a couple more days we left the sandstone bastions behind and ascended into a landscape of rolling limestone hills which became greener with every passing hour as more and more evidence of human activity began to emerge. There were small fields of wheat and barley scattered across the countryside, beside which were numerous tented communities. Rabbel told me the Bedouin here were the Huwaytat and that they owned the substantial herds of goats and fat-tailed sheep being shepherded around the hills by their young men. Some were playing haunting tunes on simple reed flutes giving the scene a pastoral loveliness all of its own as we continued our journey upwards out of the desert. After a half-day climb, we at last reached the top of a substantial escarpment and suddenly we were looking down into a gigantic tear in the landscape. The mountains abruptly fell away into what seemed like a vast and bottomless chasm, stretching never-endingly into the blue misted distance both to the north and to the south. This was what they called the Wadi Arabah, the Valley of Desolation. As we looked north along the east side of this valley Malichus animatedly pointed to a small dark green patch among a jumble of rounded summits in the far distance, slightly below us, which he said were palm trees.

"Reqem," he murmured, "that is Petra, our home!"

I felt the whole party breathe a sigh of relief. We had made it through some of the worst conditions on earth, as well as having had to deal with certainly some of the most challenging and potentially belligerent people that I'd ever come across in my life and we were all still together. We had arrived, nearly, that is.

"On the other side of the Wadi Arabah," declared Rabbel pointing westwards, "beyond the other face of those mountains over there, lies the Great Sea and your homeland, Niko. Think of that!"

Yes, I thought, in the last two or three months we'd been through a lot together, the ten of us, to get here today, through untold obstacles and unspoken difficulties, as well as some of the most unforgiving country on earth. I felt a moment of pride to have been part of this remarkable team and I was especially impressed that Calista had come through it unscathed and without a word of complaint. With Andreas' help she'd overcome every adversity. It was as though for all of us our mettle had been tested to the ultimate degree and we'd withstood the most extreme burden. As we moved off again I was looking forward to us arriving at their capital, which we would do the following day.

The next morning saw us moving slowly downhill along a road which slanted across the contours between small stone-walled fields, passing little hamlets built into every fold of the limestone, until we reached the settlement of Ain Musa, Moses'

Spring. Just below it was a seemingly insignificant narrow valley which turned out to be the way towards the entrance of Petra. As I was soon to discover, Reqem was truly swallowed up among the corrugations of the mountains, out of the sight of travellers along the nearer edge of the escarpment where we had just walked. It could be glimpsed from far away on the crest above the Wadi Arabah, as we had done, but as we had got closer it just vanished, as if it had never been there.

We entered the more open part of the valley leading down from Ain Musa and were back in the sandstone scenery of the Wadi Ramm once more and where we saw rock-cut tomb façades rising on either side of the track which led ever inwards. Some of the rock faces had been chiselled back into pyramid-like decorations, whilst in other places they had been carved to create large, free-standing stone blocks. Though the designs were unfamiliar to me, these were clearly evidence of a sophisticated people and a cultured history.

But as we turned a corner a little further down it looked for the world as though we were heading towards a blind alley ending in a solid impenetrable wall of rock of the same towering red sandstone cliffs. I couldn't make out what was happening until we got very close when miraculously a constricted entrance opened up in front of us, not visible until we were right upon it. Without breaking step we entered its sombre interior. I have never in my life seen anything as remarkable as that narrow gorge. It bore a pronounced resemblance to a lofty, elongated, twisting subterranean passage, though open to a sliver of sky way above us. So deep was it and its width so restricted that in parts by stretching out your arms, you could almost touch both sides at once and from time to time the meanders and turns in its direction entirely blocked the blue of the heavens high overhead. Out of the glare of the sun's rays the rocks could be seen for what they were - sandy layers of a muted rose-madder, alternating with those of a rust colour and interspersed with narrow bands of bleached pallid grey, from time to time shot through with thin, sharply-angled seams of an intense russet. Even with the sun at its zenith at mid-day, in the depth of that cleft it was dark and cool, clothed as it was in the profound shadow of what felt like the dull light of a late afternoon.

Our footsteps echoed on the stone flags that had been laid as a pavement for this thoroughfare through the rock. Here and there a small shrine had been set up along the wall beside the roadway, with offerings of flowers placed alongside them. Looking at the cliffs above us, we could see where at some time in the past during the creation of this wondrous passage water had carved its way violently into its sides. However it had been formed, this gorge provided the main access into Reqem and effectively locked the city away from preying eyes. For maybe half an hour we continued along this remarkable ravine until quite suddenly the view opened up into the strong sunlight again. There before us had been carved an immense rock-cut tomb many times our own height soaring up on the opposite flanking cliff, so large that the camels looked like ants in front of it. This, Rabbel said, was the tomb of one of the most famous of all the Nabatean kings, Aretas, who had lived and died here some three hundred years ago.

Andreas, Calista and I gazed at the magnificence of this remarkable stone façade, with its pillars and registers of designs of what I took to be statues of gods and goddesses carved out of the living rock. It clearly had echoes of the Classical orders of architecture with which I was familiar, but it was distinctively Nabatean, certainly not Doric, nor Ionic and nor yet Corinthian. It spoke for itself. But finally here we were in the realms of civilization, having been released from the adversities of the wilderness and its desert dwellers. Thinking of the date of the king who was celebrated by this tomb, it occurred to me that this would have been carved at about the time of our Lord, when Jesus was preaching in Judaea on the other side of the Arabah, bringing the good news to the people of that country for the first time. I looked up again at the tomb and saw a central statue of a female figure which dominated the whole frontage. She was naked from the waist up, standing in a carved rotunda and holding a cornucopia.

"That is Al Uzza, our mother goddess," whispered Rabbel. "She is like Astarte, goddess of love, of procreation, of life itself. I think in your world they call her Aphrodite."

“That may be true Rabbel,” I replied, “but we are Christians. We believe in the one true God, in the death and resurrection of our Lord Jesus and that he died for our sins.”

“Ah yes, we thought you might be, watching the three of you on our journey. We have a Christian community here in Petra. Would you like me introduce you to them?”

And so saying we continued our progress into the heart of Reqem, still for a short distance hemmed in between two rock walls, but now on a wider roadway, with people and animals, donkeys and camels, jostling up and down carrying their heavy loads. After a few minutes the way began to open out more and more, becoming ever more spacious, with scores of smaller tombs crowding the rocks on either side as they angled away above us. A little further on there stood the most amazing sight - a complete theatre, its curved seating fashioned in tiers entirely out of the rock. The backdrop of the theatre was certainly the most dramatic I'd ever seen.

“We stage performances here,” observed Rabbel, “all kinds of traditional plays and pageants. It can hold up to six thousand people when it's full.”

We walked a little further on and the whole city appeared before us. It was still constrained within two towering rock faces, but they were now far apart and the plan of the city had been cleverly laid out between them, a complete, hidden metropolis.

Huge monumental tombs graced the distant hillsides on either side, carved with quasi-classical decorations, but the centre of the city was constructed like many others I had seen, even in Lycia. There were splendid atrium style villas of Petra's wealthy merchants rising up the hillsides. I could see that there must have been recent earthquake damage to some of the buildings, but this had been quickly repaired and life seemed to be going on as normal.

At the bottom of the road we reached the banks of an incised channel, along which a stream flowed through the lower part of the town, having been cleverly diverted through a man-made tunnel away from the gorge which formed the entrance to Petra. Beside the stream and running across the width of the city was an entire colonnaded street, with a central road-way for pack animals and elevated columned walk-ways on either side onto which opened the shops and offices of Petra. It began with a nymphaeum, a Classical public fountain decorated with marble statues, in front of which was a pool where the people of the city were drawing water. Looking at that urban scene we could have been in any one of the cities of Asia Minor.

But at this point we had to say goodbye to our caravan. Our journey through the desert had finally come to an end and we bade farewell to our travelling companions as they led the camels off over a bridge to a market on the other side of the stream. It was an emotional parting as we declared our abiding thanks to them all for their friendship and tolerance. We would never forget them, of that I was sure. Waving them on their way, the three of us then strolled with Rabbel down the main street. Silk, incense and spice importers had laid out their goods in the covered part of the colonnade, just as they might have done in Patara, though the merchandise here was much more exotic. However, the many sounds and aromas of this market street were familiar to me, even if the shoppers and the traders looked and dressed differently. In a way it was rather comforting. We stopped at one shop which sold bales of cloth and Rabbel motioned us to follow him inside.

"This is Simon," Rabbel introduced us to the owner. "Simon, these are my guests who have travelled with us all the way from South Arabia. They are Christians."

Turning to us he explained, "Simon and his family are also Christians. I'm sure you will have a lot to talk about together. Niko, Andreas and Calista, I have to wish you good-bye too at this point. I have much to do with our newest consignment. It's been our great delight travelling with you and I wish you good fortune with your onward journey, wherever that may lead you. I leave you in Simon's company. He will take care of you I'm sure."

So saying he walked into the street and was soon lost among the crowds outside. We turned to Simon who indicated we should follow him up the stairs at the back of the shop. On the upper floor he waved us towards seats set along the wall.

"May the Lord be with you! Welcome to my humble home. Please, be seated." He called to a young girl on the other side of the room, "Mary, do bring refreshment for our guests." Turning back to us, he continued, "How was your long journey? It must have taken many months. I have heard the desert is a really wild place. And what were you all doing in Sheba, so far away from home? Was it very foreign? How did you meet up with Rabbel and his caravan? Did they rescue you from terrifying strangers? Sorry! I apologise; too many questions all at once. Perhaps the first thing we should do is to give thanks to God for your safe arrival here in Petra."

I think we were all a little over-awed by Simon's fulsome approach. We had learnt such circumspection during our desert travels that we had perhaps forgotten how to conduct ourselves in civilized society. It took me a minute or two to get my urban bearings, so to speak.

"It was my idea," I ventured. "My family has been in the incense trade at Patara in Asia Minor and I thought it might be interesting to see where frankincense came from. I didn't realise just what a remote place it was going to be. Andreas and I started our journey together in Alexandria where we had been with the Christian community there and we picked up

Calista on the way, in Berenike in fact, after which we have travelled together throughout."

I could see Simon giving Calista curious glances; she did look rather out of place in her male outfit, which had also become very dusty on the journey. He was about to make a remark when Andreas headed him off.

"Please forgive me, Simon," Andreas interrupted, "but might I make a suggestion? I think it might be an idea if Calista were to be allowed to change out of her travelling clothes into more suitable attire. Whilst we were in Arabia, you see, we were in a way travelling incognito."

Calista effected the broadest of smiles; this was clearly what she had wanted to do since we had first arrived. She went with Mary into another room taking her few possessions with her. Meanwhile, Andreas, ever mindful of the information he'd picked up at Hegra, asked Simon directly, "We understand that there has been some trouble between the emperor Diocletian and Christians in the legions. Do you know anything about this?"

"Ah, so you've heard about it. Well, yes, that was at the end of last year. A number of high-ranking officers were dismissed, although naturally it made no noticeable impression on the people of Reqem at the time. But it's got a lot worse since then. Just a few months ago, Diocletian published what was called an 'Edict against Christians' which has made everything considerably more difficult. It hasn't exactly affected us here yet, but in the Province of Asia, at Nicomedia, which as you know Diocletian has made the new capital of the east, they've pulled down one of our churches and burnt many of the scriptures. Some private property has been confiscated. In many cities Christians have been forbidden under punishment of law from meeting or from holding services and I understand that some of the senior bishops and elders in that part of the empire have been arrested for speaking openly. They say that Diocletian is trying to avoid all-out bloodshed, but it seems to us that it won't be long before someone gets seriously hurt."

"What are we to do in the face of this threat?" questioned Andreas.

"We've discussed it amongst ourselves here in Reqem and we think we should witness for Christ even more than before!" suggested Simon. "We don't think there is anything like as much support for the emperor and his madness as he believes, certainly not here in the east. Our numbers have grown enormously over the last few years. Our message of good-will strikes a resonance with people from all walks of life. No-one wants to return to the old religion. As you are well aware, philosophically and socially it's totally bankrupt! It offers no comfort at all for our people."

When we had finished the tea and sweet cakes Mary had brought in and Calista, restored to her sunny feminine beauty, had joined us, Simon suggested that we accompanied him to the meeting house and we naturally agreed. Walking back into the main thoroughfare we turned left and continued along the colonnades towards a Roman triple ceremonial archway which had been erected at the end of the street. On our way we passed a prominent staircase rising up to the left from the middle of the footpath. I asked Simon where it led.

"That's the way up to the Temple of Dushara, the Nabatean equivalent of Jupiter, or Zeus if you prefer. Dushara has always been the patron deity of Reqem. The high mountain behind us which overlooks the whole city is named after him too. It's an amazing building, by the way. Just slip by and poke your nose into the Great Court. You'll be astonished."

I walked up the steps and through a vestibule into a huge courtyard with colonnades all around it shining in bright colours in the sunlight. But what made it incredible, if not totally absurd, was that surmounting each of the hundred or so columns was a capital carved to look like four trumpeting elephants, trunks raised. Where had they got that idea from, I wondered, as I ran back down the steps to join the others? Amazing! We continued through the arch, more evidence of Roman influence and past another temple to a villa up the slope which had been converted into a meeting house for the church in Petra.

During the evening a service, the bishop, Jason, asked for compassion and patience to prevail over the persecutions in Asia and for forgiveness for the excesses of the Roman administration there. Speaking to Bishop Jason afterwards he made it clear to us that we should try as much as possible to help and support our brothers and sisters in the heartland of Christianity, in the Holy Land, and it was this conversation that made my mind up as to what to do next. I'd actually been thinking about it for months, especially as we were travelling day after day through Arabia. I would go up to the other side of the Jordan, to Bethlehem and Jerusalem, to Capernaum and to Nazareth, where Jesus had been brought up. I would make a pilgrimage in search of the holy places of our Lord, just as our maid Irene had wanted me to on the day I left Patara.

That night, staying at a rest house in the city, I told the others of my plans. I fully expected they would want to leave me at that point, no doubt having also had an equal time to think of their own futures. But Andreas and especially Calista were both for coming with me. Calista in particular clung to me and speaking with great seriousness said that she would never leave me. My rescuing her and her own conversion to Christianity had made her a new person, she said, strong in faith.

"Please don't ever send me away, Niko. As I've said before, you are the first person to ever have shown me any kindness. I have no other life now. I will follow you everywhere and," she added quickly, "so will Andreas, won't you?" Andreas smiled approvingly.

"Of course, Calista!" I assured her. "I'm not going to leave you. Don't be frightened. I would never do that to you. Now, let's work out how we negotiate the next part of our journey. We'll talk again in the morning and see what we have come up with."

I slept fitfully that night in such luxurious surroundings. I'm afraid I had become accustomed to the austerity of the desert and was unused to a proper bed and the newly laundered sheets that went with it, so waking early next morning I went out into the city. I walked down to the colonnaded street just as the shop-keepers were setting out their goods for the day. I stopped at a baker's to buy fresh bread for our little party and falling into conversation with the owner discovered that there were two ways we could travel to the Holy Land. One was to descend to the floor of the Wadi Arabah and to go along the side of the Dead Sea, a vast salt lake which separated us from Judaea. This was not recommended; it would be oppressively hot and totally lacking in amenities, he said. The other was to stay on the eastern side, on the edge of the escarpment and walk through the ancient kingdom of Moab to Dhiban and Medabeni and on to the cities of the Decapolis.

"You should aim for Philadelphia," said the baker. "It's a wonderful Greek city and a great centre of Christians, if you're interested. From there it will be easy for you to cross the Jordan River and get up to Jerusalem if you wanted to."

That gave me the information I needed. Some, if not most, of the way we would be walking up Trajan's 'New Road', albeit with its somewhat negative military connotations. Once we had made up our minds to start, it would take us about a week, I learnt, but it would a pleasant journey with an ample number of villages and towns along the way. I went back and reported to Calista and Andreas who were sitting together in the rest house. There would be time enough to think about setting off north to Philadelphia and the Holy Land later. For the moment that could stay and enjoy the delights of Petra.

CHAPTER FOURTEEN

CRISIS IN PHILADELPHIA

However civilized and enchanting we found Reqem to be, and it had certainly appealed to us after our months in the desert, there was actually nothing to hold us there for more than a few weeks. So having exhausted its superficial delights and with a renewed energy and, most importantly, fresh clothing more suitable to the country life to which we were aspiring, we said our goodbyes to Petra and set off northwards towards Philadelphia and ultimately the Holy Land. Simon's news about the Roman maltreatment of the Christian community in the Province of Asia had filled me with considerable anxiety. It was, after all, my own province, albeit that my city, Patara, being part of Lycia in the south, was a long way away from Bithynia in the northern part of the region where the incidents had taken place. But Nicomedia, the capital in the eye of Diocletian's storm, was a metropolitan city and the clergy who had been arrested there were very senior members of the Christian church empire-wide. In private I felt the Greek in me wanting to rebel against the unimaginative idiocy of imperial Rome, though I feared that my own natural timidity would not allow me such freedom in public.

No matter! The sun was shining and the weather good on that early summer morning as we walked out of Petra and took the road north. We were high up here on the eastern side of the Wadi Arabah and the temperature was cooler at this altitude. What's more, the whole region had clearly received substantial rains during the winter months. Everywhere we went we could see that the harvest was just beginning; men were in the fields with sickles cutting the ripened wheat whilst their womenfolk were walking behind stacking the stooks and gleaning the fallen ears. Skylarks were singing, the black irises were in flower and the evergreen oak forests offered ample shade among the folds of the rolling limestone hills whenever we wanted to rest awhile. The pastoral tranquillity of the scenes as we passed by was most agreeable and it quickly dispelled any depression I might have felt.

We made our way from village to village along "Trajan's New Road" which, though slightly eroded in places, was still generally very serviceable. The milestones the Romans had erected two hundred years ago were largely intact and the highway itself was being used regularly by local drovers and waggoners alike. The further north we walked the more fertile the land became. The Bedouin encampments we had encountered south of Reqem had largely disappeared, giving way to neat mud-brick settlements surrounded by extensive field systems and we began to see the dark green of fruit trees nearby. In particular, there were large numbers of almond and fig trees among the field walls. The almond trees had blossomed at least three months before and now their filigree of leaves created islands of shade along the road. Many of the village houses had trellises alongside them covered with vines in full foliage, showing the beginnings of minute bunches of grapes starting to form among their shadows. Further on still we saw the blue-green smudges of olive orchards in the distance. The whole appearance represented a lush antithesis to the desert we'd become so used to.

On the fifth day of our journey, we suddenly came across a precipitous wadi dramatically cutting across our path and running westwards towards the Dead Sea. This, we'd been told at the last village, was the dry valley of the River Arnon, traditionally the border between the ancient land of Moab southwards, through which we'd just travelled, and the land of the Amorites to the north, in which lay Philadelphia. The road zig-zagged down the slope in front of us and we could see it winding its way up the other side far in the distance. The layers of the limestone hills which surrounded it lay exposed on its deep flanks and we thought we glimpsed the occasional small herd of ibex bounding about on the bare ledges.

When we finally reached the floor of the wadi, the heat within the bowl of the mountains had become palpably more oppressive, but nevertheless, even here enterprising farmers had built up field-systems, laid out just above the channel, itself still showing a diminishing trickle of water along its sandy bed. We toiled up the other side of the wadi, back to the top of the escarpment, and soon afterwards arrived at the small settlement of Dhiban, a flourishing little market town on the road towards Philadelphia. We were to stop here for a night and in so doing we quickly learnt that Dhiban was very much a Christian community. It took pride in having two churches, both of which we visited and struck up conversations with the people there. They told us the town had been larger during the time of the Nabatean kingdom and it had benefitted greatly from the trade that they had generated. But they also gave us darker news, that Diocletian's oppression of Christians had now reached the eastern part of the empire. There were reports of arrests in Antioch and in the northern Syrian city of Beroea and there were disturbing rumours that some of their prominent clergy had just vanished.

"We are very afraid that this persecution will spread south to the Decapolis cities of our area," one of the church members lamented, "especially to Pella, Gerasa and Philadelphia. You know the history of the ten cities, don't you? They were deliberately created by Alexander after he had conquered the east six hundred years ago and they were filled largely with Greek colonists who lived alongside the local population. The plan was that these newcomers would act as a leaven, encouraging Greek culture and Greek ideas to flourish in our part of the world. So the cities were founded very much on Greek lines, originally with a strong Greek atmosphere, which is why we like to think they are still today so much more forward-looking than other towns."

He paused for a moment and then continued, "More especially, they have always enjoyed a certain amount of autonomy. You see, Philadelphia prides itself on its independent government, even though for years it's been part of the Roman province of Palaestina. I suppose you could say that the population ought to have become romanised through and through, but because of its Greek origins the city has become very Christian. Our people there venerate their connection with Jesus' own ministry."

We sympathized as best we could, not really knowing enough about it. When we said that it was Philadelphia to which we were actually travelling, another member continued rather gloomily,

"If you do go, you must be careful when you're there. Keep your eyes and ears open. I mean, even in our sleepy little town, right here in Dhiban, we've seen more soldiers than we ever normally see. We've noticed whole phalanxes of them marching up and down the main road in the past few weeks and we're left wondering why? What are they doing? Perhaps it's just meant to intimidate us, I don't know! You might learn more when you reach Medabeni, which is in the direction you're going anyway. Our community there is large and very active and many of them frequently go up to

Philadelphia to do business. They'll know the latest news. You must ask them there. It's all very distressing."

We left Dhiban very early the next morning and reaching Medabeni in the late afternoon, putting up at a rest house for the night. When we talked to some of the local people we discovered that almost the whole population was Christian and we were eager to meet them. In the morning we walked around the town and quickly found a number of meeting houses, at all of which we were at once made very welcome, so much so that we decided to extend our stay in Medabeni for a few days. It was Calista especially who persuaded us. She'd found out that the crest of a ridge nearby afforded incredible views over the Holy Land and she encouraged us to go and have a look.

"It's only just over an hour's walk there," she told me enthusiastically. "Andreas and I were speaking to one of the women and she told us that if we get to Mount Nebo, that's the place to be by the way, well, if we get to the crest of the ridge really early in the morning before the heat haze builds up, it's the best time to see the whole panorama; she said that there's a slim chance we might even see Jerusalem!"

That made our minds up. So, the following morning, with a guide from the rest house, we set out just after the sun was up and walked along the stony track to the top of the escarpment overlooking the valley of the Jordan River and, on the opposite bank, the Wilderness of Judaea. The air was relatively clear in the early morning light. The guide pointed out the dull indigo ribbon of the Dead Sea below us and the city of Jericho way off to the right.

"Near Jericho is the place where our Lord was baptized by John in the River Jordan," he told us. "And over there in the far distance and slightly to the left, you can see a village just below the horizon; that's Bethlehem, where our saviour was born."

"So can we see Jerusalem?" asked Calista.

"Not exactly," he replied, "but you see that small rise all the way on the skyline in front of us, that's the Mount of Olives over the other side of which is the place where our Blessed Lord was crucified. That is where the Holy City is."

Then he continued, "You know, this has always been a special place of pilgrimage for Jews as well as Christians. The reason is they believe it was from here, on the summit of Mount Nebo, Moses first saw the Holy Land. Actually, I should tell you though, most of the Jews who used to live in Medabeni have converted to Christianity several generations ago."

We must have spent more than an hour peering hard at the view, but as the sun rose higher the panorama became progressively mistier and eventually the outlines of the hills merged with the blue of the sky. Turning, we made our way back to the town.

We were invited to celebrate eucharist at one of the meeting houses later that day, following which we talked much about the news coming from the north.

"I think we have to conclude that this is a full-scale persecution," said one of the members, seriously. "There is no point in trying to disguise things. The intention seems to be systematically to eradicate Christianity from the whole of the Roman empire. If we ask why do it now, I think it's because the empire itself is in deep trouble, the economy is in total disarray and the emperor, or should I say emperors, fear they are losing control, especially in the provinces. I'd say they're deliberately externalizing their own problems onto innocent people and wrongly blaming the Christian community for bringing their own short-comings into high relief. The latest news we have heard is that some of the presbyters and officers from more of the churches in Asia, including some bishops, have been imprisoned without trial and there are rumours that some have even been summarily executed."

This was grave news indeed, but we didn't let it let it depress us for long. In the end, we enjoyed being with the local community at Medabeni so much that we spent several months with them. We got on so very well with some of the elders of the various churches and stayed with them in their homes and we visited each of their meeting houses by turns. Knowing that I was a priest and having heard of our adventures in Arabia and our visit to the frankincense mountains, several of the deacons asked if I would preach to their members, which I did, each time using as my text Matthew Chapter 2 verse 11:

> "And when they came into the house, they saw the young child with Mary his mother and fell down and worshiped him: and when they had opened their treasures, they presented unto him gifts; gold and frankincense and myrrh."

I referred to the three magi from the east who had followed the star which led them to the stable at Bethlehem where Jesus was born and what that really would have entailed, travelling through the unforgiving deserts alongside the Nefud. I paralleled their story with our journey through Arabia and I explained why frankincense was considered to be so very precious. They were most interested and listened attentively to what I had to say. We also went around with some of the church members to visit the infirmed and the sick and to hand out food to the poor people of the town. Although everyone in Medabeni had heard about the excesses of the Roman state against Christians, no-one seemed in any way frightened by it.

"We believe that Christ is our saviour and he taught us that if we believe in him, we shall not perish but shall have everlasting life. What is there that can possibly make us afraid?"

That was the universal response we met. We could only admire their courage.

It was while we were staying with one family, Thomas and his wife Elizabeth, that Thomas mentioned that he had to go up to Philadelphia at the end of the week and he invited us to accompany him. We thought it was an excellent idea, knowing that he would introduce us to the Christians there, which would ease our onward way considerably. So on a fine late summer's day we travelled leisurely along the section of 'Trajan's New Road' that connected Medabeni with Philadelphia. Thomas had arranged donkeys for each of us and the ride took about five hours. By the time we were approaching the great city Thomas had told us much about its history, how it had once in ancient times been the capital of the Amorites, how it had been totally rebuilt by the Hellenistic king Ptolemy Philadelphus as a new Greek city, hence the name, and how the Romans had rebuilt it yet again in their own style with their own inimitable cumbersome architecture.

We entered Philadelphia through its western gateway and at once were struck with just how busy it was, its streets crowded with people. On a hill in the middle of the city, on what they called the citadel, we could see what looked like the ruins of a huge temple. I asked Thomas what it was.

"That was intended to be a temple to Hercules," Thomas informed us. "It was built during the reign of Marcus Aurelius over a hundred years ago. Or I should say they tried to build it then, but they failed. It was planned to be one of the biggest temples ever built in the

Roman world, certainly bigger than anything in Rome, and they had paid for an absolutely massive marble statue of Hercules to be carved and placed in the cult room. It would have been one of the biggest figures ever created; you know what these Roman are like – bigger and better than anyone else."

"So what happened?" I asked.

"The whole thing fell down in an earthquake before it was completed; we get many of them here. That's why anyone who knows anything about this area never builds anything remotely that large. The statue toppled to the ground and was smashed to pieces. You can still see bits of it lying around to this day. So the ruins stand as an unfinished reminder of Roman folly. I suppose you could say it was a metaphor for Roman hubris."

Then he whispered. "And you could also say that's what comes of putting your trust in false gods!"

As we continued walking deeper into the city, Andreas pointed out that there were Roman legionaries everywhere on the streets, all fully armed.

"It's unusual. You wouldn't normally see that; ordinarily as far as I know they'd be confined to barracks at this time of the day. It's almost as though they have been told to circulate with the city-folk to make a display of Roman strength. If I see one looking rather more at ease, I'll go and talk to him."

Within five minutes, that's exactly what he did. We waited a short distance away as though we were browsing among the shops.

On his return, he said, "He was a bit ill-mannered, but I did get some information from him. They're from the Xth Fretensis Legion which Diocletian has ordered to take up station at Ayla, near Reqem, ostensibly to cover the Scorpion Pass on the other side of the Wadi Arabah. But they've been told to expect trouble in all the eastern provinces too, especially among the Christians. Can you credit it? That doesn't make any sense. We're not in any way violent or threatening. But it does explain what the people of Dhiban told us when we were there, about troops marching up and down the main road, which connects Ayla with Philadelphia. By the way, rather worryingly, they're mainly pagan, these soldier, barbarians under the control of Roman officers. The army doesn't seem to be able to recruit enough native Italians to join their ranks these days."

"Come on, let's go and talk to some of our friends here and ask them what they think is happening," suggested Thomas. "They may have a better idea what's going on."

We walked through the city, observing its Roman design, its main street with the colonnades, the side streets leading off at right angles, a large Roman theatre and a smaller odeon, even a nymphaeum I noticed with a huge pool in front of it; the Romans always liked lots of water in their cities. We reached the meeting house that Thomas knew and met a few of its members inside. At once we could see that they were all extremely anxious. They reported that although they hadn't been directly affected yet, some of their friends from one of the larger churches in the city had told them that two of their own elders had been arrested some days before and taken by soldiers for no good reason and had not been heard of since, despite repeated enquiries.

It was while we were talking together that a detachment of armed legionaries suddenly burst noisily through the doors and surrounded us, shouting that we were all under arrest for being there in the first place. One of the members scuffled with the soldiers and was knocked to the ground, bleeding profusely. Otherwise we all stood in silence while the soldiers just glared at us. No one seemed to know what to do next. It was Andreas with his military experience that came to our rescue. He went up to the man who seemed to be in charge and speaking in his immaculate Latin, he asked him if he could see the warrant which would have had to have been issued for the arrest. The soldier looked confused, so Andreas very politely asked him again, going into greater detail as to the military procedure that was to be followed in such cases. The man who was their leader looked puzzled and then, rather sheepishly, he ordered the whole lot of them to turn around and leave, making a mumbled statement to Andreas as they went.

"He rather implied that he was sorry and said he thought that they may have entered the wrong house by mistake! I'm afraid these people are not known for their superior intelligence. But I do think it might be an idea if we were to disperse, in case they change their minds and come back. I'm afraid I think that it was here they were meant to be."

I suggested we said a quick prayer of thanks and went our separate ways back into the city, perhaps to meet again later at another place. One of the members quickly furnished the address of a villa and we all streamed out of the building. Calista was almost in hysterics by this time and Andreas put his arm around her and spoke quietly to her for a long time to calm her nerves.

"I was so frightened, Andreas," she confessed. "I didn't know what to do or why those dreadful men were here. I was terrified that we'd all be parted. Oh, forgive me; I'm so faint-hearted aren't I?"

"Nonsense, Calista!" Andreas reassured her. "You are with me now as well as Niko and always will be and while it is in our power to direct events we will never be separated. Don't be afraid. Put your trust in God; he will look after us all!"

That evening we made our way with Thomas to the address we'd been given. Thomas knew the way and we eventually stood outside the entrance to a villa up near the citadel. After we had given our names to the guard on the door we were allowed in and were shown into a large reception room where I recognised one of the men from the church this morning.

After the introductions were made, he said to us, "Greetings in Christ's name Nicholas and Andreas and Calista. I do apologise for that incident this morning. Our city is not normally as rough and unwelcoming. I would hate that you should form a bad impression of us here. We are normally very civilized."

"I understand fully," I responded, "but these are not normal times, I fear."

When all the people who had been in the meeting house that morning had assembled, an impromptu prayer meeting was held at the end of which we all sang a hymn and said the Lord's Prayer together before our host gave the blessing on our party. After that, refreshments were brought in and we sat talking about what had happened and more importantly, what was happening throughout the eastern empire. Our host, Athanasios, said he had very recently been in Bostra, the capital of the Province of Syria and there, he said, things had become much worse. Many people had been seized and with their families they had been put in prison. They'd then been taken to makeshift courts where they were confronted with their beliefs, the magistrates telling them they could redeem themselves only if they sacrificed to Jupiter there and then on a hastily erected altar. One or two of the more timid members had done that, but many refused and were taken out and lashed to huge pyres to be burnt alive.

This random terrorisation was absolute and total madness to me. The Roman administration, in trying to make itself more secure by these persecutions, was instead fatally weakening its own position. What they were failing to grasp, it seemed to me, was that in this half of the empire, all the way from the Adriatic Sea in the west to Mesopotamia and the borders of central Asia in the east, the populations considered themselves to be Greek, well, if not actually Greek, that they had enjoyed six hundred years of advanced Hellenistic free thinking. Diocletian, in obdurately trying to secure his position through these alarming acts, was in fact achieving the diametrically opposite effect by permanently alienating at least half his subjects – millions of people. Whether he liked it or not, Christianity was becoming the dominant religion in this part of the world and there was nothing he nor anyone else could do to stem that tide.

When we'd exhausted all our discussions but had reached no real conclusion Thomas suggested that it might be better if the four of us returned to Medabeni at once. We knew everyone there, it was a lot quieter than Philadelphia and we would be able to cross over the Jordan River and travel up to Jerusalem just as easily from there as from Philadelphia. We happily agreed and although it was already late in the evening, we decided immediately to walk back to Thomas' house. It was a fine night and the stars shone in a huge silvered skein above us as we retraced our steps of that morning, leaving the great city of Philadelphia and all its problems behind us.

How grateful we all were that we'd escaped the wrath of Diocletian's persecution, this time at least, and each one of us in our own way felt it had strengthened our faith, making us stauncher in our beliefs than we had ever been. Although I'm sure it was not the intended outcome that indeed was the end result. By comparison, my confidence in Roman government, never very strong in the first place, had now more or less totally evaporated!

CHAPTER FIFTEEN

TO THE HOLY CITY

When they heard what had happened to us in Philadelphia, our friends in Medabeni were horrified, worried too no doubt that the tide of world events was lapping so close to their own shore. They all reluctantly agreed that matters were likely to become a great deal worse before they got any better, which indeed was what would be the case. But meanwhile, putting that distasteful experience behind us, the three of us began to make plans to cross the Jordan River and go up to the Holy Land, and in particular to Jerusalem. I remembered that I'd heard some rumours about what Jerusalem was like, that it wasn't quite what it had been at the time of Christ, but I was not prepared for what had actually transpired there. It was Thomas who described it to me when I asked him.

"To tell you the truth," he confided, "it's not really there at all any more, not as Jesus would have known it anyway. It's been deliberately destroyed, or rather, altered beyond recognition."

"But what on earth happened?" I queried in astonishment. "How could such a thing take place in such a short space of time? Was it an earthquake?"

"Well, a Roman-induced one maybe! It was all brought about by the fierce arguments the Romans had with the Jews and it happened in two separate waves. You've probably heard of the first one; it was only about 40 years after Jesus' crucifixion. During the reign of Vespasian the Jews revolted against Roman domination and especially against Roman taxes. They'd had enough. They actually started the uprising just before Vespasian acceded to the purple, but the moment he did, he sent his son Titus with four legions to quell the rebellion." Turning to Andreas, knowing his interest in things military, he added, "They were the Vth Macedonica, the Xth Fretensis, XIIth Fulminata and the XVth Apollinaris, by the way."

Then he continued, "They do say that Titus didn't actually intend to destroy anything in the city, but rather that it happened almost by accident and that the temple, which was so holy to the Jews, was burnt to the ground by mistake. I think Titus' idea had originally in fact been to rededicate the building as a Roman temple. Anyway, the net result was that tens of thousands of people were killed, many of them Romans. According to Matthew's gospel, we think that this was the destruction Jesus predicted when he said, 'Truly, I say to you, there will not be left here one stone upon another that will not be thrown down.'"

Thomas continued, "But that wasn't the devastation which really did the damage. It was the second wave, more than sixty years later, during the reign of the emperor Hadrian. Hadrian was visiting the eastern provinces to rearrange the grain tithes and for some odd reason the Jews got it into their heads that he was going to rebuild their temple for them. But he had no intention of doing any such thing, which made the Jews so disillusioned that they angrily fomented another insurrection - they call it the Bar Kochba revolt - and the aftermath was much worse for them. This time Hadrian sent ten whole legions to Judaea. Can you believe it? Sorry Andreas, I can't remember them all at this point. Jerusalem was again over-run and over half a million Jews were put to death. A significant number of legionaries died as well; they say that one legion, the IXth Hispana I do seem to remember Andreas, was almost wiped out altogether!"

Thomas waited a moment for us to assimilate this, then he resumed. "As a result of what he considered an assault on his army Hadrian became absolutely infuriated and issued a decree that there should be no more Jews anywhere near Jerusalem ever again. He had already totally obliterated what was left of the city, as much as he could anyway and built a brand new Roman one over the top of the ruins; he then decreed that even the very name of the city itself should be entirely eradicated! He erected a Roman sanctuary on what had been the temple mount and went on to dedicate it to his chief Roman god Jupiter Capitolinus. He ordered that the name 'Judaea' was to be removed from all their maps and that the title 'Province of Syria Palaestina' was to be substituted in its place. He then gave his version of Jerusalem a new Roman name, 'Aelia Capitolina.' And that's what it's still called today. Everybody is supposed to refer to it as Aelia. Hadrian went on to recreate it as a purely Roman colony and any Jews left in the area were permanently excluded."

"But is there nothing from Jesus' time still standing?" I asked in amazement. "What about the place where he was crucified, or the tomb in which he was buried? These must be sacred site for Christians, mustn't they?"

"Ah, yes, they would have been, I mean, extremely so, if they were still there. But Hadrian had no love for Christians either and he ordered a temple dedicated to the goddess Aphrodite to be built right over the place where Jesus had been buried; that was Joseph of Arimathea's tomb, so they say. And that temple is what's there today."

I was stunned. "But what about Bethlehem?" I asked again. "We saw the village from the top of the escarpment of Mount Nebo when we first arrived. Is there nothing there either?"

"Ah, yes there is, but it's not what you think. There is a cave which was said to be the one belonging to the stable where Jesus was born and there was originally a small Christian building erected around it. People used to go and pray there. But as I said, Hadrian had no love for Christians and he had it reconstructed as a temple to Adonis, which, by the way, everybody thinks was a slightly veiled allusion to his friend Antinous, this beautiful Greek boy he was supposed to have been in love with and who also might have been with him at the time."

I was greatly disappointed by Thomas' descriptions and felt in a way that the Christian community had again been wrongly punished for something with which it hadn't been involved, though obviously I hadn't studied the history well enough to find out if I was right. Thomas did give us a little bit of good news, in that he mentioned that the northern part of the Holy Land had remained relatively unchanged during the last three hundred years, though I suppose it would have been impossible for even the Romans to have removed the whole Sea of Galilee! Whatever had befallen it we were going to take a look at the Holy Land anyway and we made our plans accordingly.

A couple of weeks later, early one winter's morning, with much sadness and many promises to write to each other, Andreas, Calista and I left the people to whom we'd grown so close and walking out of Medabeni we started our descent of the rocky track down the side of the escarpment and into the Jordan Valley. Even though it was cold when we took our leave of our friends, as the morning wore on and we got lower and lower, the sun's heat began to feel warmer and by the time we'd reached the Dead Sea it had really became quite hot. We went to the edge of the lake to have a look; it was a strange landscape, a colossal sheet of very saline water ringed with small pools edged with salt crystals and from the shore we could look across the Sea to the dry Wilderness of Judaea on the other side. After a while, we walked a short distance north to the point where the Jordan River entered the Sea and where someone had lashed together a rather rickety bridge of boats. Once on the western bank we walked to the small oasis of Jericho, which for us felt like abruptly and unexpectedly being back in Arabia. It was a mud-brick village amid totally arid scenery overlooked by sterile mountains, but dominated by huge groves of date palms and other trees surrounded by green fields which were fed from a massive perennial fresh water spring.

We'd been given the details of someone to contact in Jericho by our friends at Medabeni, one Isaac by name, who was a butcher in the town. We found him easily; he was in his shop cutting up a goat carcass.

"Welcome, my friends. Welcome to Jericho. Despite what the Good Book says, none of us here are thieves you know," he said disarmingly. "As you see I am but a humble butcher." He was referring to Jesus' parable about the man who was set upon by robbers on his way to Jericho. "And I believe in Our Lord Jesus Christ who died for our sins," he continued. "So what can I do for you?"

We asked if he could show us where Jesus had been baptized, to which he said he would do so gladly and wiping his hands on his apron and calling to his assistant to mind the shop, he asked us to follow him. We walked a short distance out of the town and down to the Jordan again, where there was what looked like a fording point and waving at the pebble bank he said that traditionally this was the place where John baptized his followers, including our Lord. I could see Calista was deeply moved by the experience, gazing hard at the flowing river as she no doubt remembered her own baptism. Isaac then pointed to the stark pyramidal mountain rising above Jericho to the west and said that locally this was called the Mount of Temptation, where many believed Jesus had been tempted by the devil.

"Now, I understand that you, Nicholas, are interested in incense. Did you notice the large orchards as you came into Jericho? Those are balsam trees. Our balsam is famous, so much so that the Romans have even fought pitched battles over it. They say our balsam is the only one that works. It's very similar to myrrh."

"So what do you use it for?" I asked.

"Oh, many different things," Isaac replied enthusiastically. "Women use it as an ointment, to make themselves more beautiful and also as a perfume to attract young men; they won't admit to that, but privately they swear by it! But its main use is as a medicine. You can cure just about anything with balsam oil – everything from sciatica to snake-bite, that's what many of the great writers say, anyway. You've heard of Galen, the well-known medical doctor from Pergamum? Well, he was very keen on our balsam!"

We spent the rest of the day with Isaac relishing the fresh greenness of the oasis and the sensation of seeing cool water bubbling along its irrigation canals. Jericho seemed so tranquil too, away from the military pressures and the harassment of the big city like Philadelphia, or even the tenseness of the community at Medabeni. Walking back to Isaac's house, he pointed out a huge sycamore fig which he said was thought to be the one in which Zacchaeus the tax collector hid in order to see Jesus. The whole town was very evocative of those historic times and we were all enthralled by it. That evening we enjoyed relaxing with Isaac's family and breaking bread with them. Calista was especially taken with Isaac's wife and their three lovely daughters.

It was quite difficult to tear ourselves away the next morning and to follow the road Isaac had pointed out to us which led up to Jerusalem, the road along which, according to Isaac, Jesus himself had walked several times. Outside the oasis but before we ascended into the mountains we passed through the extensive ruins of Kypros, once a winter palace of Herod the Great which had been designed with all manner of luxury pavilions and pools. It had recently been refortified by the Romans as a garrison fort. Beyond it we began climbing up the steep track away from Jericho, the one which Isaac had told us was the Roman road; it ran alongside and gradually rose above a deep and ever-narrowing ravine, the Wadi Qelt. He had mentioned to us that recently many Christian hermits had taken up residence in caves among the rocky cliffs along its sides. They somehow survived there, he said, harbouring the notion that because they were close to the site where of Christ himself had been tempted, they would through their own rigorous asceticism be able to emulate our Lord and resist all evil.

After two or three hours the track curved out of the wadi and into the empty, rolling limestone hills of the Wilderness. We walked onwards, descending first into the dry Og Valley before beginning to climb once more. On the horizon far ahead we eventually saw the Mount of Olives, the sight of which gave us extra heart. The road curved round a dry ridge, ever upwards, but at this time of the year a slight flush of green was appearing along the slopes. We passed goatherds tending their flocks and here and there we glimpsed the red-coloured flash of newly-flowering poppies. Small bushes growing out of the bare earth were coming into new leaf and in one spot there were even a few tiny fields of wheat. Finally, just below the crest of the Mount of Olives, we came upon the little village of Bethany, where Jesus used to come to visit Martha and Mary and where he performed the miracle of raising their brother Lazarus from the dead.

After pausing awhile to reflect on these stories, we walked on up to the top of the ridge and suddenly there in front of us was our first sight of the Holy City, across the other side of the Kidron Valley. Even if this wasn't quite the city it had been in New Testament times, for us it was still spellbinding to see it; this was the city where Jesus had preached, where he'd been crucified and where he had conquered death and risen in glory. As the city lay there partly profiled in the low-angled afternoon sunshine, I felt it exuding an extraordinary primordial magnetism. Since we had become Christians, this was the place which for us held such immense potency and evoked such powerful emotions. Calista, who had been standing close to Andreas, came over to me and in silence held me tightly for several minutes as the tears welled up in her eyes, from time to time glancing sidelong at the scene across to the heavy walls which had once been part of the platform of Herod's temple. She was clearly profoundly moved by her experience.

"That is where our Lord spoke to Mary Magdalene; over there, that's where it took place," she whispered, in total awe. "Oh, Niko, what he did for her then he has done for me today; my demons have left me and I am transformed by what happened here!"

Such is the dominance of the message, I thought, still as compelling for our generation as it has ever been. No Roman emperor could ever diminish its power, no phalanx of Roman legions could ever extinguish its flame and no intensity of persecution could ever obliterate its dynamism. I knew then of a certainty that long after Rome had gone from here, that message of love and forgiveness would still reign supreme. But most important of all, Christ is not in this one place alone, but in our hearts and in our minds everywhere, for ever. That, I realised standing on the Mount of Olives looking across at the view was the true miracle of Christianity. Thinking of Diocletian's recent attempts to eradicate Christians, I remembered Jesus' own teaching during his 'Sermon on the Mount,' "Blessed are they who are persecuted for the sake of righteousness, for theirs is the Kingdom of Heaven." With a promise like that, any attempt by Rome to abolish Christianity would always be totally futile, of that I had absolutely no doubt.

We stood there for many minutes staring at the sight before us and suddenly an idea came into my mind so powerfully it was as though someone was standing next to me and speaking into my ear. It was the confirmation of my ordination in Alexandria; I knew at that moment that I would be given the strength to dedicate my whole life to disseminating the Christian message, whatever might befall, into whatever danger it took me and whatever hardships I had to endure; that would be my role in life from now on. That is what the sight of Jerusalem had done for me. Suddenly, just like Calista, I too felt transformed.

It was Andreas, ever the practical one among us, who pointed out a squad of soldiers marching up the road towards us.

"I think it might be best if we moved on," he suggested. "We're looking a bit conspicuous just standing here."

Jolted back to the here and now, we quickly picked up our belongings and walked down into the valley, below the ruined walls which the Romans had attempted to destroy, and we continued up the other side.

"I would think that because this is a Roman colony," Andreas observed, "it's going to be totally policed by the army. Before we go anywhere near it, let me have a look around first and find out what I can about what we might do while we're here. I would hate us to be arrested at the first garrison check-point!"

We readily agreed and deliberately walked off on a road which led north of the city to a small suburb where we found a lodging house.

"Don't say anything to anyone," Andreas warned us. "We have no idea yet what is happening. Just wait here until I get back. Niko, look after Calista for me."

And with that he strode off, assuming what I thought to be a somewhat more military bearing than usual, like an off-duty legionary perhaps. He was gone for over an hour and came back with a rather depressing description of what he'd found out.

"Right, what's going on is that the city is indeed a Roman colony. I've spoken to a couple of soldiers near one of the gates.

They are from the Xth Fretensis again, the ones you remember who were garrisoned at Ayla. Well, this is their central headquarters. There's still quite lot of the legion here. They've got their camp right inside what was once the Herodian city. They are forbidding any Jews at all from entering. They've got detachments on all four gates and they've been ordered to stop and search everyone going in. They're not too keen on Christians either, fearing that somehow we'll create a protest and upset the good order of the city. But they have to allow traders in and out or the city would grind to a halt."

He paused for us to absorb this and then he continued,

"This is what I propose we do. Tomorrow morning all three of us will present ourselves at the Column Gate on the north side of the city and I'll get us in. I can speak Latin better than most of the sentries I've met - as I told you when we were in Philadelphia, they're a rough lot, the Xth Fretensis; most of them are barbarians anyway. I'll say that I'm an off-duty military attaché from the IIIrd Cyrenaica coming to visit friends of mine at the barracks. They won't know any different. You two can be my brother and sister. I think that will do it, but don't appear too keen to look at anything, don't dawdle about when we're inside and again don't speak to anyone. Is that clear?"

We agreed and after a frugal supper went to bed. The next morning we dressed very simply and followed Andreas to the Column Gate. A couple of fully armed garrison guards approached him and he chatted volubly with them for a few minutes, joking, as far as I could tell, about life in the army. In the end he pointed to the two of us and the legionaries just waved us through and strolled back to their post. We were in.

"How did you manage that?" I asked.

"Easy," replied Andreas quietly, "I just talked about how lousy the pay was. These men are only too aware of that, more than most because being barbarians they're actually paid less than their Italian counterparts. As you can imagine, they're always willing to grouse about it to anyone who will listen. See, it distracted them!"

Inside the gate was a semi-circular piazza dominated by a huge column which had been erected by Hadrian when he had rebuilt the city. From here the cardo, the main Roman street of the new city, ran straight and slightly downhill into the heart of the place they now called Aelia. It was a wide boulevard, wider than many I have seen and it was built as usual with colonnades on either side where the merchants were displaying their goods in the shade of its porticos while men with frames strapped to their backs transported piled-up goods from one place to another and a few heavily laden donkeys were being driven along the centre of the street. From that point of view I suppose it could have been anywhere in the Roman empire, though, because of their own restrictions, it was nothing like as crowded.

The city had been built on two hills and a central valley. To the left of the cardo the ground fell away into what they called the Tyropoeon Valley, the Valley of the Cheesemakers and the eastern part of the city rose up to the left of that. We could see in the distance a large, typically Roman temple on the summit of the hill. That must be the temple of Jupiter Capitolinus, built on the site of the Jewish temple which Titus had burnt down, the one in the court of which Jesus had overturned the tables of the moneychangers, I recalled. The ground also rose to another hill on the right, to the west, and the cardo ran slightly at an angle downwards along the side of this one. Streets ran at right-angles on either side away from the cardo, at the far end of which the main Roman cross street, the decumanus, led down from the right hand hill across the cardo and then continued eastwards up to the temple of Jupiter.

At the junction of these two main streets was a wide forum, the Roman market-place, beyond which was the legionary barracks. To the side of the forum and slightly back the way we'd come was another sanctuary courtyard, the one in which Hadrian had erected the temple to Aphrodite. We paused very briefly at the entrance to this sacred area and peered in. If Thomas had been right, this was the site of Golgotha, the place where Jesus had been crucified and also where the tomb had been, the Holy Sepulchre. There was nothing to be seen and Andreas didn't let us linger here. He'd noticed a detachment of soldiers lounging on the opposite side of the street and he was concerned that they may have been eyeing up Calista. Anyway we couldn't take any chances and walking away rather more smartly, we retraced our way back up the cardo and out through the Column Gate again.

That alas was our only visit to the Holy City, not very enlightening to be sure and certainly not very spiritually uplifting, but at least we'd been there and when we talked about it together later we all felt a certain pride that we'd run the gauntlet of the Roman army and got in and out with impunity. Our next thought was that we should try to visit Bethlehem, which Andreas maintained ought to be considerably less stressful. He'd learnt that the army was not so vigilant at policing outside the capital. So in the early afternoon after gathering our belongings we walked the short distance to the village of our Lord's birth. We took the road that led south towards Hebron and after a little over an hour we saw Bethlehem on a hill in front of us. There were soldiers scattered about who were obviously meant to check on passing travellers but they didn't bother to stop us and we were able to walk into the village unchallenged.

We discovered that there wasn't much to see here either. The village looked rather run down, characterized by a number of ruined houses. There was a small Roman-style temple in the middle which we took to be the one built over the grotto of the stable, as we'd been told in Medabeni. We didn't approach it but instead walked over to a small food stall in one corner of the village square to observe it from a distance. Whilst ordering tea for us, Andreas spoke to the owner who said that if we walked a little further on, just outside the village, we could look across the hill country. There, supposedly, were the fields where the shepherds had been tending their sheep on the night when they heard the news that Jesus had been born. We thanked him for the tea and ambled unhurriedly beyond the houses and just as he had described shepherds were minding flocks of sheep, exactly as the event had been described in Luke's Gospel. We found a quiet spot beside a rough field wall and together recited a short prayer of thanksgiving.

As I thought about the whole story in its wider context, I felt that Bethlehem couldn't have been much different three hundred years ago to the little settlement we saw that afternoon. It's likely that there would have been Roman soldiers here too, on the very night that Jesus was born, because, unimaginatively as far as the people of Judaea must have thought, Joseph and Mary had been forced to come to Bethlehem all the way from Nazareth merely for a Roman tax census, one which had been dreamed up by Caesar Augustus' bureaucrats over one and a half thousand miles away.

The more I mused over it, the more pedestrian in its thinking imperial Rome seemed always to have been and the more it lacked imagination or basic astuteness, then as now. Seen in such an unflattering light, it was little wonder that the current emperor Diocletian was at this very moment trying to stop the unstoppable. Like all his predecessors, he really didn't want to try to understand what was happening in a world beyond his own rarefied vision, in the world where most of us lived and where Christianity was spreading so rapidly. Surely, I thought, things couldn't go on like that, could they? They must eventually change. And as it turned out, after not too long I found I was proved right.

CHAPTER SIXTEEN

LIFE IN JUDAEA

Surprisingly, although somewhat downcast following our unsatisfactory visits to Jerusalem and Bethlehem, we were to spend the best part of the next three years in the Holy Land, sporadically visiting cities from Gaza in the south all the way to Nazareth in the north. We met many Christians on our travels and heard a great deal more about the effects of Diocletian's excesses. We made our home not far from Jerusalem, at a beautiful little village in the hill country just to the west side of the Hebron road, a tiny settlement called Apezala where our house, like many in the region, was built against a limestone cliff face in front of a small rock overhang which always reminded me of the cave of our Lord's stable in Bethlehem. The population of the village was made up entirely of Christians and it had been that way for some generations. We had stumbled upon the village while looking for somewhere to stay following our afternoon in Bethlehem and found the people were all very welcoming. We met Philemon, the leader of their community and he introduced us to all the families there.

Making a living from their extensive olive groves and excellent vineyards festooned over the surrounding hills, I would have thought that the people of this small community were remote enough and detached enough that the intimidations and the torments being carried out around the large centres of the population would have passed them by. I couldn't have been more mistaken. Philemon unburdened himself to me almost immediately, about how they had got to know a young man who had been a Roman soldier billeted locally, a man named George. His father, Gerontios, was from Cappadocia in Asia Minor but his mother Polychronia was from a village not very far away called Lydda, just on the coastal plain below Jerusalem, and that's where George had been brought up. The family were Christians. Gerontios had been in the army, rising through the ranks and had even been well thought of by the emperor. After his father had died somewhat prematurely, George had also joined the army and was quickly elevated to the position of tribune and as luck would have it he was posted for a time to Syria Palaestina and was actually in charge of the garrison at Bethlehem. During quiet periods he would allow the people from Apezala to go into the grotto of the stable to pray.

"He spent all his free time in our village. In the end we all very much felt that he was one of us!" Philemon said.

Regrettably, by sheer happenstance it seems George found himself at Nicomedia in Bithynia simultaneously with Diocletian ordering the removal of all Christian officers from the legions and Nicomedia of course turned out to be the epicentre of that edict. Instead of leaving quietly and perhaps arguing the point later, George complained vociferously at the time and despite his rank and his connections, or maybe because of them, who knows, the local powers decided to make an example of him. He was immediately brought before a magistrate and asked to sacrifice to Jupiter and to swear he had given up Christianity. He refused point blank, very loudly proclaiming Christ as his saviour. The result was he was immediately seized, dragged through the streets, tortured and finally beheaded.

"This was at the end of last year!" Philemon continued. "We only heard about it here a few weeks ago. We are all naturally totally devastated by the news. George was a very good friend to us and we all loved him dearly. We shall always remember him. Obviously there are many others in the army who all suffered at the same time, but to us in our village George will be the one we shall never forget; for us he will be a martyr for ever. What has taken place since then we know is perhaps even worse, but in a way George was one of our own. It touches us very deeply!"

* * * * *

During the period we stayed with the villagers, with all the catastrophes happening in the world, we thought it prudent only ever to make brief trips to the other places in the Holy Land. The news of George's execution had made everyone so despondent that they had become unable to see their way forward, but Andreas and I spoke often to the men and Calista witnessed many times before the women, to inspire them. In the end, they asked me to be their priest and after consulting Philemon I agreed. Gradually, through prayer and encouragement, the atmosphere among the whole community became more tranquil and morale slowly improved.

We'd been in the village for some time when Andreas came to me one morning and rather self-consciously confided to me something I had suspected for a while.

"Niko, it's about Calista and me; you've probably noticed that we've become very close during the last few months and well, not to be too cryptic about it, we should like to get married. We wouldn't dream of doing so without your permission, but we would really like to if we can."

"Why, Andreas!" I exclaimed. "First, I'm really very happy for you both and second, you don't need my permission."

"Well, Calista thinks we do. As you know, she's very sensitive and she's so mindful of her past mistakes; she feels she owes you everything, her whole life in fact. So we agreed we would only do it if you consented and if you performed the ceremony of course! Shall I call her?" he concluded, rather relieved.

Calista came in looking somewhat embarrassed.

"Oh Niko, I do hope you don't mind," she said rather sheepishly. "Andreas and I are so much in love. What I mean is, we've found each other through this extraordinary journey we've all made. I really didn't think anyone would be interested in me anymore, not after all I've been through, all the mistakes I've made and at my age too, but Andreas is so strong and reliable he makes me feel safe and he says he wants to marry me. Do say it's alright, Niko! Say you don't mind!"

"My dearest Calista," I reassured her, taking both their hands in mine, "nothing would give me greater pleasure than to see my two best friends joined together. I'd be delighted."

Andreas looked at me proudly and Calista smiled through her tears of joy.

And so it was a few weeks later I performed the marriage ceremony of the two people who were the most important to me in the entire world. They both looked so happy on the day it is hard for me to put into words what we all felt.

* * * * *

Life moved on. It was during the late autumn olive harvest towards the end of our second year that rumours reached the village that all was not well with the emperor Diocletian. He'd been campaigning somewhere on the Danube and had evidently fallen ill. Whatever ailment had struck him down became progressively worse, so much so that he had to be carried about in a litter. His fellow tetrarchs didn't help at all, ambition being what it is and some weeks after we had celebrated our Lord's birth we heard he had retired through ill health to his palace at Aspalathos, near the Dalmatian provincial capital of Salona on the Adriatic coast where he'd been brought up.

Not unnaturally everyone rejoiced at the news, believing that the persecutions would now come to an end. Alas it was not to be. Galerius became the new augustus in Diocletian's place and the level of oppression against Christians substantially increased. It became apparent too that he had been the one encouraging Diocletian all along; it was actually Galerius' policy in the first instance! We heard harrowing stories of meeting houses being burnt to the ground, some with men, women and children still locked inside them. There were other horrific tales of people being tortured, crucified and even dragged into their local theatre and attacked by wild beasts as an example to others. Yes, it made us afraid when we heard of such terrible things happening, of course it did, but it didn't dampen our spirit; we prayed the longer and sang hymns the louder. We felt our faith was unshakable.

* * * * *

It was about the end of our third year at Apezala that I happened to be in Bethlehem with Andreas one morning when I noticed a small group of people I thought I knew. They were clearly not local inhabitants; they were trying to make themselves as inconspicuous as possible and although they didn't go right up to the Roman temple which had been erected over the place where the cave of Christ's birth was located, it was obvious that this was their focus of attention. As I looked at them, to my absolute amazement I recognised Irene among them, our old housemaid from Patara. I was about to go across to speak to her when a small section of soldiers suddenly marched around the corner, strode over to them and started pushing the group out of the square. There was a scuffle at which point the soldiers drew batons and laid into both the men and women with some violence. I spoke quickly to Andreas and we ran into the mêlée. Grabbing Irene by the arms we dragged her struggling around the corner out of sight. She looked at us wide-eyed and in total terror, believing we were the instigators of the affray.

"Irene!" I said urgently, "You must come with us at once. Don't make a noise, don't shout, or they'll hear us."

She was so completely startled by what I'd said, she stood stock still for a moment, looking at me open-mouthed, then at Andreas and then back at me.

"Who are you? What do you want? How do you know my name? Let me go!"

She began struggling again so that Andreas had to pin her arms to the wall.

"Irene," I persisted, "it's me, Nicholas. Irene, you remember me, from Patara. You brought me up. Irene, you must remember me. I'm Aquila's son."

She stopped squirming and glared at me as though she'd seen a ghost. She was trembling with fright.

"You are Niko? You are Aquila's son?" She was completely stupefied. After a long silence, she said slowly, "I don't believe you! If you are Niko what are you doing here? Why are you in Bethlehem? And who's he?" she asked suspiciously, pointing her chin towards Andreas.

"I'll explain everything in a minute. Just for now let's get away from here; it's not safe for you Irene. Andreas, let's go back to Apezala, quickly, out of harm's way."

Still with obvious deep misgivings Irene allowed herself to be hustled away from the side street into which we'd dragged her and we walked swiftly along a small path through some vineyards towards our own village. Once we'd reached Apezala we took her to our house and closed the door. In some confusion we turned to face one another.

"What were you doing in Bethlehem, Irene? Had you come to see the place where our Lord was born?"

"You really are Niko, aren't you? But you're so manly. I didn't recognise you. And why did you say 'our Lord?' Are you Christian? Is that it? It can't be can it?"

And as luck would have it that was the moment Calista came into the room. Irene did a double-take and if she had been frightened before, she was now absolutely terrified and shrank back in pure horror.

"And what's she doing here? She's dead! She drowned years ago with that awful man, what was his name, Chronos. Yes that's it! You are all spectres, all of you; you are all phantoms, that's what you are. I have got to get out of here now! Let me go! You are all from another world. O God, protect me!"

Andreas held her by the arms as she started to struggle again.

"We are not ghosts, Irene," I spoke very quietly and slowly. "We are as real as you are and yes we are Christians, including Andreas and Calista here, who by the way are man and wife; Chronos has been dead for years. We live in this little village. Everyone here is Christian. We saw you in the square in Bethlehem and thankfully we managed to get you out of what could at this very moment be turning into a very tricky situation with the soldiers there. They react nervously at the first sign of any trouble; they're very suspicious of strangers and they're under orders to arrest anyone showing any sign of reverence towards the shrine of our Lord's birth. Now why don't we all sit down and we'll explain everything to you. Don't be afraid, Irene; you are among friends."

Still shaking, she allowed herself to be lowered into a chair. For a moment or two she mumbled to herself; I think she may have been saying a prayer. While she did so, she stared at me for a long time and then she looked at Andreas and then at Calista. She was obviously totally bewildered by what had so abruptly happened to her. Within only a few minutes, her whole life must have felt as though it had just imploded, almost as though for her it was the end of the world. Calista went into the other room to boil some water. In a minute or two she handed round hot sweet tea to us all. Irene by this time was slightly calmer, perhaps because she could see homely things going on around her, but she still regarded me with a very questioning look.

"What's going to happen to my friends? The friends I've travelled with from Patara. What will happen to them?"

"We'll deal with that shortly. First of all, let me explain how we all come to be here, so that you can appreciate that we are not some ghoulish apparitions."

With that I began a narrative of my life over the past six or seven years, how I had been taught by the Christian scholar Eusebius of Caesarea in Alexander, where I had met Andreas and we'd been baptised and I'd later been ordained. I described our journey down the Nile and through the mountains to

Berenike where we had found Calista and that she, too, had become a Christian. I gave an account of our journey down the Erythraean Sea to Shabwah and of our time in the incense mountains and the long caravan journey with the Nabateans through the deserts of Arabia to Petra. I talked quite a lot too about our time in Medabeni and of the incident with the soldiers in Philadelphia before explaining why we were in the Holy Land and how we came to be living in the village here.

Finally, I said, "I am the leader of the Christians here at Apezala, where we have been staying for the past three years. We are very much part of the community."

Calista added, "Nicholas is very well thought of among the people here, Irene; everybody reveres his knowledge and his sanctity. If you stay with us for any length of time, you will see for yourself how highly regarded he is. And thanks to my own salvation, I think of myself indeed many times blessed to be counted among his followers; Andreas too."

Andreas had left by this time to see what was happening back in Bethlehem. By the time Irene and I had finished catching up about our intervening lives she had become much more composed and actually began to regard me with some fascination.

Even more so when I added, "I suppose you could say that we could trace the reason why all this has happened back to you, Irene! Do you remember? It was you who told me, on that night before I left Patara years ago, how wonderful it would be to visit the places where Jesus had lived. It was that enthusiasm which you instilled in me then which is really why we're here today. You presented me with a remarkable gift with which to travel."

After that Irene and I talked animatedly while Calista prepared a meal for us all. Just before we sat down to eat, Irene again brought up the problem about her travelling companions back in Bethlehem. I told her that Andreas had already gone to find out what had happened to them and to see what he could do.

"He'll be back with news shortly, Irene. Let's wait until he returns."

A few minutes later Andreas came in again looking rather serious.

"They've all been arrested, the whole lot of them and been taken to the army camp on the edge of the town. They haven't been charged with anything yet and that gives me some hope. I spoke to Trebonius, the centurion we know fairly well, who luckily is officer of the watch today. I think we may be able to get them released before tomorrow morning, but it's going to cost us a bit. We'll need the usual mixture of encouraging friendship on our part and administrative corruption on theirs! I'll go back this evening while he's still on duty and see if I can make an arrangement with him."

After we'd eaten, I went into another room with Andreas and we spoke about what monetary settlement we were talking about.

"I've got quite a lot of gold belonging to our community here. In that some of it is earmarked for charitable purposes, I suppose I can use that."

I gave him the amount he'd asked for and he returned to Bethlehem. He was gone for about four hours. I knew he was likely to buy drinks for the section at one of the wine shops on the square. When they were feeling more amenable he would leave them the agreed amount 'for the army benevolent fund', knowing full well that they'd probably drink that all away. Finally, after it had already grown dark outside he came back to our house leading a rather bedraggled group of men and women. Though they all showed signs of having been roughed up a bit they were otherwise none the worse for wear after what I am sure had been a rather narrow escape.

Although they didn't recognise me, I knew nearly all of them from when I was younger and after Irene had introduced me they became quite animated. Mercifully, few if any knew who Calista was and certainly no-one made any remark about it. I repeated the story of how we'd come to be in Apezala and I quietly suggested that we held a Eucharist here in our house to give thanks for their release. So, after they'd had a chance to draw breath and tidy themselves, Calista set up the table with the bread and wine. We said prayers and sang hymns before we came to the moment when I blessed the bread and wine and gave them each their portion. Afterwards we gave thanks to God for their safe deliverance and I concluded with the doxology.

"Glory to the Father, and to the Son, and to the Holy Spirit: as it was in the beginning, is now and will be forever. Amen"

Following a few minutes of personal silent prayer, the group started asking me a whole variety of questions about my life in the village, how I had come to be the leader of the Christian community and what went on here. I answered as best I could and in turn I asked them about Patara. They told me that they too had suffered under Diocletian's oppression. Two of their senior men, both presbyters, had been arrested one Sunday during a service and forcibly removed; they had not been heard of since. The rest of the members of the church felt deeply intimidated by what had happened and were now leaderless. This group had decided to come to the Holy Land to seek guidance as to how to proceed but they now realized things were equally if not more oppressive here as they were at home. They were naturally very shaken by what had just happened to them outside the place of our Lord's nativity and I sensed their despair about what they should do next. The person who seemed to be in charge of the group was a man named Petros whom I vaguely remembered from my earlier days and I addressed my remarks to him.

"Petros, I understand you have been staying at a rest house outside Jerusalem. Well, it's too late to get back there tonight and I wouldn't advise it anyway, after the incident in Bethlehem this morning. You know how news can spread and the Holy City is a hotbed of rumour and repression. I think you should stay here tonight and in the morning we'll see what to do next."

So saying, Calista, with the help of the women in the group, started distributing blankets and she showed people where they could bed down; it would be a full house. But after a few hiccups the night passed peacefully and Calista was up early the next morning baking bread and laying out olives and cheese for us so that we could have as a communal breakfast. After we had eaten, Petros came up and spoke to me.

"Nicholas, we can't thank you enough for your kindness to us. If you hadn't intervened yesterday, I don't know what would have happened to us. It was extremely frightening. We've been talking among ourselves and were wondering if there was any possibility of you assisting us more. As we told you yesterday, since the arrests back home we are now leaderless; we have no-one to look after us. Would you consider coming back with us to Patara to be our priest? You have your Christian education from Eusebius in Alexandria and your pastoral experience here in this village; but if I may speak rather boldly and point out that Patara is your home too. We would be eternally grateful if you would think of us and help us."

I must say that at first I was totally taken aback by the suggestion. But strangely, after a moment or two, it did strike a chord in my mind. I had been thinking for some months about possibly returning to my Lycian roots, that, because of the persecutions and torments they were suffering in the province, I really should witness my faith in the land of my birth. I had been feeling a little guilty that I had become too comfortable in the village here and that attitude of complacency had given me cause for concern. I felt that God was challenging me to speak out more against the gross injustices which were taking place but I wasn't able to do so effectively here in Apezala; it was too small. But also I faced a dilemma. The village life had become familiar to me and I did not want to compromising people who had become my close friends in the community. I thought hard for a few minutes and confided to Petros that I would have to consult the people in the village as well as my companions in the house.

I took Calista and Andreas aside and spoke to them at length about Petros' suggestion and of my own feelings, which they already knew. We'd been talking about it for some time now and they were familiar with the arguments, but I still thought they might be taken aback.

Andreas said, "Niko, you know that Calista and I will follow you whatever you decide to do. We've always said that and so it shall be. If you think you ought to go back to Lycia, then we are ready, but you'll have to talk to the people here, to Philemon and the others. They would miss you greatly were we to leave, but I'm sure they will understand the driving force behind such a decision. Why don't we call them together at midday and put it to them?"

And that's what we did. They all gathered in Philemon's house at noon and we walked over to put before them the possibility of my leaving. It was Andreas who opened the proceedings, telling everyone how happy we'd been among them but he told them how I'd become anxious about what I felt I was being called upon to do. I then stood up and outlined my thoughts on the matter.

"You all know what troubles we are going through and I don't want to emphasize that any more than I have to. But you also know that in the province of Asia things are considerably worse. The church is weaker, but the persecutions there have been even more severe. I hope you can all understand that in these extreme times I feel it is my duty to go and assist my fellow countrymen, that God is calling me to help them. Does that make sense to you?"

The discussion went on for an hour, back and forth through the various pros and cons, but in the end Philemon stood up and said, "Nicholas, we realise that you have to leave us. In our heart of hearts we have always known this moment would come but

I'm sure you realise we shall be so downhearted once you have gone. You have been like a father to our children as you have to us all over the years and you have brought us out of darkness into the light. But we always knew that you were destined for higher things. We have privately talked about it a lot. What more can we say but to thank you eternally for your help to us? We have been grateful for your courage and compassion and we wish you God speed on your next mission and may God keep you safe in this next task he has allotted you. We shall never forget you."

The whole community nodded their agreement with those sentiments and it was left to me to bring the meeting to a close with a final benediction and a wish that God would keep them all safe too in the forthcoming times. I told them I had one gift I wished to leave with them, so that they might remember me and I reached into my bag and drew out the small packet of frankincense I had bought when we were in Shabwah all those years ago.

"I want to leave this small thing with you as a token of my love and respect for you all. It has come all the way from South Arabia, as did the three kings at Jesus' birth and I would like you all to have it against the day that you can worship once more at the stable where our Lord was born. Let it ascend to heaven in thanks to him who has redeemed us all and in memory of the time we have spent together."

It was a very moving moment, but with that I went around and said goodbye to each of them in turn, many of them showing how much they had valued my presence. I left them and we walked back to our own house where I spoke again to Petros and told him that yes, I would come back with them to Patara and we would see what would happen next. The group was overjoyed at the prospect. I told them that there were some administrative matters that I had to attend to first, but after that we should leave very soon, perhaps even as early as tomorrow morning. I wanted us to be on our way, so that I had no further time to reflect too deeply on the matter, I suppose in case I should change my mind.

So began a process of adjustment in my life which was to change it irrevocably, in some ways for the worse and ultimately in other ways for the better. We all have to trust in the dear Lord that our conscience and our upbringing will in the end be the elements which lead us in the right direction and bring us to a proper understanding of our correct place in the world.

CHAPTER SEVENTEEN

RETURN TO LYCIA

By mid-day the following morning, rushed though it was, we had completed our plans to leave Apezala to set off for Patara. As we knew would be the case, it turned out again to be an emotional farewell to all our friends among whom we had been made so welcome for three years, to Philemon and all the other families with whom we'd shared such spiritual times; with a heavy heart, we set off north towards Jerusalem, bypassing the rest house where they'd been staying and continuing on through the hills to the coast. We had decided to take the shortest route, travelling via the port of Caesarea, despite the fact that it was the centre of local imperial power, largely because we felt that among the crowds of Romans milling about we would be the least conspicuous. Who would willingly go into the lion's den if they feared the persecutions with which the imperial house was manifestly involved? The hope was that at Caesarea we'd quickly find a boat sailing for Asia Minor and thus leave before it became known we were even there. So with some trepidation we walked down the mountain road and along the coastal plain to the sea.

We had talked extensively the night before about how we should portray ourselves to outsiders, should anyone ask;

everyone being somewhat traumatised by their experiences in Bethlehem two days earlier. A dozen or so people travelling together would be very noticeable so we decided we'd pass ourselves off as a trade delegation, trying to find information about the exports of frankincense and silk fabrics between the east and the Aegean. I had the knowledge of the incense market and someone else in our group, Philip, had once dealt in textiles and could pass himself off as an expert to anyone who didn't know better. Naturally, we would keep our religious beliefs strictly to ourselves and if asked we would say that we hadn't really given the matter any thought. It was a rather spineless thing to do, but we wanted at least to get as far as Lycia without suspicion and the fear of being arrested on the way weighed heavily on us all.

And it worked. We were stopped at check points, albeit by a few fairly desultory soldiers, but by saying as little as possible and minding our own business we reached the outskirts of Caesarea in two days. As expected, the city was bristling with army personnel, which every one of us found profoundly unnerving. There were squads of legionaries everywhere in the streets, all in full uniform and fully armed. Officers sped by in chariots and imperial symbols were to be seen on every building. I could sense that our little party was feeling greatly intimidated by such a show of military might. By shuffling through the city we made our way as far as the harbour, itself heavily guarded. When we got there we saw it was filled with naval vessels and yet more military staff. I suggested we went to an ale house and send Andreas to reconnoitre the docks for a suitable boat. He was gone almost an hour before he came back and reported that miraculously he had found a local ship sailing to the Aegean that night. They would take us, he said, but the price was exorbitant.

"I don't think we have an option," I ventured. "The sooner we get out of here the better."

Everyone agreed and with everyone pooling their resources we collected together the sum. Andreas returned to the ship to make the arrangements, coming back with the marginally worse news that they had increased the price because we numbered more than ten. As the sun began to go down, we made our way over to the quayside and went aboard. To say that there were no luxuries on board would be an understatement. The ship was carrying bales of ox hides which absolutely reeked from the compounds used in the tannery and there was nowhere for us to sleep except on the open deck. The crew turned out to be a surly threesome from somewhere up near Byblos who grumbled at us the whole time for being there in the first place, for getting in their way and for eating their food. But whatever the hardships were going to be, we were all relieved when the ship was warped out to the harbour bar. In the fading daylight, the sails were set and we left the Holy Land for the open sea.

By noon the following day we were somewhere close to the northern shores of the island of Cyprus. In a brisk wind the old ship wallowed and creaked its way past the western tip of the island and after two more desperately uncomfortable nights at sea we reached the coast of Lycia near the little town of Teimioussa. During the voyage we had quietly comforted each other with the notion that we were travelling the same route that Paul the Apostle had sailed all those years before. I suppose the idea made matters marginally more bearable, but everyone was more than happy when we began to recognise our own coastline. Soon after we passed Simena the captain informed us he would have to put in to the town of Antiphellos for water. Although this was still some distance from Patara, we all agreed we should disembark at Antiphellos and walk the rest of the way. Our collective relief at leaving the boat was palpable.

From Antiphellos our road home took us over old familiar Lycian mountain paths, with towering peaks rising above us and haunting panoramas of the silvered sea and the islands far below us as we climbed. We were only too happy to travel together in our own country again, among our own kinfolk, passing the time of day with people who spoke in our own tongue, our own dialect of Greek. I pointed out the landmarks to Andreas as we went - the ancient tombs of our ancestors carved in the cliff faces, the Hellenistic aqueduct as it threaded its way around the hillsides bringing water to Patara far in the distance. To him it was all new and keen to learn about our homeland, he became increasingly enthusiastic as we travelled. For Calista, however, I could see that she was becoming progressively more and more unsettled the nearer we came to her village and to the city which naturally she felt she had so ignominiously and thoughtlessly abandoned. The very scenery seemed to bring all the ghastly memories back to her.

"Niko, what do you think we should do?" she asked rather disconsolately. "People know me here. They will all know what I did, that I left your father and ran off with another man. And anyway, they probably think I've been dead for years and yet now I will have to face them alive. I'll be shunned and we'll be made a laughing-stock. I'm not so worried for Andreas and me, but won't it be a bad beginning for you?"

"Don't be anxious for one moment, Calista. You are both with me, where you belong. You know you've always had my forgiveness, if it were ever needed, but much more importantly, you know that God has forgiven you; you are in no wit the same woman who left all those years ago. You are totally different, a living witness to his loving kindness. Be that witness Calista; be strong in his love."

"But where are we to go when we get there?" she asked apprehensively "Where are Andreas and I going to stay? I have so shamed my family and dishonoured my home; what will become of us?"

"We shall all stay together in my house, as we did in Apezala. You and Irene will be like sisters together and you will look after your husband and hopefully me too, just like you have been doing. You know I have much to do in Patara. You must be my buttress, my support in these difficult times. Be that for me Calista! Be my help and my family!"

The tension visibly left her and relief flooded in; her face said it all. I realised then that she must have been deeply troubled by these anxieties since the day I had so unexpectedly agreed to return. I knew too it would not be the easiest of times for her, not at first anyway, but soon people would have to accept that we were a loving family and that she and Andreas were an integral part of it. She gave me such a loving smile and a look of such innocence and peace that I knew only God's grace could have bestowed it upon her. I squeezed her arm and we walked on together. I had every hope too that Irene, after her initial disbelief in the Holy Land, had finally accepted Calista as a Christian and an equal and as such the two would live easily in each other's company. So it was that we reached the turn off on the road which led up the Xanthos Valley and walking the short distance around the last bend, we passed the row of ancient Lycian tombs at the entrance to the city, through the ceremonial arch and on into the place of my birth. There laid out before me was Patara, just as I had remembered it. We were home.

We walked along the familiar streets up to my old house. It looked just as I thought it would. Irene had kept it exactly as I had left it and I came back into it as though I might have only stepped out for a short morning walk. Eurymachus, my father's old manager, was sitting in the kitchen. He had aged considerably in the intervening years and his eyesight had dimmed as he'd got older.

It took him a while to notice that there was anyone there at all but when he did he walked over and asked, "Can I help you sir? I'm afraid there's no one here at the moment. Irene's abroad and the family all went away a long time ago."

"Eurymachus," I said gently, "it's me, Nicholas. I've come home."

He misunderstood me. "Nicholas? Oh no sir, he's been gone nigh on seven years now. You'll not find him here."

"No, Eurymachus, it's me. I am Nicholas. I've come back to Patara."

"You are Nicholas, you say? Well I never!" He was speechless for some time. In the end he continued, "Is it really you Nicholas? You've come back to us, after all this time?"

When he had got over his astonishment at my presence, he was excited and apologetic by turns.

"Master Niko, or, sorry, perhaps now I should call you Nicholas, seeing as you are a man of some years, I've looked after the business for you while you've been away, so I have. It's developed a lot. And I've kept all the profits hidden for you, all in gold pieces, against the day that you returned to us. It's worth a tidy sum now, a very tidy sum."

When he told me how much I nearly had a seizure.

"How much?" I asked incredulously.

He repeated the amount and then said, "You'll be coming to take over the business, now you're back will you?"

"Actually, no Eurymachus. Circumstances have changed a great deal since I've been away. I have much else to take care of now. Perhaps it would be better if we sold the business; you could retire, put your feet up. I'd naturally go on paying you an allowance. How would that be?"

"Well, if you do that, the amount you could get when you sell it would add much to your already substantial worth, Nicholas, what with all the accumulated stock and the warehouse. As for me, yes I would be happy to stay at home. Alas my eyesight isn't what it was and I'm getting older. Would you really give me an income? I hadn't expected that; I have a bit saved against my old age just in case, you see."

I looked at Eurymachus, faithful servant to my father for many years and keeper of the business in my absence.

"I'll buy a new house for you and your family and give you more than enough money to live on, you have my word. Why don't you see if you can find someone who will buy the whole thing? I'll even give you a percentage of the sale price. Would that be fair?"

And so it was. Within only a few weeks Eurymachus had found a buyer, a family from Telmessos, the business was sold and he retired with his family to a modest villa near the harbour so that he could be near his old friends and acquaintances. That chapter of our life closed once and for all. But it left me with an embarrassment of riches which I knew I would struggle to give away. But that problem would have to wait while I settled into my own new life.

* * * * *

Shortly after our arrival in Patara, Petros had introduced me to the other members of the church. It was with some surprise that I once again met Nicodemus, the man whom Irene had taken me to meet after my father had died and who had I suppose been my first exposure to the Christian faith. He'd heard about the contretemps in Bethlehem and the way we'd rescued his fellow members and how they'd then asked me to come back to lead the church at Patara.

"My dear Nicholas," he said at our first meeting, "little did I think all those years ago that you would come back to us as our spiritual leader. You are twice welcome then and we shall give you our whole-hearted support. We desperately need someone like you to stand for us in these troubled times. We are too weak and ineffectual."

We discussed how matters were developing. Nicodemus had himself narrowly escaped being arrested by dint of being away from Patara when the other two presbyters of the church were seized. He talked about that and also brought us up to date with events in the rest of the Province of Asia.

"There are reports from Ephesus and around that part of the province that holy books are being confiscated and burnt and can you believe it, even writing itself is being considered an ungodly magic or something akin to the dark arts? Scribes are being arbitrarily imprisoned and even some non-Christian books are being treated as anti-government propaganda and destroyed. It's truly incredible. Even more disturbingly, many senior judges have been removed from office and their positions given to illiterate manual workers and ruffians off the street. In some cases they've actually been accused of treason, just for questioning the harsh punishments handed down to Christians. It's awful. If it continues, we will be reduced to a nation of ignorant idiots."

We all agreed. The patently crass stupidity of the imperial decrees led us all to the inevitable conclusion that Rome must be feeling its influence increasingly weakening in the provinces. Why else would they issue edicts which instead of strengthening their position drove any residual support for them into oblivion? They had also embarked on a policy of imposing more and more taxation on their subject people. In certain cities, the inhabitants were reduced to penury, having had to sell their farms and their livestock to pay what was being levied. Left without the wherewithal to buy seed-corn, fields were left fallow, food supplies were dwindling and whole populations were beginning to starve to death. Farmers were reduced to begging and we even heard that people found asking for hand-outs in the street had been rounded up and drowned en masse in the sea. Surely, we felt, it couldn't go on like this.

Despite all these alarms the church at Patara had grown considerably since the days when I was there. Ironically there was no doubt that it was the depredations of the imperial officers themselves, in enforcing punitive taxes and destroying valuable cultural material, which persuaded many people to become Christians. For them, the Christian message unflinchingly offered love instead of hate, hope instead of despair and eternal life instead of ignominious death. Families were drawn together by the adversities they were collectively suffering and the new focus of devotion to the stories of the risen Lord gave everyone a fixed purpose and a new inner strength.

As my congregation multiplied, I found I had to speak out more and more against the entirely negative values being pedalled by Rome. Our people needed to hear a message of optimism in the face of the torment offered by the empire. As a result, I became drawn ever deeper into political controversy and inevitably ever closer to a clash with the authorities. It was not long in coming. It was on the emperor's birthday the following year when the blow finally fell. For weeks there had been imperial agents in the city trying to bolster support for special celebrations that had been arranged, loudly declaring the usual public holiday and promising free wine for those who took part. There was to be a show of solidarity for the imperial house to take place in the theatre, that's what they announced, with public entertainments and all manner of other inducements giving the otherwise cheerless festivities a partial veneer of respectability. In the end, however, it was a dismal failure. Only a few dozen citizens bothered to turn up to see what it was all about and most left after only a few minutes.

As it transpired, the day on which this supposed public adulation was to take place happened to be a Sunday, the day when we always held our main eucharist of the week. By eleven that morning, our meeting house was full and our service began in an atmosphere of defiant prayerfulness. I had decided to preach a rousing sermon on the quality of Christian values and the supremacy of the Almighty but in the middle of my delivery an unholy scuffle took place at the doors and a squad of rather shabbily-clad soldiers burst in, swords drawn, and jostled their way through the crowds to the front where I was standing.

"Are you Nicholas?" one of them asked curtly. Without waiting for a reply he announced, "You're under arrest for defaming the emperor's birthday."

"And in what way was I doing that?" I countered, calmly.

"By not turning up at the theatre to celebrate his name day and by persuading all these people to listen to you here instead of watching the entertainments on offer, that's how!"

"I had no intention of being disrespectful to the authorities, none whatsoever. Do please tender my apologies to the military tribune or whoever sent you if I have offended him."

As I said this, the congregation gathered more closely around me, thereby challenging the soldiers to carry out some act of violence with their weapons whilst the people themselves were unarmed. Had they made a move there would have been a blood-bath and the leader of the squad realised it. Mumbling abuse at me he ordered his squad to retreat back into the street, but I could see they were not going to withdraw completely. They were going to wait until our service had ended and then they'd carry out their orders. The people in the congregation were incensed, angry with the interruption and outraged by the implication that our service had constituted some kind of civic delinquency, with me as its figurehead. I called for calm and offered prayers for the city and for the country in the face of this naked aggression. Although I hadn't yet been arrested, I knew I was only postponing the inevitable. I would have to face the wrath of the local governor and the might of imperial Rome, even if they were both by now utterly discredited.

Sure enough, at the end of the service, I walked out into the clutches of the soldiers and was bundled off unceremoniously to the city prison where I knew that further argument was fruitless. These were paid mercenaries, probably from Gaul or somewhere the other end of the empire. Their understanding of local feelings must have been negligible, even if they gave them any thought at all. Once at the prison I was pushed and prodded through heavily studded doors and finally thrown into a dark, underground cell and the lock was shut noisily behind me. I had become the latest victim of Galerius' persecutions, right here in my own city. From what I knew was happening elsewhere, the future looked bleak, not only for me, but for us all.

I remained in that stinking cell for many months without any communication with the outside world except peremptorily with the old man who was my jailer and who from time to time brought me bread and water. Inevitably I had ample time to consider my position, to pray for my immortal soul and perhaps too to think about my last days. I had chosen this path voluntarily and I would not have done it any other way. I felt God had called me to witness and that is precisely what I had done, obedient to his will. Many times I remembered the sufferings of our Lord, of his questioning supplications in the Garden of Gethsemane the night he was arrested and taken before the Roman prefect Pontius Pilate. His own dignified opposition to the hostility of human authority at his so-called trial gave me great inner strength. Although I was only another believer who had been wronged by an unfair government, I felt that my purpose was just and I hoped my stand would set an example, as thousands had done before me, even if my end would be wretched in this dreadful place.

It's extraordinary how we take freedom so much for granted in our day-to-day lives. We move about as we please, speak to whomsoever we wish and do just about anything within reason as day follows day, without giving it another thought. When that liberty is taken away, however, a heightened sense of being alive comes into one's mind, a deeper appreciation of the preciousness of every hour and of the warmth of human contact. This was particularly driven home to me when I was befriended by a small family of house mice who lived under the brickwork somewhere outside my cell. They came to visit me frequently and I shared some of my bread with them. Normally so reviled, as I watched them eating, the only part of the living world to which I was exposed, I felt that more than ever I was becoming at one with the greatness of God and his creation. Their scurrying movements in and out of my cell acted as my notional freedom. They were my talisman of the world outside. Somehow, we came to exist together in our own tiny universe.

In all my somewhat self-centred soul-searching, I rather forgot that the outside world would not be standing idly by. My arrest had been extremely public and with the vast groundswell of support for Christianity in Patara, there were moves afoot almost immediately to challenge my incarceration. The first inclination I had of it was one morning, when I heard an argument in the corridor outside my cell. I could hear the old jailer asking to be shown documents, followed by a voice I knew only too well. It was Andreas, demanding he be allowed to visit me. In the end, the lock turned and in strode Andreas, with a full military swagger, carrying a bundle of papers and a basket which I later discovered was full of things to eat.

As the door closed behind him he dashed across the cell and embraced me for some minutes, rocking back and forth with emotion. He then put his finger to his lips to indicate we should sit quietly and that in the main he would do the talking.

“But how did you get in?” I whispered first, disbelievingly.

"I waited until the guard changed on the main gate. For some reason the replacement didn't turn up on time today, so I marched in and told the jailer I was a supernumerary from the local governor. He's some old chap with no real clout, so it was easy. I showed him some spurious credentials betting correctly as it turned out that he couldn't read. Anyway, quickly Niko, let me tell you that the whole city is up in arms about what has happened. Your arrest has become a rallying symbol for the stand against the oppression that everyone is suffering and you have now turned into the beacon of resistance for the whole region.

"The bad news is that the authorities are reluctant to make any decision at all in case they enflame emotions in Patara any more than they already have, which is why you're stuck here. And that's also the good news. They daren't do anything desperate in case the whole province erupts in open revolt. It's been close to that already over the last few months, I have to tell you. Now I must go. Enjoy the pies. Calista and Irene made them with all the love they could put into them. They miss you mightily, by the way. Keep your spirits up. We are doing all we can to get you released. Oh and incidentally there are rumours flying about regarding a change at the top. I'll get you news as soon as I can."

And with that Andreas knocked for the jailor to open the door and he departed leaving me alone with a hamper of fresh food, for which I must say much thanks.

CHAPTER EIGHTEEN

HOME IN PATARA

Andreas was not wrong that changes were afoot. I didn't know at the time why it happened, but one morning a few days after Andreas' visit the old jailor came to open my cell and without explanation announced that I was free to go. Although I asked him why, he said nothing and just motioned me out into the street, filthy as I was and, I have no doubt, stinking like a rat's nest. There was a small crowd gathered outside who cheered long and loudly as I appeared blinking into the sunlight. Despite my unsavoury condition they hoisted me on their shoulders and carried me in triumph up the hill to my home. More and more people joined the throng as the commotion grew until the street outside my house was packed with a rowdy mob shouting slogans in my favour and against Roman rule.

Once inside, Irene and Calista ran to embrace me, holding me for a long time before letting me go. There was a stream of questions, both from them and from me, but first I called a halt and said that I had to wash and change my clothes before anything else happened. They rushed about and heated water and they brought me sweet-smelling oils to rid myself of the stench of that foul prison; and they arranged fresh clothes for me to wear, wine to drink and sweet cakes to eat. Soon I felt comfortable in my own household once more as they sat me down to listen to my experiences. But I kept my description short; there was after all not much to tell. I rather wanted to know why there had been this extraordinary reversal of events. I told them quite honestly I had fully expected never to come from that prison alive and I was anxious to find out what had changed.

It was Andreas who gave me the news. Constantius Chlorus, who had been the augustus of the west, parallel to Galerius in the east but actually the more senior, had been at the head of a large army campaigning against the Brythonic tribes in northern Britannia when he fell ill. Galerius with his venal ambition for power was fully expecting to take over complete control from his co-emperor, but Constantius, lying on his death bed, named his own son, Constantine, as his successor and most importantly this was confirmed by the legions at Eboricum, where he was stationed at the time. Galerius was devastated, to say the least.

"On being declared augustus," Andreas declared jubilantly, "one of Constantine's first announcements was that he was going to tolerate Christians in his empire. Galerius meanwhile, whose health has taken a distinct turn for the worse, by the way, to the extent that he believes he is dying, has totally changed his tune in response to events swirling around him. He's actually had the nerve to ask Christians to pray for him, can you believe it? After all he's done against us!"

I must say I was rendered speechless by this information.

"There has been a panic response to the news, I can tell you. Suddenly no-one wants to be discovered persecuting anybody. That's why you were released with such haste this morning. Nobody wants to be found responsible for doing any harm to Christians in case the powers-that-be suddenly come down on them with the whole might of the new empire! Amazing, isn't it?"

I thought for a few moments and then I said, "It had to happen, Andreas, it really did. They couldn't go on holding back the inevitable tides of change for ever. I must say that in prison I prayed and prayed for something like this to occur, for some miraculous change of mind, but I didn't expect anything so dramatic, or so swift. We must give thanks to the Almighty for his infinite mercies in showing this new man Constantine the path to righteousness. Let us rejoice at his wisdom and power."

As the story began to unfold, some said that Constantine had quickly realised he had had to bow to the inevitable, so great was the influence of Christianity at all levels of society, not only in the east but also in Italy and the west. He could see the obvious direction events were taking and he gave in to it. Others said it was his mother, Helena, who persuaded him. Indeed in the coming years she was to be a powerful influence on the course of events throughout the empire. She was an interesting woman. It appears that she came from a very humble background, the daughter of an inn-keeper from somewhere up near Pontus. Her husband, the emperor Constantius, Constantine's father, if indeed he was actually ever properly married to Helena, and some would dispute they ever were, divorced her soon after the boy was born in order to make a more politically advantageous marriage. It meant that the shunned Helena and her young son grew very close to one another and they say that it was she who was the Christian and who influenced the lad accordingly.

* * * * *

Whatever had happened, the change left me free to carry out my duties as leader of our church at Patara without hindrance. The first thing I had to think about with an ever-growing congregation was where we were going to meet? The villa that had been modified to act as our meeting house was clearly too small; every time I held a service there crowds spilled into the street outside. I spoke to other senior members of the church and we decided to buy the old law courts which had stood almost derelict for years – they'd built a newer building about a decade earlier. I went to have a look at it. The building was certainly a lot more spacious, being a basilica with two rows of columns creating a central nave and two wide side aisles. All we had to do was to add an atrium and a vestibule to the western end and set up an altar at the eastern and it was ready to be used.

I spoke to a number of house decorators who had experience working with frescos and they created a series of wall paintings on the inside of our new church, with scenes from the Old Testament near the entrance – Adam and Eve being expelled from the Garden of Eden; Noah and the ark; Moses receiving the ten commandments on Mount Sinai. Near the eastern half they painted scenes of Christ's ministry – the miracle of turning the water into wine at Cana; the raising of Jairus' daughter from the dead; the feeding of the five thousand. At the end of the basilica they painted the Theotokos, Mary with the child Jesus and an impressive picture of Christ in Majesty. Those who could not read among our community were thus able to see what they believed, an essential re-enforcement of their faith.

As we became more and more open with our devotions, the more people came and wanted to join us, until once again our church was full. So many families, both young and old, wanted to be baptised and become members it was hard for me to keep up with the teaching and the services required. I took on two young men as assistants to help me cope with the constant backlog and that eased things for a while. Young couples wanted to be married in our church and old people said that they wanted to be given a service of remembrance when they died. In that way our church was becoming a vital part of the family life of the city and it was to be the centre of my existence for years to come.

* * * * *

Speaking of families, a year or two after I had accepted the leadership, I came across an elderly man in our congregation by the name of Bartholomew, who lived with his three daughters over on the east side of the city. He had been a wealthy man once but had lost all his lands through a combination of reckless investment and Galerius' swingeing taxation policies. He had thus become impoverished almost to the point of penury. Tragically, he had lost his young wife to disease some years before and his financial losses meant that he was now struggling to keep the household together. He barely had enough money to keep his own head above water, let alone manage to feed and clothe his three blossoming girls. They were a lovely trio, Angelica, Paloma and Sophia, and they were all now reaching marriageable age, which would take them off his hands and make life so much easier for him. The problem was that he had no money to offer as a dowry, not even for the eldest, Angelica, who was now already 23, let alone the two younger ones, and without a marriage settlement the chances were they would continue to be spinsters.

Bartholomew was an exceptionally proud man and had naturally once been a person of some standing in the community. As such, he would not consent to any of his three daughters marrying beneath them despite the fact he couldn't afford anything to induce any young man of whom he might have approved to court them. I watched this sorry story unfolding month by month and I saw the faces of the three girls growing ever sadder whenever they accompanied him around the city. I spoke to Irene and Calista about this unfortunate man's plight and they confirmed that since he was so intensely stubborn he would never be persuaded to change his attitude. Alas, the girls would therefore have to remain unmarried.

It was then that I had an idea. I still possessed what I considered to be untold and, as it transpired, unwanted riches from the old incense business; I had not yet found any means of distributing it, except for some small sums to the poor and needy. Why shouldn't I provide the dowry for each of the three girls, I thought? But when I suggested this to Irene, she told me that Bartholomew was such an overbearing and stiff-necked person that there was no way in which he would accept what he would consider to be charity, especially from me, his priest. It would be too severe a blow to his dignity, she said.

"He is so set in his ways, Niko," Irene continued. "He was once a wealthy man, that's the trouble and he would feel he was demeaning himself and belittling his family name if he were to accept any hand-outs, and from you of all people. It would only confirm to himself and to everyone else that he was now to be counted among the poverty-stricken. No, he wouldn't consent to it. It would take a miracle to change his mind, like the money turning up out of the blue, as if from heaven or something. But

I tell you, because of his intransigence and pig-headedness, if he continues like this the three girls will end up on the streets either begging or offering themselves to men for money. I can't see any other way around it."

I thought about this for some time; if only I could alleviate their suffering in some way. I was appalled at the notion that the three girls might end up in prostitution however remote a prospect that might be; it was a truly terrifying idea! And then I hit upon it. If I could provide the dowries anonymously, making them look like a divine gift, he surely couldn't refuse that and the problem would be solved. I talked it over with Irene and she very cleverly suggested a way of doing it. She told me the family employed an old woman, Thalia, who went to the house every Thursday for a few coins to clean up and to cook a hot meal for the four of them. Why didn't we get her to take the money into the house surreptitiously when she was next there? Bartholomew wouldn't know where it had come from; he certainly wouldn't suspect Thalia the cleaner as the source, she being demonstrably impoverished herself.

I asked Irene if she could find the old woman and bring her secretly to our house, which she did that evening. I had put a goodly number of gold pieces in three linen bags, each with the name of one of the three girls, 'Angelica,' 'Paloma' and 'Sophia,' written on a label tied around the neck. I put the three bags into a basket and Irene gave it to the old lady and told her to leave them in their house by the family shrine, in the atrium next to their main living room. That way perhaps Bartholomew might think it had come as a gift from his ancestors, an answer to his prayers.

And that's what we did. Thalia was given the basket, not knowing what it contained, although it was quite heavy. On the next Thursday afternoon she took it to Bartholomew's house and saying nothing to anyone she laid out the three bags alongside the shrine set up to honour the spirits of the household. The following Sunday in church I saw Bartholomew and he made a point of coming over to talk to me; I thought for a moment he'd rumbled my stratagem, but not a bit of it.

"Oh, Father Nicholas," he began excitedly, "I have to tell you something. A miracle has happened to us, in our own home. I have been worrying for a long time about what I must do for my three daughters. You probably don't know this, caught up as you are in religious matters, but they have reached marriageable age you see and I thought I would be unable to provide dowries for them. I have been praying for many months and seeking guidance from the Almighty for a solution to my problem and behold my prayers have been answered. The dowries appeared as if from nowhere the other night, three of them. God has indeed been generous to me, poor sinner that I am. The girls will now be able to get married – you will officiate won't you? – and I can hold my head up again. I can't tell you how miraculous this has been for us."

And with that he went out and told as many people as would listen. I don't remember having seen him so animated as when he retold over and over again the 'miracle' of his daughter's dowries. And in due course I married all three girls to 'suitable' young men and their families thrived to the extent that I was later over the years to welcome several of their offspring into the church.

There were a number of moments like that when I was able secretly to give away my fortune - I had no need of it – and our community continued at peace with itself. On the political front, I was already emboldened to speak out against any iniquities perpetrated by government officials, though whilst Galerius was still living we could never be sure he wouldn't revert to his previous anti-Christian policies. However, during what was to turn out to be his last illness he issued an unequivocal statement, he called it his 'Edict of Toleration', in which he said that 'Christians ought to pray to their God for our safety, (meaning his own of course!) that the empire may continue uninjured on every side and that they may thus be able to live securely in their homes.' It didn't do him any good. He died shortly afterwards of a painful condition, un-mourned by the vast majority of his subjects and certainly unmissed by us at Patara.

On Galerius' death, the tetrarchy, which had been created by Diocletian some thirty years earlier, began to unravel. The eastern half of the empire was under the control of Licinius, supposedly an old friend of Diocletian's. Meanwhile Constantine was already theoretically the augustus of the west, as declared by his father. But it was a usurper, Maxentius, who seized control of the city of Rome and he had set himself up in opposition to Constantine. Paradoxically Maxentius was Constantine's brother-in-law, Constantine having married Maxentius' sister Fausta before all this had blown up. With Galerius dead, there was nothing standing between Constantine and absolute power in the west except Maxentius. Almost exactly a year after Galerius' demise the expected confrontation took place. Constantine led his armies south through northern Italy and marched on Rome. He hoped to engage Maxentius' forces outside the eternal city near the Milvian Bridge over the River Tiber and he camped there overnight thinking to attack the city the following morning.

It is said that the night before the ensuing battle, Constantine had a dream in which he saw a symbol written in the clouds showing the letters 'Xhi Rho,' the first two letters of the Greek word 'Christos.' He took it as an omen that if he embraced Christianity, he would surely be victorious. Some say he heard a voice saying 'In this sign conquer'. Whatever the case, he woke before dawn and ordered his officers to see that all his soldiers painted these characters on the front of their shields. He had expected Maxentius to stay inside the city thus forcing a siege.

Maxentius had certainly stock-piled enough food for such an event. However, Maxentius' own omens had indicated that if he personally fought he would that same day destroy an enemy of Rome. He sallied out with his troops and crossing over the bridge took up a position against the bank of the river where after fierce fighting his army was soundly defeated. He himself was driven into the Tiber where he attempted to swim back to the safety of the city, but he was captured and beheaded, leaving Constantine to enter Rome in triumph.

After that, there began an eight year uneasy truce between Constantine and Licinius, respectively emperors in the west and east. The change in leadership was for us best expressed only a few months later, early the following year. It was a proclamation by the two co-emperors known as the Edict of Mediolanum, which gave total legitimacy to Christianity as one of the official religions of the empire. It further stated that all property which had been seized or confiscated from Christians during the persecutions of Galerius had to be returned forthwith. This was an amazing step forward for us and, once and for all, it lifted the weight of fear under which we had been struggling for the past decade or more.

For me, it meant I could preach whatever I wished in our church without fear of intimidation and we could be totally open in our adherence to the worship of our Lord. There were still some old diehards in the province who continued making sacrifices to Jupiter and to other pagan gods, though not too many in our own city, but that was their affair. They didn't bother us and over the next few years our membership grew and grew. Privately we were never quite sure whether Constantine had declared himself a Christian, or whether he just tolerated Christianity, but that toleration was more than enough for the present, compared to our previous activities which a lot of the time had had to be carried out in secret.

* * * *

As much as possible I was keen to encourage children to come to our church. They were our future after all and I did my best to inculcate Christian behavior among them. It was not always easy. There were some seemingly intransigent problems between the young boys and the older members of the church. One I particularly remember some years after I'd come back to Patara was a spat which developed between some youths from one of the neighboring villages and a butcher in the city called Remus, somewhat of a bear-like figure with a temper to match. Three of the boys in particular used to go down and taunt him, calling him names for being obese and throwing stones at his shop. He in turn hurled invective at the boys, saying that if he ever caught them he'd slaughter them like cattle and put them into his brine barrel with the other cuts of meat. It became a well-known problem in our city. On one occasion the squabble became so heated that it ended with Remus running down the street after the boys wielding a meat cleaver. One of the boys tripped and fell over and it was as much as his friends could do to drag him to safety.

It was the boys' parents who came to me in the end and asked if I would intervene to prevent a really serious incident occurring. I went to see Remus and spoke to him quietly about the boisterous nature of young children, but he was having none of it. He felt he was being constantly abused by the boys and he wanted redress. I then brought the boys together and asked them why they were being so unkind to the butcher, to which they said he deserved it. He was a malicious man, they declared. And then having thought about the problem I made a proposition to Remus. His wife I knew made some remarkable meat pies which he sold in his shop and knowing that boys are forever hungry, I suggested to Remus that I paid in advance for a year's supply of the pies and that he should appear to give them to the boys whenever they came near. Although he grumbled at first, the inducement of the money made him change his mind and I personally supervised the first hand-out of the meat pies to the lads, which I must say they ate with relish. From then on peace was restored and the boys went frequently to see old Remus and receive their pies. They even helped in his shop from time to time and he actually took one of them on as his apprentice. The local people said it was a miracle that they now got on so well together, but I'm pleased to say that no-one guessed the real motivation that saved the boys from the brine barrel.

* * * *

In my position as leader of the church at Patara, I used to travel about Lycia quite often, preaching to other communities, going to conventions about our faith and meeting many other church leaders from around the country. About twice a year I would go to Myra, the metropolitan city of Lycia, where they had erected a rather magnificent church building decorated with wonderful frescos of the apostles and saints of the church on the walls to encourage the congregation in their worship. It was while I was there, maybe nine or ten years after I'd returned to Patara, that the presbyters at Myra cornered me after I had delivered a sermon on Christian tolerance and brotherly love. Their leader, Joseph, spoke for them all.

"Father Nicholas," he began, "over the years we have always been more than impressed by your spirituality and your learning. You have clearly studied the gospels and the epistles very deeply and your devotion shines through your every preachment."

The other murmured in agreement.

"You will be aware, no doubt," he continued, "that our beloved bishop Honorius has recently been gathered to his fathers. God has seen fit to take him from us and we are bereft without him, I must confess."

I wondered where on earth this conversation was leading.

"We have recently had a meeting with the patriarch who knows of how matters stand with us and we were wondering whether you might consider the position in Honorius' stead, that of bishop of Myra? As you will appreciate we are a devout community but we cannot function as we should like without the spiritual direction that someone like you can offer us. We realize that it would mean leaving your home in Patara where you have been for so long, but we would do our very best to make you and your household very comfortable in our city. What do you think?"

"Well," I answered, totally taken aback, "I had never thought of being elevated to such a position. Becoming an episcopal servant of the church would be a huge step for me, especially since as you already know I was born and brought up in Patara and I have been familiar with all the people there since I was a child. They are all my family so to speak and it would be hard for me to leave them."

"We realise this would not be easy for you," Joseph admitted. "It would be a big change, we have no doubt, but would you at least consider it? Take your time to weigh up the pros and cons. We won't pressure you for the moment, but shall we say we might expect an answer in two or three weeks' time? Would that give you enough leeway to think it over and come to a decision? Should you accept, the patriarch is certainly prepared to ratify your position."

I told them I was deeply moved by their proposal and their faith in me and I agreed to think it over and to talk to my own household, to Irene, Andreas and Calista, as well as to the members of my congregation.

"Yes," I concluded, "I am indeed most honored by your offer and will let you know after I have consulted with those that would be affected, if that's alright."

As I rode back to Patara, I was full of trepidation about what I would say when I got there and what the response would be. I need not have worried. The response I received was overwhelming.

CHAPTER NINETEEN

BISHOP OF MYRA

By the time I reached home I was still undecided as to how I should broach the subject of the offer that had been made to me at Myra. On the one hand I considered it a remarkable honour to have been invited to take up the bishopric, yet on the other I felt I owed my allegiance to the people of Patara who had supported me for well over a decade through all the trying and the difficult times we had collectively endured. They had been my inspiration and my ship in the troubled oceans through which I had navigated. How, I asked myself, could I even contemplate leaving them? And there was my own household to think about, Andreas and Calista, as well as Irene. They probably didn't want to be torn away from the society where we'd all put down such deep roots. We'd been a team for a considerable time now and our connections to the community as a whole were very strong. I spent several hours in prayer, turning the whole thing over in my mind, until eventually I knew I had to confront the issue head on.

I began by calling the three others to me. I had decided that if any one of them was not happy with the move, that would be the end of the matter and I need ask no further.

"As you know," I began, "I went to Myra last weekend and while I was there the elders of the church made me an extraordinary offer."

"Don't tell me!" interrupted Andreas. "They've asked you to become their new bishop! That's what's happened isn't it?"

"How on earth did you know that?" I countered, astonished.

"Well, we all know that his holiness Honorius has recently died and you are the most senior priest in Lycia and if you ask me, probably the most respected clergyman in the whole province by far. You are the obvious choice, I would have said."

"That is what has happened, I must confess," I replied, "but I'm very much in two minds about accepting the position, not least because of us all here. We have become a fundamental part of the community here, have we not? Everyone has given us their support through the best and the worst of times. How can I, or should I say, how can we leave them now? No, I feel we owe the people of Patara a great deal and I don't want to go thoughtlessly to Myra just because it would be an elevation for me. I think that would be desperately unfeeling and frankly socially unacceptable."

Irene spoke at this point, "Niko, may I say something? I have known you all your life, even longer than Calista and Andreas. I know your restless spirit of adventure and I have seen you rise to every challenge. Why else do you suppose you made those incredible journeys through Arabia and the Holy Land all that time ago? That is very much your character. If you ask them, I am sure the congregation here will be immensely proud that you have been invited to ascend to this high office."

And Calista elaborated, "We will go anywhere with you Niko. We are your family and you will always be our head. Whatever you want to do, we'll support you and travel any road with you, you know that don't you? You can always count on us, as you have done these many years."

The other two nodded in agreement. I felt humbled by this show of absolute solidarity and I thanked all three of them for their support. Armed with this unanimity, I knew I now must face my congregation and see if they could shed any light on the decision that was still very much weighing on my mind. I decided that I would broach the subject at the end of next Sunday's eucharist, the time when we normally saw the largest number of members present. How would they react to such a move, I wondered? I prepared a sermon based upon the parable Jesus told of the sower, that some of his seed fell on poor ground and yielded nothing while some fell on good ground.

Sunday came and I was full of anxiety, wondering what the people would say. I concluded the sermon reminding the audience that the seed that falls on the good ground ends by bringing forth a manifold crop. I completed the service with the doxology and then announced that I had something to say to them all, something of a personal nature that I would like them to hear. I told them of the proposition that had been put to me by the church at Myra. To my total amazement and considerable embarrassment, the whole church erupted simultaneously into enthusiastic applause which continued for some minutes, over which I could hear cries of "Well done!" and "You will be our bishop too." When it finally subsided, many people came up to me to shake my hand and congratulate me, as though my acceptance had been a foregone conclusion.

"You deserve to be there, Father," one said.

"You can be a remarkable influence on our church from such a position," said another.

"We are not losing a priest so much as gaining a bishop!" said several others, which sentiment seemed to sum up the general feeling of the meeting. I was overwhelmed by their support. What a remarkable community, I thought. On the following day I sent a messenger to Myra with a letter accepting the elevation. At this late stage of my life everything was about to change again.

I thought it would be a straightforward task to move from one city to the other, but not a bit of it. I had accumulated so many books and papers, as well as associated bric-a-brac, that it actually took weeks to clear everything, to pack and send it by mule train across the mountains, even with Calista and Irene helping. I'd sent Andreas ahead to organise things at the other end; he was going to act as my private secretary, which was an enormous comfort to me. He knew all my little foibles and ways of doing things. I naturally made Irene head of the new household; she if anyone knew how to run our home. Calista I appointed as my personal assistant, getting me ready for events and arranging all the vestments that were needed. I resisted any attempt by the good people of Myra for them to manage my affairs, apologising in advance for keeping my own people around me instead.

* * * * *

On the face of it, Myra was just like any other Lycian city, with many similar monuments to Patara for example, but there were significant differences. To begin with, although it called itself a port, it actually wasn't. It lay inland a few stadia from the coast up the very fertile valley of the River Myros. The actual port for Myra was Andriake, built at the mouth of the river, which like Patara was dominated by huge granaries constructed during the reign of the emperor Hadrian. The port itself was a busy one and interestingly enough had strong connections with Christianity. The Evangelist Luke, author of the Gospel which bears his name, as well his book on the Acts of the Apostles, had come here, and the Apostle Paul changed ships here on his final journey to Rome. Myra, which it served, had been the seat of a bishopric for a considerable time, since sometime shortly after Hadrian's reign in fact, so I was taking on a very historic position.

The approach to Myra by ship offers perhaps the most exceptional seascape in the whole of the Great Sea. Navigating between clusters of beautiful islands and tiny islets, the spectacular mountain backdrop rises up range upon range, ascending through a kaleidoscope of ever higher ridges which run parallel to the coast. Their lower slopes are clothed in ancient pine and oak forests as they reach skywards, and their barren, undulating peaks are covered in snow every year from the autumn until well into the following early summer. It is a vista that once seen is never to be forgotten, superb in its appearance and singular in its majesty and scale. The city with all its outlying villages nestles in the narrow valley at the base of this dramatic panorama.

Unlike some of the cities of Lycia which displayed more ancient buildings, Myra very much has a Roman feel to it, largely because it had been rebuilt after suffering an earthquake at about the same time the granaries were being constructed at Andriake. The magnificent theatre which dominates its centre is very Roman in style, erected as it has been against the steep mountainside with the seating cantilevered out on huge, flanking barrel vaults. Its massive auditorium faces impressive, purpose-built, heavily decorated scenery buildings three stories high. But there is also a necropolis on the side of the theatre dating back to a period long before the

Romans, the cliff faces carved with many rock-cut tombs. There is another similar necropolis further along the mountain. Many of the chambers of these tombs have recently been adopted by religious hermits as monkish cells. Otherwise, the city has all the features you might expect in such a large, modern metropolis – the colonnaded streets, the temples to various pagan gods and a whole host of other civic buildings which complete its urban profile.

The members of the church at Myra arranged for us to live in an imposing villa on the slopes of the hillside overlooking the city and Irene wasted no time in organising it to suit our needs. Besides an impressive tablinum decorated with beautiful mosaics on the floor, the villa featured an striking atrium planted with sweet-smelling bushes set around a large fish pond, off which opened a whole series of reception rooms and bedrooms and there was even a small Roman bath-house alongside the main part of the villa complete with underfloor heating and a plunge pool. Two young girls came with the villa, Vanna and Mala, who had their own quarters at the back of the house and Irene soon had them working hard cleaning the whole place ready for us to move in.

By the time I arrived, having sailed down the coast from Patara, Calista had sorted out all the splendidly embroidered vestments and had even ordered new ones for me; she thought the existing robes might be too small. She'd also discovered other equipment which I would need on ceremonial occasions

– although personally I was never one for finery. Andreas had spoken to the elders of the church and arranged for them to organise an enthronement at the earliest opportunity. When it took place it was a grand event to which it seemed the whole of Myra turned out. I preached on the unity of the church and asked that we should show tolerance towards our fellow man. The idea came to me because I was becoming only too well aware that there were fierce and growing schisms dividing different groups of believers around the empire and that as a bishop of Christ I would be drawn into the various debates and would have to face up to what this meant. I was not looking forward to the heated discussions that I knew were raging in some cities.

But before even that impinged upon my new life, another and for me far more immediate problem arose much closer to home. I'd already heard a little about it from Andreas, who always kept his ear close to the political ground. It concerned three men from a neighbouring village in the mountains, a village which actually belonged to the 'demes' of Myra. These men had been accused of fomenting insurrection against the city council of Myra. They were alleged to have turned the people against the legitimate government, of setting up an alternative council outside the city and most importantly, of stealing vast amounts of money from the public purse. Feelings among the city fathers were running high. The three men had been arrested and with indecent haste they had been given what I understood to have been a travesty of a show tribunal, following which without further ado they were sentenced to be executed for treason.

Several members of the men's families came to see me to make frantic representation on their behalf, saying that the three were entirely innocent and that the charges against them had been totally trumped up. They had been critical of the council, yes, they said, but the council members were demonstrably corrupt and it was they who had purloined the city's funds to cover up losses they'd sustained in a recent fraudulent property venture. The families maintained that the trial and conviction of the three men was meant to divert attention from the main perpetrators of the swindle, the councillors themselves. There had already been intense arguments all over the city regarding the matter when I joined the debate, suggesting, I thought quite logically, that the three men should be allowed to speak freely at a properly-constituted legal trial.

Disturbingly, shortly thereafter, a number of henchmen from the councillors involved came to see me to warn me off interfering in matters that they said didn't concern me.

"Your Grace," opened their spokesman, "you are new here and don't really understand the intricate workings of our city. We feel sure that if Bishop Honorius were still alive he would have been certain to let things take their natural course and we strongly urge you to do the same. It would be quite unfortunate if you were seen to be meddling in things about which you really don't know a great deal, if we may put it so strongly. Leave it to us, your Reverence; I'm sure you'll find that this is the best way in the long run."

But I couldn't let it rest and the more they tried to persuade me, the more I suspected that they were in some way complicit in a colossal deception for which the accused men would take the blame and pay with their lives. I campaigned vociferously for the three to be tried properly, with witnesses, in a magistrates' court, but my entreaties fell upon deaf ears. No one of any influence wanted to hear the alternative point of view and I got the impression, wrongly perhaps, that maybe many of the rank and file citizenry were in some way peripherally involved in the whole deception as well.

"It would take a miracle to save these three men," people were saying. "They always looked guilty from the very outset."

No one was prepared to consider that there might have been a deliberate miscarriage of justice. They would rather sweep the whole affair under the carpet, let things take their course and forget all about it. But I persisted in my call for a proper trial, even as the day for the execution of the three men drew near. I prayed about it both in private and in public, quoting the ninth commandment, 'Thou shalt not bear false witness against thy neighbour,' but it seemed as though I was not going to prevail. Then, just at the very last moment, a young secretary whom I knew to be a faithful member of the church came to me with some papers. It transpired that he actually worked at the council offices and had found the papers secreted behind a cupboard. They related to the bogus property deal and contained figures actually outlined on one of the pages showing how money had been surreptitiously abstracted internally from the city's coffers. I thanked him profusely and ran to the magistrates' office to show them the proof. They in turn stayed the order of execution upon the three men and ordered the arrest of the councillors concerned.

A proper trial followed, revealing the truth and the extent of the dishonesty involved and two of the councillors were imprisoned for a considerable number of years, while three more, no doubt with someone's connivance, somehow managed to flee the city, never to return. The good news for me was that the three young men were released without further charge. Obviously I could never reveal where the papers had come from for fear of implicating the young secretary, which thus left people with the mistaken impression that a miracle had indeed taken place and that somehow I was its author, a notion that I was unable for secrecy's sake to refute. At any event the whole affair proved to the people of Myra that I wasn't simply a religious cypher and that I was prepared to become involved with the daily life of the city and its inhabitants at every level, which worked very much in my favour. Slowly, the people began to respect me more and more and listen to my message of good will to all, men, women and children.

* * * * *

I was always to be seen about the streets of Myra, visiting the sick, supporting the weak and comforting the bereaved. I felt that no part of that community was beneath my dignity and I cared for them all, rich and poor alike. As I had done at Patara, I was particularly keen to encourage the young children to join in our church activities and I created special schools where they could be taught about the life of Jesus and of the promises he had made to mankind. It became a legendary feature of my ministry and I made it clear that, unlike many other senior clergy who considered that dealing with the youth of their parish was beneath them, little ones were always welcome under my jurisdiction. I loved sitting in as some of the Biblical stories were being told, watching the children's entranced faces following the familiar tales of the feeding of the five thousand, or the parable of the shepherd and the lost sheep, or the story that they all loved most, the birth of Jesus in the stable at Bethlehem and the subsequent visits by the shepherds and the wise men. When I told them that I had for a time lived very close to Bethlehem and actually knew the cave where Mary had laid her baby in the manger they were always transfixed.

* * * * *

Political events beyond our borders in Lycia were stumbling on from one imperial crisis to another leading to endless confrontations between the two co-emperors, Licinius and Constantine. But as representatives of the Christian church, we were becoming more and more concerned with the contradictory statements Licinius was issuing. Although ten years before he had been a co-signatory to the Edict of Mediolanum, as his rivalry with Constantine grew Licinius was seen more and more to represent the old world pagan values of the empire in contra-distinction to his fellow co-emperor. Constantine and the Latin west were totally in favour of the freedom of Christianity and this aspect of Constantine's emperorship led Licinius to begin to interfere in church matters in the east, demoting some senior figures and getting rid of others. It wasn't so much a return to the persecutions of former days as it was of Licinius making an anti-western statement of intent. An uneasy relationship developed between his administration and the church.

For most of the time, we were dealing with not so much a shared, co-operating government as an uneasy truce between two belligerent halves of the empire. For some years peace appeared to prevail, but then came an incident which became the unrelated spark which ignited the already-dry kindling of mutual suspicion. Constantine was being plagued with incursions along the Danube by the Sarmatians, illiterate raiders who came from north of the Pontus. He eventually commanded his army to drive them out, which they did down through northern Greece and Thrace and thus accidentally into Licinius' territory. In response Licinius accused Constantine of breaking their treaty of non-aggression by sending his army east and thus prompting him in turn to adopt a correspondingly bellicose posture. War was never far from the surface with these two.

Finally, after a short period of comparative inactivity, the two sides of the empire fell to blows in earnest in what soon became all-out civil war. On two separate occasions Constantine's ships skilfully attacked and defeated Licinius' superior fleet in and around the northern Aegean and the Hellespont, a stretch of water which some people wrongly thought was effectively the boundary between the two leaders. After the second of these sea battles Licinius himself was captured. Although having been soundly beaten, he was spared the death penalty owing to the intervention of his wife, who was Constantine's sister. Instead of being killed he was interned under house arrest in Thessalonica. But the following year Constantine had him hanged anyway. It transpired he had surreptitiously been trying to initiate hostilities all over again by raising an army even whilst in captivity. With Licinius' demise the tetrarchy was finally in ruins and, more importantly, it left Constantine in sole charge of the whole Roman empire.

* * * * *

Constantine lost no time in consolidating his new position. He felt it most important to bring the two sides of his dominion back together, the Latin west and the Greek east and he did this in a very bold and revolutionary way. Rome had for almost five hundred years been the nexus of world power, both during the time of the republic and certainly during the last three hundred and fifty years of the empire. It had enjoyed enormous imperial patronage to such an extent that to be a citizen of Rome was deemed to be an elevation to a superior style of life in every conceivable way, financially, legally and socially. What Constantine now proposed, however, was moving the capital from the west, where it had always exerted an eccentric influence on affairs, and building a new first city in the east; well, if not actually in the east, more in the centre, thus acting to unite the empire and refocus people's loyalties.

He considered several urban candidates. Serdica in Thrace was one of them and some people said at one point he was even looking at the city of Thessalonica on the north Aegean coast. In the end, he chose the old Greek trading colony of Byzantium, at the opening of the Bosphorus. I suppose this was the nearest place he could find to a half-way point between the extreme east of the empire in Mesopotamia and the extreme west in Britannia. It also offered the advantage of having already been extensively rebuilt on a Roman plan during the preceding hundred years or so; as such it was ideal for developing into his 'New Rome'.

Byzantium lay on a spit of land with the seashore of Propontis on the one side and the inlet called *"Chrysokeras,"* the Golden Horn, on the other. It was between the two that Constantine was to create his magnificent new capital, to act as the *"omphalos,"* the navel, of his reformed empire. It was going to outshine Rome many times over and would act as the focal point for all the citizens of the world. He would instigate the building of magnificent churches, palaces, a hippodrome and many other remarkable features of this his personal creation, for indeed personal it was going to be. He was going to rename the city "Constantinople," Constantine's City, not so much for his own aggrandisement but rather to keep his disparate people's imagination focused on this pinnacle of the new order, with him as its head.

Having heard about it, I wondered if I should ever see Constantine's new city. I was feeling my age by this time and liked nothing more than relaxing at home after ministering to the citizens of Myra and the surrounding countryside. My idea of voyaging any distance was to return to Patara for a few days to see my old friends and privately to relive the memories of my youth. I was always welcomed back there as a part of what I still considered to be my wider family, a comforting feeling that suited me perfectly. I liked nothing better than to sit on the quaysides of the harbour, watching the ships being unloaded and hearing about how things were progressing, just as I used to when I was a boy. At three score years and ten my travelling days were over, or so I thought.

I was sitting there as usual during one of my frequent visits when a couple of the local fishermen came over, "We heard how you rescued them sailors the other month, your Holiness. They was real scared, so they was and you brought 'em safe out of the storm. It was a miracle, so they say!"

The incident to which they were referring had taken place about three months earlier, when I was sailing back to Myra from Patara. We happened to be navigating too close to the shore near Teimioussa, an area known for its sudden and fierce downdrafts funneling off the high mountains, especially in the late spring, as this was. Dramatically, part of the sail ripped and the boat canted over and started to take in water. Counter-intuitively, I told them to steer the vessel further out to sea, where I knew from experience that the winds would be lighter. For a few minutes they had been extremely frightened, but it was simply seamanship they lacked, not divine intervention, as I explained to the fishermen.

"It was local knowledge that saved them, no more than that," I countered. "You would have told them to do the same thing if it had been you there instead of me!"

But they wouldn't have it. Maybe it's because they didn't expect a man of the church to know about the ways of the sea. Whatever the case might have been, the idea that this was "yet another of Nicholas' miracles" wasn't going to go away. Once again, I was the talk of Lycia.

CHAPTER TWENTY

THE COUNCIL OF NICAEA

It was not long after Constantine had assumed full control of the empire that I was summoned in my capacity as bishop of Myra to a convocation of senior members of the world-wide Christian church. It was to be held at the city of Nicaea quite near Constantine's new city, Constantinople. Constantine's intention in convening the council was that it should hammer out a creed, a statement of belief upon which we could all agree. The more generous younger clergy that I spoke to praised Constantine for his breadth of vision, for his political generosity and for his manifest support of the Church of Christ. But for me, old hand that I now was, what did I think? Well, cynically, I am sorry to say, whilst I rejoiced that our church was so openly supported by the emperor after all the upheavals I had experienced, I perceived somewhere in this move the sinister hand of political intrigue and vain ambition. I had seen enough of the machinations of the imperial house to have lost any vestige of faith I might once have had in their innate altruism and public spiritedness. I decided I would go along to Nicaea anyway and see if I could make a contribution to the scholarly debates that were likely to ensue.

At my age it was going to be quite a journey. I would have to take a ship up the coast of Asia Minor to the Hellespont and then into Propontis, the Marble Sea. It was not the easiest time of the year to do this either, just at the beginning of spring, when winds could be contrary and seas could run high, but there was no alternative. The land journey would have been too difficult.

I spoke about it to Andreas, "You and Calista will come with me, won't you? I will need your moral support, but I'll also need your physical help too. I'm not as young as I was and such a long journey will no doubt be exhausting."

I recognized that Andreas, being the same age as me, was no longer a young man either. What with him looking after my secretarial affairs and Calista taking care of my domestic matters and accompanied by a few other supernumeraries from Myra, we set sail westwards towards the Aegean. Irene was too old and infirmed by this time and stayed at home. Our journey took us close to Patara and then across the gulf to the island of Rhodes, where we spent a day or two enjoying their fine wine and the spring sunshine. From there we sailed past the islands of Symi and Tilos to the city of Cnidus at the junction of the Great Sea and the Aegean.

The winds being somewhat contrary off Cape Crio, we put in to the commercial harbour at Cnidus and spent the next couple of nights enjoying the hospitality of that beautiful city. It occurred to me that when St Paul was sailing on his journey to Rome, having set off from Myra as we had done, he too had experienced contrary winds at this point. The idea that we were following in the wake of his last voyage seemed to give us extra heart. Two days later the gusting north-westerly wind abated allowing us to sail up the side of the island of Kos, past Halicarnassus and on towards Miletus where Paul had stayed during one of his earlier missionary journeys and from where he had called the elders of the church at Ephesus to him.

From Miletus we continued northwards to Ephesus itself, the city from which Paul had once beaten a hasty retreat when assailed by those supporting the cult of Artemis Ephesia. The temple of Artemis was still there, though rather dilapidated after having been damaged by a series of earthquakes. We were pleased to see that the old Roman corn exchange was being transformed into a rather magnificent basilica in honour of the Theotokos, the Virgin Mary, whose one-time presence here had supplanted the worship of Diana, the wild goddess of the hunt. After a few days communing with the church at Ephesus we carried on northwards. Bypassing Smyrna and Pergamon we sailed across the gulf to Assos, where again we had to wait until contrary winds once more calmed down. From Assos we sailed around the cape and towards the Hellespont, calling in at Alexandria Troas, the port from which Paul and Silas had set sail for Philippi in Macedonia when they were called to bring the gospel to Greece.

We entered the Hellespont the next day, a strait which has featured so much in ancient history. It was across this narrow strip of sea that the Persian king Xerxes had built his bridge of boats to take his armies across to Europe when he invaded Athens, having first had his task masters thrash the waves for being so unruly. I'd read about it in Herodotus' "Histories" when I was a boy. It was not much more kindly to us that day and the going was slow. The captain told us there was a strong current coming down the channel against the direction of travel. After a trying time tacking back and forth for hour after hour the straits opened out at the beginning of the Propontis. Alas once more the winds turned against us, a strong, late-winter gale bringing cold, stormy weather down from the Bosphorus, so we had to put into harbour once more, this time on the south shore of Propontis in the port of Cyzicus, once the capital of Mysia. I became rather irritable while we waited here for a day or two, before Andreas suggested to me that as we were not that far away from Nicaea at this point, we might as well continue by road.

"It will only take a day or two, three at most and I'll arrange an enclosed carriage for us so we won't have to brave this awful weather on the roads. How would that be?"

Leaving the boat was a good idea, and as Andreas had indicated, after a not too uncomfortable three days, a journey made more enjoyable by the riot of spring flowers we saw along the roadsides - the huge daisies, giant fennel and blood-red poppies in particular - we approached Nicaea, one of the most important cities of Bithynia. The city had been heavily defended by a polygonal wall built by the Romans during the reign of the emperor Hadrian, but that hadn't stopped it from being sacked by the Goths only 70 years ago, signs of which could still be seen in one or two places. Once inside, we made our way to the imperial palace where we were told the council was to take place and we were assigned rooms in one of the wings of the complex.

I met several bishops whom I had got to know during my time at Myra and on my second day, before the council sessions had begun, I came across Eusebius of Caesarea, my old teacher who had induced me into Christianity all those years ago in Alexandria. He was a venerable old man by this time, as I suppose I might well have seemed to him, but he was very much more senior in the ranks of the church than I was. He was very pleased to see me, as I was he, and we exchanged several stories about our varied experiences during the intervening decades.

As I had come to expect over the years we had been together, Andreas had taken himself off and done some investigating as to how the council was to be convened and what subjects we were likely to debate. That evening, he told us what he'd discovered.

"The emperor is very concerned about schisms in the church. As we know, some alternate interpretations of our faith have developed in different parts of the empire and Constantine is keen that we all adhere to the same Christian tenets. He wants everyone to agree to a single statement of belief, a 'credo' he calls it, which we should all follow."

We had already heard rumours regarding this; it was how we were going to achieve it which interested me.

"Well over one thousand bishops have been invited to Nicaea," continued Andreas. "It's supposed to be a meeting of the 'most eminent men of our generation', but seemingly only about three hundred have actually turned up, mostly from the eastern provinces of the empire. The real sticking point seems to be the ideas of this presbyter from Alexandria, the man called Arius. Remember him? Now, I have found out that this chap is a Berber from the deserts of Africa and a strict ascetic. In various papers he has published over the years and through his teaching he has been promulgating the idea that since Christ is the son of God, he cannot be on the same level as God. Someone taught him this when he was young. He's managed to create a huge problem with this divisive doctrine, but at the same time he has accumulated quite a following. It's causing a great deal of political unrest in the cities around the Nile and elsewhere in North Africa. This is the main thing that you have to debate, this so-called Arian heresy!"

"But what concerns me," I interrupted, "is what Constantine's real motive is for wanting us to do this? Is it the heresy itself or is the unrest he's worried about? Don't forget that although he sees himself as the new supreme emperor, it was only a year or two ago that one half of his domain was at the other's throat and that was purely political. I don't remember it having too much to do with Christianity."

"Well," replied Andreas, "you'll find out about everything tomorrow when the council opens. Constantine is going to be there in person and I've been told that he will introduce the whole thing."

The following morning we all met in a splendid audience chamber in the centre of the palace, where a magnificent manuscript of the gospels was left open on a table to remind us no doubt of what the focus of our deliberations should be. At a prearranged signal, the rear doors were thrown open and in walked the imperial procession. First were members of Constantine's immediate family, followed by various worthies from his court and finally, after a brief pause, the emperor himself. We all rose in deference to him and he strode through our midst, head held high, wearing a robe of Tyrian purple adorned with strands of pure gold and rows of multi-coloured precious stones which glinted in the shafts of sunlight beaming through the clerestory windows. It was reminiscent of a procession of heavenly angels, so impressive they seemed to be, but this undoubtedly was his intention.

He bade us all be seated and then in a deep and sonorous voice expounded that we were here as the guarantors of his empire; it was our influence through our faith that would hold the whole edifice together. In that we were mainly eastern bishops I wondered what the people of Rome might think of that. We all had to agree, he adjured us; we had to come up with a common set of beliefs, namely that God is supreme and rules with Christ and the Holy Spirit indivisible, that is, the doctrine of the Holy Trinity. There could be no place for a heavenly hierarchy, he insisted. After placing considerable emphasis on unity, he begged us to finalize a formula that would bind the church together as one, and by association, I thought privately, his own political sphere as well.

He continued, "Let, then, all contentious disputation be discarded; and let us seek in the divinely-inspired word the solution to the questions at issue." He waved pointedly to the open gospel on the table.

He ended with a series of extraordinary statements, that his empire was the new Rome, that it was God's will that it should be so, and he finally implied that he had thus been divinely appointed as God's vice-regent on earth, that this too was God's will. Eusebius, who was very much a supporter of the emperor, confirmed my suspicions that Constantine considered himself divinely elected to his position when he wrote in his account of the Synod, which was circulated a few days later:

"Thus then the God of all, the Supreme Governor of the whole universe, by his own will has appointed Constantine to be prince and sovereign: so that, while others have been raised to this distinction by the election of their fellow-men, he is the only one to whose elevation no mortal may boast of having contributed."

There you have it, I mused rather irreverently, the ultimate political combination of church and state. That's the real reason we're all here, I concluded. It was all very clever!

When he and his entourage had finally made their grand exit, we got down to the detail of agreeing a creed, led by one or two of the eastern patriarchs. From the discussions it was obvious to me that those bishops and presbyters who were present were all deeply impressed with the way events had moved. After three centuries of periodic persecutions instigated by various Roman emperors it was little wonder. Some still carried the scars of recent imperial torture; one priest from Egypt was missing an eye while another was crippled in both hands as a result of being subjected to a trial by red-hot irons. None of these was going to question the veracity of Constantine's message or his motives. As far as my ideas were concerned I thought the best policy was to keep my own counsel.

Discussions went back and forth for some days. Twenty two bishops, mainly from Egypt and North Africa, initially supported Arius' claim that Jesus was God's son and therefore was not of the same substance as the Almighty and must be subservient to Him. Many others were violently opposed to that idea, saying that it called into question the very divinity of Jesus and thereby belittled his message. After the arguments had swung this way and that, some of Arius' writings were read out before the synod and it became obvious to us all that they demeaned the whole notion of Christ as our saviour. The more vociferous bishops went on to denounce Arius' theology as nothing less than blasphemous and most other participants had to concur. It was finally agreed that Christ was co-eternal and con-substantial with the Father and from there we proceeded to create the statement of belief that Constantine had decreed we make.

At first no two bishops could agree. The discussion was interminable and it went on for nearly two whole weeks. But the result was to be known as the Nicene Creed.

"We believe in one God, the Father, the Almighty, maker of heaven and earth and of all that is seen and unseen. We believe in one Lord, Jesus Christ, the only Son of God, eternally begotten of the Father, God from God, Light from Light, True God from true God, begotten, not made, one in Being with the Father."

There was more to it, but that was the main nub of the statement. 'One in Being with the Father,' was the crucial phrase.

The Council continued for a further two weeks, discussing various other schisms, working out when the Christian Easter should be, when we should properly remember Christ's crucifixion and his rising from the dead and a few more similar ecclesiastical problems. Eventually one of the patriarchs brought the discussions to a close and with a final Eucharist, our deliberations came to an end. It was none too soon for me. I was feeling tired and out of sorts after being away from home for so long.

Andreas suggested that if we had the time we should cross the Propontis to Constantine's new capital to see how he was transforming it, but I said I felt too exhausted to make the extra journey and that as far as I was concerned the sooner we set off for Lycia the happier I would be. Andreas graciously gave in and went off to organise a ship to take us back to Myra.

It was now late summer which usually brought with it the favourable daily etesian winds for those wanting to sail south. It was a dry wind which during the mornings would blow briskly from the north, curving around the coast of Asia Minor into the eastern parts of the Great Sea. But it could also be a dangerous wind. Instead of normally dying back as evening approached, it could blow more and more vigorously, sometimes for days on end, when to be caught in the wrong piece of sea could prove disastrous. All the sailors that I ever knew had a very healthy respect for these summer winds and tended to seek shelter by the middle of the day until early in the evening rather than brave them out.

Andreas found us a sturdy ship to transport us back home. It was a vessel from Pontus, with the tall prow and wide sails which characterised that type of design. It was built to counteract the high waves and the wild winter weather of those northern parts, but it also meant it had plenty of space and a couple of cabins which we could share. We went aboard one evening and the following day set sail down the Propontis towards the Hellespont. This time the current worked in our favour and the following day we were in the Aegean sailing in a sprightly wind down the Mytilene Channel alongside the island of Lesbos. Two days later, we'd reached Ephesus where again we stopped in the harbour to take on water. Parts of the city were being reconstructed after yet another damaging earthquake, but we hoped to enjoy their hospitality.

Alas I felt very unwell while we were there and the doctor whom they called confined me to bed. I was distinctly ill for some weeks and while the good people of Ephesus ministered to my every need, I didn't feel like moving very far. Andreas and Calista were becoming anxious for me, I knew. They were keen to get me home, to our own house. Andreas kept eyeing the weather, which worsened as the autumn wore on and it wasn't until December there was a calm period, light winds and even some sunshine. He arranged that we should sail on while the quiet weather lasted, so finding a new ship, we set sail south again.

We passed through the narrow channel between the mainland and the island of Samos before rounding Cape Crio again at Cnidus and sailing east towards Rhodes and home. Because of the possibility of strong winds, we hugged the shore and put in several times en route for fear of being caught unawares. We stopped briefly at Caunos before continuing to Telmessos in northern Lycia and from there we set off around the coast for the last leg of our journey to Patara and Myra. As we came around the aptly named Devil's Point, the wind began to rise again and the sea became very heavy, with uncomfortable winter swells hurtling in from the direction of Rhodes. By the time we could see the mountains along the western coast of Lycia the wind was howling and the captain had had to reef the sail to almost nothing to prevent us being capsized.

"I'm afraid we're going to have to seek shelter," he announced. "This could blow stronger and stronger for several days."

I told him we were not very far from where I had been born and that I knew of an island around the next headland where there was a well-protected anchorage.

"If we can reach that we'll be safe to ride out the storm," I said.

With great skill he rounded a group of rocks jutting out into the sea and we cruised on behind the lee of the small elongated island which the locals called Partridge Island, presumably because of the abnormal numbers of red-legged partridge that breed there. In the narrow sound we found calm water. The storm was mounting as we did so and we were lucky to have somewhere to shelter; I knew from experience that there was nowhere south from here for many hours sailing where we could have escaped the fury of the weather until we got as far as Patara. The captain dropped the anchors overboard right against the northern shore of the island and made the prow safe with ropes tied to myrtle trees growing on the bank.

My fever had returned on our journey and by this time I began to feel really wretched. What I would not have given for a proper bed in my own home. But here we were stuck behind this uninhabited island and there was nothing to be done but to wait and wait. We had no option.

THE NARRATIVE ENDS

PART III

LOOKING FOR NICHOLAS

THE WRITINGS

CHAPTER TWENTY-ONE

READING ABOUT NICHOLAS

What you have just read is for the most part pure fiction. It's an imaginary reconstruction of the life of St Nicholas based loosely upon legend, hearsay and accumulated and unsubstantiated stories which have from time to time eddied about the academic and ecclesiastical ether relating to one individual or another called Nicholas. Here they have been woven together around a framework of historical facts, in so far as even these can be relied upon.

The story is not intended to be a true reflection of the life of the venerable saint for one very good reason. Despite many scholarly works dealing with Nicholas of Myra, which discuss in depth the sources and their veracity, debating the miracles he was supposed to have performed and the contribution he may have made to the history of the early church, there is in truth no contemporary written evidence that he existed at all. That should be kept firmly in mind when considering the tales which were supposed to make up his life - that there may have been no such person in the first place and that the whole composition may just be an accretion of fanciful anecdotes spuriously attributed to someone bearing that name.

I have no doubt that there are some clerical scholars and church historians who would vigorously dispute this interpretation. They would quote, critically or otherwise, various sources, having convinced themselves that the stories do have some validity and that such a person really did exist. After all, the claim I have made to the contrary impugns the reputation of one of the most popular figures in the annals of Christendom, Nicholas of Myra. He is, probably more than any other figure from church history, far and away the one about whom today every layman knows, whose name is in any given year on everyone's mind, Christian or otherwise, not to mention on most people's lips. Nicholas is of course the exemplar for Santa Claus, Sinterklaas, Father Christmas, Père Noël, call him what you may. Who would dare dispute the fact that this kindly figure was not real, when he is manifestly present at the apogee of our annual feasting and good will, the yuletide celebrations?

I am not a historian but I have enough critical apparatus to make some evaluation of such written records as are available. I have also read the inherent scepticism of other scholars who know better than I the value and authenticity, or lack of it, of the individual texts. The main and interestingly the earliest document upon which much of today's story depends is the so-called biography of Nicholas by the Byzantine theologian Methodius which dates to around the middle of the 9th century AD, some five hundred or more years after the events were supposed to have taken place. Methodius, together with his brother Cyril, felt the calling to become Christian missionaries. Born in Thessalonica, the two of them considered their task was to bring the faith to the uneducated Slavic people of the Balkan states and on as far north as Moravia. To do this, among other things, they created the Cyrillic alphabet, a form of which is still in use today. But while their excursions into literacy might have proved valuable, Methodius' history of Nicholas is almost universally thought to be fictitious. This is the one in which the so-called miracles are first described, including the gold given for the dowries, the brine boys, the release of the three men from execution and the rescue of the sailors. Subsequent church writers invariably quote this biography, with or without attribution, thus compounding the fabrication.

By the time of the First Crusade at the end of the 11th century, fascination with eastern saints had grown exponentially and had firmly taken root in western Europe. Byzantine holy men and women who had previously enjoyed only local significance in church history became globally important. One such instance was St George, with accompanying dragon. Christian pilgrims returning from the Mediterranean brought with them not only tales of miracle workers of the eastern Church but also various articles of veneration and even physical fragments attributed to the individuals concerned. The intention no doubt was to re-locate their transformative capabilities westwards. For example, there are several versions of the veil with which St Veronica was said to have wiped Jesus' face when he reached the sixth station of the cross on his way to Golgotha. It is believed an imprint of his visage miraculously transferred itself onto the fabric. Catholic churches in Italy and Austria and two in Spain all claim they actually own the one true and legitimate imprinted material, sometimes known as the 'Holy Face.' Or take the 'genuine' pieces of the true cross on which Christ was crucified, all of which were said to be imbued with miraculous powers. So many churches in the west claim to own one of these that the choleric theologian John Calvin actually refuted the whole lot when he wrote:

> "There is no abbey so poor as not to have a specimen (of the cross). In brief, if all the pieces that could be found were collected together, they would make a sizeable ship-load!"

Any eastern saint who was said to have exhibited miraculous powers during his or her lifetime, however far-fetched, was fair game to be espoused by the gullible, not to say grasping, churches of the west so that their efficacious faculties could then be transferred and exploited by their adoptive occidental foundations. When Methodius' stories about Nicholas began to circulate, the commemoration of St Nicholas became even more popular in Europe than it had been in the east, he becoming by degrees patron saint of all the Russias, a figure of enormous reverence in the Netherlands and a personage of huge importance even in Britain. (There are several hundred churches dedicated to Nicholas in England alone, so pervasive is his influence).

And there are many other claimants to the Nicholas legacy too. It was during the same 11th century that the Selçuk Turks, newly converted to Islam, swept out of the steppes of central Asia and appeared on the borders of Anatolia, at that time part of the vast Byzantine Empire. In 1071, its emperor, Romanos IV Diogenes, underestimating the power of the Selçuk leader Alp Arslan, engaged him in battle at Manzikert near the northern shores of Lake Van, where not only was Romanos soundly defeated but he was also taken prisoner. The Selçuk Turks lost no time in annexing a large portion of Byzantine lands in what today is central Turkey to create their Sultanate of Rum, centered on the old city of Iconium. Some activists in the west were seemingly outraged by this move, especially since the newly acquired Selçuk domain included sites of Christian significance.

By this time various emergent city states in Italy had been trading with the Byzantine Empire for many decades and took great interest in what was happening there. Ships from such ports as Genoa, Pisa, Bari and Venice were plying back and forth as far as Cyprus as well as up into the Pontus, the Black Sea, exchanging commodities with their eastern counterparts. Late in the 11th century, sailors from Bari, seemingly concerned about the security of Christian religious relics in southern Anatolia, navigated as far as Myra. In 1087 they perforce removed the bones purporting to be those of St Nicholas from the church where seemingly he had been interred and took them back to Bari for safe-keeping. However, there is some suggestion that these seafarers were not bona-fide mariners, nor yet the anxious Christian devotees they are sometimes portrayed, but a bunch of unscrupulous Italian pirates hoping to turn a handsome ducat or two from selling any 'miracle working' relics they could find to the highest unsuspecting bidder.

Whatever the case, the citizens of Bari were most pleased to receive the relics. They instigated the construction of an impressive new cathedral, the Basilica di San Nicola, to house Nicholas' remains, a building which stands to this day. According to Bari's own justifying legend the saint, whilst passing by the city on his way to Rome at some point in his life, elected Bari to be his final resting place. The clergy at Bari uphold that Nicholas must be happy in his new home because it appears his bones annually exude an efficacious effluvium, described as 'holy manna,' which is collected in May each year and sold in small glass vials.

But the matter did not rest there, nor it seems did the remains. There was great competition for the Nicholas relics between Bari and its arch rival Venice. Not content with having half-inched the remains of St Mark from Alexandria some two and a half centuries earlier, the Venetians also maintained that it was they, not the people of Bari, who had received St Nicholas' actual bones. And they assert that they still have them, in the Chiesa di San Nicoló al Lido across the lagoon from St Mark's Cathedral. Bizarrely, in the middle of the 20th century, pseudo-scientific analysis of the fragments from both locations declared that the two groups were a perfect match, each establishment holding complementary halves of the same skeleton. Which is odd really, because other disembodied parts of Nicholas have also turned up in many other churches across Europe in places as far apart as Greece, Germany, France, Denmark, Spain, Switzerland and Russia, and even in places of worship on the other side of the Atlantic, both in Canada and the United States. All claim to have in their possession small fragments of the relics of St Nicholas. If all these were authentic, at the very least it would make Nicholas abnormally multi-digited, many of the relics being said to be of his fingers.

So how did this obscure Lycian cleric come to be canonized in the first place and then so venerated throughout the world? The canonization is relatively straightforward, if somewhat suspect as reported. Many saints of the Eastern Church had in one way or another been caught up in the persecutions of Diocletian, the so-called 'Great Persecution.' Some had been soldiers in the Roman army who were done to death for not relinquishing their Christian faith while serving in the legions.

Examples include Sts Sergius and Bacchus of Resafa in Syria, St Demetrius of Thessalonica and St George of Nicomedia, modern day Izmit. For the church they immediately became martyrs and were canonized shortly after their deaths.

Nicholas, too, was considered a martyr to his faith when he was imprisoned during the same persecution, but more significantly, he survived that ordeal and went on to attend the Council of Nicaea. It was this dual activity which was later recognised as a fast track to beatification. However, such a sequence of events is questionable; we have no plausible evidence that anyone of this name was ever present at Nicaea. The only contemporary list, the one compiled by Eusebius of Caesarea as part of his panegyric to Constantine, doesn't mention him. In fact Nicholas doesn't appear in any roll of attendees until about the 12th century. This makes one suspect that his putative Nicaean participation has been introduced anachronistically into the record to give his persona a promotional appeal it doesn't actually deserve. We shall never know.

What is slightly more certain is how St Nicholas became synonymous with Christmas, largely brought about by one almighty co-location of festivals at this time of the year. We can go all the way back to the Neolithic Period, five thousand years ago or more, to see that the middle of the winter was always extremely important to European peoples dependent upon agriculture for their sustenance. Stonehenge in Wiltshire and the recently discovered Goseck Circle in Saxony-Anhalt, Germany, amongst others, are aligned in such a way that they mark the winter solstice, December 21st, the date in the year when the sun rises and sets on the shortest day. Such a moment has since time immemorial been associated with feasting. It's the time when the last of the beasts were slaughtered to avoid having to feed them through the deepest part of winter.

By the Roman era, a mid-winter season of indulgence and general jollity was celebrated during the Saturnalia. There were banquets, parties, role-reversals between masters and slaves and an atmosphere of general licentiousness. The Roman philosopher Seneca described it in a letter to a friend:

"It is now the month of December, when the greatest part of the city is in a bustle. Loose reins are given to public dissipation; everywhere you may hear the sound of great preparations, as if there were some real difference between the days devoted to Saturn and those for transacting normal business!"

After the Reformation there were still vestiges of a pre-Christian mid-winter festival in Western Europe. The Yule, which was originally a pagan Germanic commemoration, again observed in December, was a period of feasting meant to induce a brief euphoria before the grimmest winter weather properly closed in. Here is the origin of evergreen plants being used as decoration, the celebration of life at this moribund time of the year, and banqueting, the idea of plenty in dearth. Both elements acted as harbingers of the hoped-for spring which one could perhaps be persuaded was not too far distant.

So how did Christmas come to be melded with the great mid-winter anniversary? There is no actual Biblical information reflecting what time of the year Jesus was born, but it suited society to syncretize the two ideas, to mix together the two beliefs of the mid-winter merriment presaging spring and new growth in the future and the promise of new life for mankind through the Christ child, thus perfectly harmonising two totally disparate concepts. It was in the 16th century that such a fusing of ideas was further characterised by the introduction of the patriarchal figure of Father Christmas. If you now add that St Nicholas' Day is in December, it is only a short step to conflate the idea of the charitable embodiment of the mid-winter festival, Father Christmas, Le Père Noël, with the kindly personage of St Nicholas, Sinterklaas, Santa Claus and lo! the transformation is complete; St Nicholas becomes the personification of Christmas.

Some countries in Europe, especially Holland, celebrate the coming of Sinterklaas with the giving of presents and general junketing early in December (December 5th/6th). However, according to the original Julian calendar, used by the Eastern Church until the 20th century, this date should be December

19th, much nearer to the day the majority of western societies celebrate Christ's birthday. Thus St Nicholas' Day, if not exactly one and the same thing, is certainly very closely related to Christmas and the mid-winter solstice. During the Victorian era, especially in Britain, with its emphasis on family and gift giving, the framework for the modern Christmas was finally put in place – the yule log, the feasting and the Christmas carols. 'The Holly and the Ivy' is a classic case of syncretism from this time, mixing pagan and Christian beliefs.

The holly bears a berry
As red as any blood,
And Mary bore sweet Jesus Christ
To do poor sinners good.

Finally, with regard to the contemporary iconography of Santa Claus as the rubicund, jolly old man with a white beard dressed in a scarlet tunic; we have to thank Coca Cola for confirming this apparition. In 1931, the Swedish graphic designer Haddon Sundblom re-enforced an already existing image by showing Santa Claus in various poses enjoying the well-known beverage. Sundblom naturally dressed his character in the red and white livery of the Coca Cola Company. (The original art works are now on display at the company's museum in Atlanta, Georgia.) The idea that Santa Claus comes down people's chimneys and gives presents to children is a reflection of the miracle of the young girls' dowries appearing anonymously within the home.

It also mirrors the legends that Nicholas was concerned about the plight of young children, particularly emphasized in the story of the brine boys.

So, is there and sound literary evidence of a St Nicholas upon whom this whole edifice can have been founded? Sensu stricto, the answer should be "no." The written records do not bear scrutiny. What is more unnerving is that perusing the various hagiographies of the early Byzantine period, several "Nicholai" emerge from the shadows, at different times and in different places. Is St Nicholas of Myra but one of these, or worse, is he a conflation? Or is he a complete figment of later fertile imagination? Left to study the written material alone, there will never be a satisfactory answer. We could never truly say one way or the other.

But I think there is primary evidence to support the miracle-working persona of St Nicholas, the early Byzantine saint from Lycia and it comes from a totally unexpected direction. It's not literary testimony, but near-contemporary, physical archaeological data, as I shall describe.

LOOKING FOR NICHOLAS

THE ARCHAEOLOGY

CHAPTER TWENTY-TWO

DIGGING UP SANTA

As an archaeologist I have been intimately involved with Turkey, the reputed home of St Nicholas, for many years. Half a century ago it was the focus of my first overseas fieldwork (see 'Looking for Aphrodite'). My growing fascination with this part of the world led me to sail many times around the coast of ancient Asia Minor as well as through the adjacent Greek Islands. Also, both in Turkey and the Near East, I have been constantly exposed to the ubiquitous Hellenistic, Roman and Byzantine remains which abound here. From this has sprung a healthy respect for the restricted value of material remains, as to what they can and can't tell us about the past. I have always been rather sceptical about connecting archaeological data too closely to specific historical events or personalities; I have observed that they are seldom congruent. So it is with some surprise that I find myself reporting here my observations of the remains found on the deserted island of Gemiler, just off the west coast of ancient Lycia, south of Fethiye and near the present little Turkish holiday resort based on the lagoon of Öludeniz, Turkey's 'Dead Sea', dramatically overlooked by the six and a half thousand foot high Mount Cragus.

The Mediterranean at this point is not an easy piece of sea to cross. The gulf between Rhodes and the western coast of Lycia, known bathymetrically as the Rhodes Trench, is a tectonic trough some two miles deep. When the summer wind, the Meltem, blows (at this point from a west-north-westerly direction) it can make the intervening body of water very uncomfortable in normal circumstances and impossible for small craft in stormy weather; note the Turkish name for the cape just to the west of Gemiler Island, Iblisburun, 'Devil's Point'! The resulting co-location of wind and sea conditions has meant that I have sheltered behind Gemiler Island many a time waiting for conditions to improve. That is how it came to my notice in the first place. The island is a limestone mass measuring one kilometre from west to east and a maximum width of four hundred metres from south to north, bearing the central sectional outline on that axis of a wedge of cheese - a rocky, storm-lashed south-facing scarp (the weather side) and a gentler north-facing dip slope slanting from the summit down to the protected anchorage bordering a narrow strait and the mainland.

Today the cliffs on the south-facing side are conspicuously bare of vegetation, but the northern slopes are thickly screened by myrtle and feral olive trees which disguise the fact that this side of the island is also covered with a mass of roofless walls all the way to the water's edge. For the most part, it is now a wilderness, difficult to negotiate for all the undergrowth, but clamber through it I have. What follows is a memoire of my observations.

Three things are worth mentioning from the outset. First, there is no natural water on the island, nor has there ever been. The only moisture available is winter rainfall which because of the steepness of the slopes quickly disappears. Second, there is very little soil cover, even on the more moderate north-facing slope, which means that there seems never to have been any attempt at agriculture here. Third, there is no trace of human habitation on the island other than Early Byzantine. However, although the island could be described as totally inhospitable, the evidence suggests that at some moment, possibly for a brief period only, a large population lived here. It's the nature of that population and the reason for their being there which forms the focus of our attention.

From my own observation I think it is useful to describe the habitation at Gemiler in four successive phases, the main three dating from between at or just before 400 to about 650 AD, especially the last one hundred years, and a peripheral use circa 1,000 AD.

PHASE I

At some time in the late 300s or early 400s AD a four to five metre high wall, clearly intended to be defensive, was built to circumvallate the top half of the island. The wall was constructed very simply, in the Byzantine style typical for this part of the eastern Mediterranean, from rubble and mortar with no rendering on the inner or outer face. It runs almost straight and horizontally for almost one hundred and fifty metres along the contour half way up the north side of the island and then curves round and rises to near the top of the scarp on the south-facing side, thereby enclosing the summit. Three small gateways punctuate this wall, all on the straight, north-facing side, the anchorage side. One is near the west corner, approached between two wing walls, one is in the centre, the steepest part of the dip slope and is reached by a rock-cut staircase of about fifteen steps and one is on the eastern corner, this last one protected by two miniscule, integrated in-turned turrets. No detail survives as to how these three gateways were closed. For the face of the wall itself there are a few simply-made vertical embrasures irregularly spaced along its length, located somewhat curiously nearer its foundation than its apex.

The purpose of this wall seems to be mainly to delineate the top half of the island and to protect it from casual looters, rather than to provide a serious defence against any properly constituted military threat. Within the enclosed area, very close to but not quite at the summit of the island, there is a small Byzantine church. It has a twenty metre long by twelve metre wide basilica nave orientated from west to east with a simple apse at the centre of its eastern wall. I shall call this the

'Upper Church' though it is barely more than a chapel, but it does seem to constitute the focus of attention for the whole island. In origin, it's very simply constructed, for the most part with the same ubiquitous rubble and mortar.

But in one unique regard this church is very noticeably idiosyncratic. At its western end the building has been excavated out of the solid rock, leaving only the rock walls upstanding. Parts of the southern wall of the nave and the whole of the narthex (the vestibule) have been chiselled up to five metres deep into the unyielding limestone. The lower portion of the wall dividing the narthex from the nave is also of solid rock, as are parts of the platforms running the length of the nave on which the pillars of the basilica sat. There is no atrium, which would normally have been to the west of the narthex. Here instead the limestone rises unmodified from five metres above the inner face of the rear narthex wall to the summit of the island west of the church. This makes the plan very incomplete, unless there was an atrium to the north of the building, unheard of in my experience. Whatever the case, to enter the church one would have approached it from outside the north wall of the nave, turned to the right and entered westwards through an offset doorway into the vestibule and then dog-legged around one hundred and eighty degrees to turn back eastwards through a single central door into the nave. Above that door, capped by a robbed classical architrave block, was a window, which may imply that the vestibule had been unroofed.

I have never seen this design before in any of the many Byzantine churches I have visited, complete or ruined, and it begs the obvious question – why? Why should such a small church be designed so that the rear third of the nave and the whole of the vestibule had to be cut out of tons and tons of hard limestone? This is especially puzzling when, had they moved the construction just a few metres further to the east and north, there is enough flat ground to have accommodated it easily, with the inclusion of an open atrium. It could then have been set out in the usual layout – atrium, vestibule and nave in a west to east train. The only reason I can think of is that they felt compelled to place the altar, or more especially perhaps the centre of the nave, over a very precise location, a spot so imbued with sacred significance that they felt unable to position the church anywhere else, whatever constructional difficulties that entailed. We shall come back to this point later.

Suffice it to say that the church as a whole and the apse in particular in this first phase display no expenditure on decoration. The only emblems visible are three upright crosses built into the inside wall of the apse at about waist height and outlined with the narrow edges of tiles. Otherwise the building is unpretentious.

PHASE 2

Phase 2 can easily be defined by examining this same Upper Church. There is ample evidence of a substantial remake of the building, probably in the mid-6th century to judge by the style of the decoration which was added. First, the inside hemisphere of the apse was redesigned with the addition of a synthronon, a semi-circular sitting-place for the clergy, mounting in five tiers, the steps and risers of which were surfaced with imported marble tiles. This resulted in obscuring the lower parts of the three tile crosses of Phase 1 with concrete, which further implies that the inside wall above the synthronon must now have been rendered with plaster, probably painted, otherwise the upper parts of the partially occluded crosses would still have been visible.

A new altar railing was also added. Whereas the Phase 1 altar screens were set across the nave in local limestone blocks, the new ones were slotted into imported white marble footings set behind the originals, and included two central, outer-facing wings. Fragments of some of these later, waist-high marble screens were still lying around. The shapes of the crosses carved on them confirm a date to the reign of the emperor Justinian (r. 527-565). The date is further supported by the design of a new floor laid in the central nave which was decorated with coloured mosaics, including motifs of running guilloche patterns. (They can easily be compared to the mosaics of the several churches known to be of this date at Madaba and Mount Nebo in Jordan.) Parenthetically at the very least, these mosaics give us a terminus ante quem; Phase 2 cannot be later than 700, the beginning of the iconoclastic period of Byzantine history, after which mosaic floors in churches were no longer used.

So, the Upper Church at Gemiler seems to have been given an expensive make-over about 550 AD. But that is only the beginning of the changes that took place on the island. East of the apse of the Upper Church is what appears to be the addition of a vestry, beyond which is another very small chapel, also with a miniscule apse, the side walls of which were decorated with paintings of Byzantine saints. But then, the most extraordinary thing happens. Leading to the north off the vestry is an arch into a domed cubicle, which itself gives access at right angles to the beginning of a vaulted passage running for a full one hundred and fifty metres eastwards down the spine of the island. It ends at another larger church on a broad shelf half way back towards sea level. The passage, though also built of rubble and mortar, shows signs of having been plastered. It was then painted with brown lines to give the impression that it had been built of mortared ashlar block work. All the way down this covered and stepped passage, every few metres, there are large, high-arched windows on either side, open to almost ground level, obviously so designed that anything moving up and down its staircase could easily be witnessed by spectators from the outside.

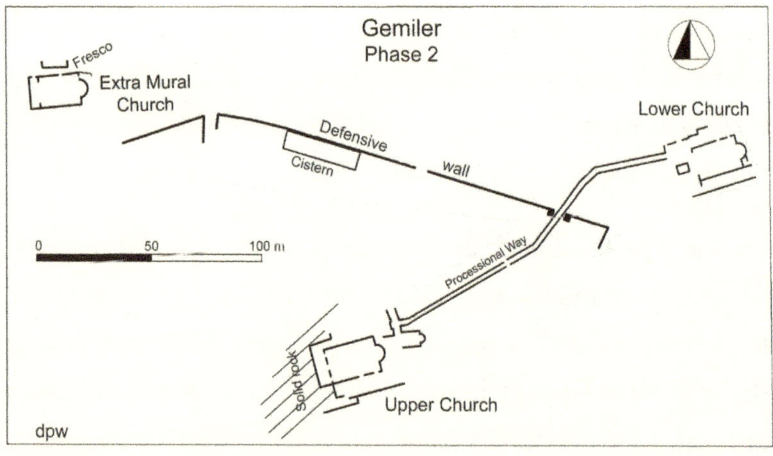

The most surprising feature of this vaulted passage, which I shall call the 'Processional Way', is that it runs right through and more or less fills the eastern gateway of the Phase 1 defensive wall without being contiguous with it and then continues down to the undefended portion of the island, thus rendering the wall protectively no longer of any value; anyone could walk in through one window and out through another. This must indicate that during Phase 2 defence was not considered important. The eastward continuation of the Processional Way ends by entering the north-west corner of the atrium of the new church, the 'Lower Church'. This church was constructed to a more traditional plan, with a courtyard surrounded by a pillared veranda at the centre of which was a pool, or rather, a cistern. The floor of this atrium was decorated with similarly dated mosaics to the Phase 2 floor of the Upper Church. This atrium leads through into what was probably a cross-aligned narthex and thence into the basilica nave and side aisles, finishing in an apse. On either side were built length-ways annexes, thereby doubling the floor area. Among the rubble of the collapsed roof can be glimpsed small marble in-post capitals.

The reason for the redesign of the Upper Church and the building of the larger Lower Church connected together by the Processional Way, in itself a unique combination, can only be speculative. But by comparison with other significant ecclesiastical sites around the eastern Mediterranean it is likely that the Lower Church includes somewhere in its plan a baptistery with walk-in pool, possibly on its north side. Such is the case at Qalat Siman in north-west Syria, the site of the magnificent, four-aisled commemorative church of St Simeon Stylites. It is connected by a processional road to a baptistery church, intended no doubt to enhance the influence and mystery of the cult of that great saint.

But the Lower Church is not the only addition in Phase 2. At least two other churches were built on the island, also outside the wall, one near the western gate, which I shall call the 'Extra Mural Church' and another lower down the slope, further west again, but now in a very fragmentary condition. Nor were these the only churches which date to this time in the area. A dramatic three-apsed church was established on the nearby island of Karacaören and there were several others set on the adjacent mainland, implying that this whole remote region had become one of extensive ecclesiastical significance, especially considering that there was no concomitant urban agglomeration to be found anywhere in the vicinity.

Back on Gemiler itself, in addition to these extra churches, many other structures were also erected outside the wall on the north slope of the island. This portion, considerably wider than the top half of the island, was divided by narrow streets and alleys crowded with buildings right down to the water's edge. Some of these were large, with two storeys, and by the appearance of crosses built into their gable ends some of these too had a religious purpose. Not only that, but remembering that prior to any occupation the island was totally without water, a number of small cisterns were cut into the rock at various points and lined with water-proof plaster to store rain. (Was the cistern in the atrium of the Lower Church intended to serve a baptistery?) But there was one which dwarfs all others. It's a barrel-vaulted cistern, also water-proofed, its north wall deliberately built against the inside face of the Phase 1 defensive wall between the western and central gateways, its south wall cut out of the solid limestone. It was thirty five metres long, five metres wide and six metres high and was capable when full of storing one million litres of water. By the water-lines on the plaster it was at some time during its lifetime at least one third full.

This cistern, together with the other constructions, speaks of a huge increase in the use of the island in Phase 2, implying the expectation of large crowds of people who for one reason or another were presumably either living or temporarily staying on the island. In that the north wall of the barrel-vaulted cistern is contiguous with the inner face of the defensive wall, it covers up what arrow slits had originally been set into it, again confirming, as with the eastern gate and the Processional Way, that the original purpose of this wall was no longer considered necessary at this time.

And there were other aspects of Phase 2 which I think are highly significant. Scattered about on the island and the mainland are a number of small windowless buildings with vaulted roofs entered through small apertures high in their end walls. These I think may be charnel houses, to accommodate the skeletons of the dead that were to be buried here. There is a large example further to the east of the Lower Church. But even more significantly, all around the Upper Church and along both sides of the Processional Way are shallow rectangular graves cut into the rock. They suggest that many people wished to be buried on the island, as close as possible to the Phase 2 buildings within the wall.

So what, or perhaps more importantly who, was so imperative to the life (and death) on the island that these extraordinary developments were required? Their purpose certainly wasn't economic, not in the accepted sense, since the island is in no way productive. But I think there is one piece of evidence which may throw light on this question, namely a fragment of carved marble found near the floor of the Upper Church. It is unmistakably a broken 'acroterion', one of four upright 'ears' that would have sat at the four corners of the pitched, roof-like lid of a large marble sarcophagus typical of the early Byzantine era. From the position where the fragment was lying, the presumption is that this tomb had once been placed in the centre of the nave of the Upper Church and by its size would have dominated it. Being so prominent inside the church it is therefore most likely that it was a reliquary tomb. If that was the case, it would imply that the Upper Church was a "martyrion church," a church celebrating a well-known martyr of Christendom whose remains and possibly other relics were kept here for all to venerate.

This would also account for the singular nature of the positioning of the Upper Church, namely, placed over the exact location where this person had died and it would also explain the large increase in the numbers of people coming to the island and the fact that many wanted to be buried here, especially near the relics themselves. In company with other sites of this period, presumably the relics were thought to have the capacity to perform miracles.

PHASE 3

I think Phase 3 relates to the sudden termination of all ecclesiastical activity on the island. It is most probably associated with the moment when the Byzantine armies and more especially navies, lost control of the coast of Lycia with the first appearance of the Arabs in the middle of the 7th century. Islam began with the first Haj, the flight of Muhammad from Mecca to Medina in 622 AD. In 636 the Byzantine emperor Heraclius lost the Levant to the armies of the Prophet at the Battle of the Yarmuk River on what today is the Jordanian/Syrian border. Shortly thereafter, Muawiya, the newly appointed Islamic governor of Syria, asked Caliph Uthman for permission to construct a sea-going fleet in the dockyards of Egypt with which he intended to harass Byzantine sea power in the Mediterranean. After annihilating the Byzantine settlements on the island of Rhodes, in 655 he engaged with and destroyed the Byzantine fleet at *Dhat al-sawari*, the 'Battle of the Masts', just off the town of Phoenix in southern Lycia.

I think that at this moment the community on Gemiler panicked. There is evidence of an attempt to redefend the island, to re-instate the defensive wall by building it higher, to block off the Processional Way and to build, or certainly to heighten, two barbicans with embrasures overlooking the western and the central gateways. There was clearly no need to re-defend the eastern gate because it was now rendered impassable by the blocked-off Processional Way. I think the attempt failed, because there is evidence of an ash-laden destruction level all around the Upper Church. The roof presumably burnt down and I would expect the same destruction level to be repeated throughout the island. The result was that Gemiler became abandoned and fell into ruins. Whether or not some of the inhabitants fled with any of their treasures, actual or symbolic, must be a matter of conjecture. There are no written records to support any interpretation, one way or the other.

PHASE 4

During the Middle Ages there is some indication of a possible renewed interest in the perceived religious potency of the ruins on Gemiler Island, as seen by two pieces of evidence. At the Upper Church at least two cist burials were dug through the rubble destruction layer and on through the Phase 2 mosaic floor to the natural rock in the nave. Presumably the efficacy of the abandoned Church was still considered potent, even if only as consecrated ground. Also the little chapel to the east of the Upper Church was modified by adding buttresses with pointed arches of Crusader design along the inside walls, maybe to support a new roof. In so doing they in part covered without regard the paintings of saints of Phase 2. Other than that, there is nothing. Let us suggest from the style of buttressing that these two features both date from the 11th century.

INTERPRETATION

So who was so important at Gemiler that they would have occasioned such extraordinary activity (and presumably expenditure) between 400 AD to about 650 AD? For whom were the upper martyrion church and all the other churches built? Who was the focus of such ecclesiastical adulation that they drew hundreds, possibly thousands of people a year to this remote and barren spot? There are monasteries of that date but whatever happened at Gemiler is far more extensive than simply monastic. Its second phase, especially for a hundred years or so until its demise, feels as though it was developed into a whole ecclesiastically-based industry, if one can use that phrase, involving hundreds if not thousands of people.

I think that question can now be answered. There is one Byzantine fresco which has avoided the depredations of visitors to the ruins over the centuries, partly at least. It is located high in a dark corner of a small vaulted passageway outside the

north wall of the Extra Mural Church near the western gateway. It shows a large haloed figure of God in the centre identified by the letters EM, for 'Emmanuel'. On his right-hand side is a smaller figure, also with a halo, above which is the title OCIOC NIKOΛAOC, the 'Devout' or the 'Holy Nicholas'. This fresco must date to no later than 550 AD (the date of the expansion of Gemiler) and has to relate to a local saint, St Nicholas, standing in paramount position at the right hand of God the Father.

All over the Byzantine world, from the 400s and on through Justinian's reign, local saints were achieving extraordinary status as 'thaumaturgists', miracle workers, in a development that has rightly been called the 'Cult of Saints'. To re-enforce their individual remembrance, many new churches were built at the locations where they had died and by extension, the places where they had ascended into heaven.

These churches housed the relics of the martyrs involved, all of which were thought to be imbued with powerful miracle-giving potency. It happens, for example, at Qalat Siman, Syria, where St Simeon the Stylite's column is placed where he had once stood, right in the centre of the four naves of the church built to his name during the reign of emperor Zeno (r.474 – 491). Another example is Resafa on the Euphrates where a church was built to house the martyrion sarcophagus of St Sergius in the centre of its nave. In this case it also prompted the re-construction of a whole city, Sergiopolis, in the middle of the desert, incidentally with the same-sized cisterns as the large one at Gemiler. Similarly too, it dates to the reign of the emperor Justinian.

But separate to the fresco there is other evidence incidentally linking the island to St Nicholas. There are rough maps made by Genoese, Venetian and Greek sailors amongst others which date from the 13th and 14th centuries, known collectively as 'portulani'. These are topographic lists of sailing instructions as to how to navigate in the eastern Mediterranean. Several of them mention an island at the location of Gemiler which is named 'Isola di San Nicola', the Island of St Nicholas. And one of the Greek ones talks about: "Το Περδικονησι όπου ἐιναι ή ἐκκλησια Άγιος Νικολαος ἀπανω εἰς την κορφη τους βουνιου," (translated as, "Partridge Island where there is a church to St Nicholas at the top of the hill"). These references are without any ecclesiastical or historical prejudice and are therefore most illuminating.

The combination of the fresco in the Extra Mural Church and the evidence of the "portulans" strongly suggests the local saint being "venerated" at Gemiler is none other than St Nicholas of Myra, one of the greatest of all miracle workers of the early church and very much a local Lycian figure, having been born at Patara, only twenty five miles away by sea and having been Bishop of Myra, the metropolitan city of Lycia. We don't know what the Byzantine name for this settlement was, but maybe by comparison to others perhaps it might have been called "Nicholopolis," who knows?

One tradition suggests he might have died in 325 AD, which if true must have been later in the same year as the Council of Nicaea and hence my ascribing the place of his death to Gemiler Island as he was returning to Lycia after the synod. Certainly, all the evidence here, both actual and circumstantial, points to Gemiler as the place of his demise. The Phase 1 Upper Church must have been built almost within living memory of his death. And his growing acclaim must also be the reason for the later major redevelopment of the site, dated as one might expect like so many others in the Byzantine world to the reign of Justinian. This expansion must have been in order to accommodate the vast numbers of pilgrims who were flocking to be near his relics as his reputation as a miracle worker spread, some of whom also wanted to be buried next to the place where he departed this life. But the peak importance of the island could have been for no more than a hundred years or so. It's noticeable that there are hardly any sherds of pottery on the surface which usually characterise the long-term occupancy of a site.

One question that follows from Gemiler's abandonment might be, were St Nicholas' remains ever removed to Myra? Maybe it was at the time of the Arab raids along the coast in 655 AD? Perhaps they were taken to a properly defended city, near the church where he had one time been bishop? Is that how the relics came to be removed again from Myra in the 11th century by the sailors from Bari, or Venice, or wherever? It hardly matters. Whether they were there or not, that is what these Italian seafarers believed they were taking and that was probably enough, especially since there is serious doubt about the properness of their motives in the first place. Who knows whether the bones being venerated today, in Bari or anywhere else for that matter, actually once belonged to a Byzantine saint of the 4th century? But Partridge Island, the Island of Gemiler, certainly does relate to this great man and feasibly with its martyrion church it is most likely to have been originally his resting place.

This then I consider is the best proof we have for the existence of such a personage, based not on dubious and late texts or on western inventiveness and mediaeval chicanery, but on the near-contemporary material remains at Partridge Island, which the Turks call Gemiler Adası, the "Island of Sailors." The rest of the story I have fictionally woven around the scaffolding of the history of the late Roman empire hoping that it will have provided an enjoyable insight into the life and times of the great Lycian saint himself, St Nicholas, best remembered today as our very own Santa Claus.

REFERENCES

The basic stories, that Nicholas came from a wealthy family involved with the incense trade and that as a young man he travelled to Egypt, Arabia and the Holy Land, are all part of the general mythology, or perhaps one more kindly should call them the unverifiable legends, which surround his life.

St Nicholas' sojourn at Apezala (Beit Jala) is celebrated by a church there today. So too is St George, to whom a chapel with wonderful Byzantine mosaics is dedicated.

Literary works of references consulted include the following:-

The oldest supposed details about St Nicholas are preserved from the beginning of the eighth century (or some say beginning of the ninth!).They are in a "letter" of Methodius to Theodore, Methodius Ad Theodorum, delivered "at his grave site" by St Andrew of Crete, who called him a "pillar and support of the Church." Most scholars think that the "historical" details contained in it are largely spurious.

The extent to which Nicholas became revered in the west is especially demonstrated by the Archbishop of Canterbury St Anselm's prayer asking Nicholas to intercede for him. It dates to about 1090 AD, the date of the dedication of the cathedral at Bari.

'The Periplus of the Erythraean Sea' is written in Greek and is an account of navigation and sea trade from Egyptian ports along the coast of the Red Sea and the coast of India. The text is probably mid-1st century AD in date. Although the author is not known, it is clearly a first-hand description by someone familiar with the area.

Eusebius of Caesarea wrote a tract about Constantine, 'The Life of the Blessed Emperor Constantine,' in which he eulogises his appointment. Eusebius himself seems to imply that he is one of the emperor's inner circle, but scholars now think this is rather exaggerated and that he had only met Constantine once, somewhat incidentally, before the Council of Nicaea.

For the atmosphere of the 'Great Persecution' conducted by Diocletian and Galerius, the only contemporary text is again from Eusebius of Caesarea in his manuscript, 'On the Martyrs of Palestine,' which claims to be an account of the events of the persecution at Caesarea, where Eusebius had been appointed bishop. However, Edward Gibbon, in his researches for his mammoth work, 'The History of the Decline and Fall of the Roman Empire,' found that Eusebius' reporting was not to be trusted. He has been followed in this by the mid-19th century Swiss commentator Carl Jacob Burckhardt, who dismisses Eusebius with the sweeping evaluation that he is 'the first thoroughly dishonest historian of antiquity'. What price accuracy now!

There are several modern descriptions of the Byzantine empire, from John Julius Norwich's eminently readable trilogy, 'Byzantium,' to the distinctly unreadable 'History of the Byzantine State' by the Serbian historian George Ostrogorsky.

The details of early Byzantine architecture largely come from the 'bible' of that subject, Richard Krautheimer's excellent tome 'Early Christian and Byzantine Architecture' in the Pelican History of Art series.

No discussion of church construction in the early Byzantine period would be complete without reference to Procopius' 'The Buildings of Justinian,' a contemporary panegyric on Justinian's building activity in parts of his empire. It probably dates to around 550 AD. Justinian is presented as an idealised Christian emperor who built churches everywhere for the glory of God.

Another reference for the beginning of Byzantine power would be Cyril Mango's book 'Byzantium, Empire of the New Rome' as well as his book on 'Byzantine Architecture.'

The history of Umayyad expansion in the 7th century is ably described in 'Byzantium and the Early Islamic Conquests' by Walter Kaegi.

Some survey work and soundings in the Upper Church were conducted on Gemiler in the 1990s by a Japanese survey team from the University of Osaka. Their surveys were published in

2010 as 'The Island of St Nicholas: Excavation and Survey of the Gemiler Island Area, Lycia, Turkey.' Their findings confirm my own prior observations. The site would undoubtedly yield more from a forensic excavation.

Incidentally, the Turkish name for Gemiler Island, Gemiler Adası, means the Island of Sailors. I've often wondered (quite without foundation) whether this might not refer obliquely to Nicholas' recognition in some hagiographies as patron saint of mariners.

GLOSSARY OF PLACE NAMES

ANCIENT	MODERN
Antioch	Antakya
Antiphellos	Kaş
Apezala	Beit Jala
Arnon	Wadi Mujib
Asia Minor	Turkey
Aspalathos	Split
Assos	Behramkale
Ayla	Aqaba
Berenike	Mina Baranis
Beroea	Aleppo
Bethany	al-Elzariya
Bostra	Busra al-Sham
Chelidonia	Gelidonya
Constantinople	Istanbul
Dyrrachium	Durrës
Eboricum	York
Erythraean Sea	Red Sea
Eudaemon	Aden
Evangelis	Suakin
Gerasa	Jerash
Great Sea	Mediterranean
Hebron	Al-Khalil
Hegra	Mada'in Saleh
Hellespont	Dardanelles
Iconium	Konya
Koptos	Qift
Medabeni	Madaba
Mediolanum	Milan
Moscha	Muscat
Mount Cragus	Baba Dağı
Mount Nebo	Ras Siyagha
Myos Hormos	Al Qusayar
Myra	Demre
Nicaea	Iznik
Nicomedia	Izmit
Omanna	Oman
Partridge Island	Gemiler Adası
Paran	Mecca
Pergamon	Bergama
Philadelphia	Amman
Pinara	Minare
Pontus	Black Sea
Propontis	Sea of Marmara
Ptolemais	Tolmeita
Reqem	Petra
Serdica	Sophia
Sergiopolis	Resafa
Simena	Kaleköy
Smyrna	Izmir
Swenett	Aswan
Teimioussa	Üçağızlar
Telmessos	Fethiye
Thebes	Luxor
Yathrib	Medina

ACKNOWLEDGEMENTS

First I must thank Harry Markos for persuading me to write this book in the first place. Without his encouragement, I may never have begun it.

I have also to thank as usual my brother John, "Yr Hen Was", for looking over the finished typescript with his professional editor's skill.

A number of people read the book while it was being written. Foremost I must thank Lynn for her eagle eye and helpful corrections, historical and literary. Her suggestions have been absolutely invaluable. And I must also thank Eleanor for her patience and for picking up some of the grammatical mistakes that I somehow had overlooked!

I am as always eternally grateful to my wife Sue who has encouraged and criticised parts of the text as it was being written and who has had to endure the constant regurgitation of the plot as it unfolded.

Kew 2017

Also by David Price Williams and available from Markosia:

LOOKING FOR APHRODITE

Knidos was renowned for its nude statue of the goddess Aphrodite. This book is about searching for Aphrodite, a memoir exploring the author's involvement with the excavation of the ancient city, while his own life was transformed from adolescent gaucheness into the beginnings of maturity. Laced with poetic evocations of the ancient and modern world, it contains hilarious stories of the people he met along the way.

Also by David Price Williams and available from Markosia:

GAZING UPON SHEBA'S BREASTS

Swaziland, a small country on the edge of Africa's Great Escarpment, is a microcosm of African environments. It was the ideal laboratory where Dr David Price Williams and a team of scientists developed a major research project to investigate the evolution of humankind from the dawn of prehistory two million years ago right up to the present. The book charts their ten year journey, along with the fascinating results of their search, and how David designed and built the Swaziland National Museum. It's full of humour and his love for Africa and its peoples.

WWW.MARKOSIA.COM

www.ingramcontent.com/pod-product-compliance
Lightning Source LLC
Chambersburg PA
CBHW030512100426
42813CB00001B/12

* 9 7 8 1 9 1 1 2 4 3 4 1 0 *